Teaching Law by Design

Teaching Law by Design

Engaging Students
from the Syllabus
to the Final Exam

THIRD EDITION

Michael Hunter Schwartz
PROFESSOR OF LAW
UNIVERSITY OF THE PACIFIC MCGEORGE SCHOOL OF LAW
CO-DIRECTOR OF THE INSTITUTE FOR LAW TEACHING AND LEARNING

Sophie M. Sparrow
PROFESSOR OF LAW
UNIVERSITY OF NEW HAMPSHIRE FRANKLIN PIERCE SCHOOL OF LAW

Olympia Duhart
PROFESSOR OF LAW
NOVA SOUTHEASTERN SHEPARD BROAD COLLEGE OF LAW

Gerald F. Hess
EMERITUS PROFESSOR OF LAW
FOUNDER OF THE INSTITUTE FOR LAW SCHOOL TEACHING
GONZAGA UNIVERSITY SCHOOL OF LAW

CAROLINA ACADEMIC PRESS
Durham, North Carolina

LIBRARY OF CONGRESS CATALOGING-IN-PUBLICATION DATA

Names: Schwartz, Michael Hunter author | Sparrow, Sophie M., author | Duhart, Olympia author | Hess, Gerald F., 1952- author
Title: Teaching law by design : engaging students from the syllabus to the final exam / Michael Hunter Schwartz, Sophie M. Sparrow, Olympia Duhart, Gerald F. Hess.
Description: Third edition. | Durham : Carolina Academic Press, 2026. | Includes bibliographical references and index.
Identifiers: LCCN 2025053551 | ISBN 9781531023140 paperback | ISBN 9781531023157 ebook
Subjects: LCSH: Law--Study and teaching--United States | Law teachers--United States--Handbooks, manuals, etc.
Classification: LCC KF272 .S39 2026
LC record available at https://lccn.loc.gov/2025053551

CAROLINA ACADEMIC PRESS
700 Kent Street
Durham, North Carolina 27701
(919) 489-7486
www.cap-press.com

Printed in the United States of America

This third edition is dedicated to:

Stacey, Samantha, and Kendra, my inspirations to be a better person and teacher
Mike

Layne, Mike, Amanda, Brittany, and Marc—my family of teachers and writers
Gerry

Chris, Kai, and Silas—the best teachers in my life
Sophie

Chris, Cai, and Christian, the whole point
Olympia

Contents

Preface to the Third Edition

In this book, we seek to apply the enormous body of research on teaching and learning to legal education. Our goal is to provide concrete suggestions about how to design and conduct all aspects of teaching law students, from sequencing a course to grading an exam. We hope that new and experienced teachers find helpful ideas, support, and inspiration throughout the book.

We invite you to read the chapters sequentially or individually, depending on your interests, competing demands, and students. We hope the book helps you and your students enjoy teaching and learning in law school. At the same time, we caution you to be selective in adopting this book's suggestions. None of us has adopted every suggestion in this book and we doubt anyone could do so. Instead, make small rather than wholesale changes, evaluate the effectiveness of every new practice you try, keep doing the things that work, discard the things that don't work, and, above all, aspire to continuous improvement.

The first chapter provides a legal education-focused overview of the research on teaching and learning. Chapters 2 through 10 focus on fundamental elements of teaching and learning: course design, class design, inclusive teaching, student motivation, teaching methods, online teaching, experiential exercises, lasting learning, and assessment. In Chapters 11 and 12 we share some of our most successful teaching ideas and our approaches to dealing with significant teaching challenges. Chapter 13 focuses on things law teachers can do to systematically improve themselves as teachers.

All the chapters and accompanying appendices from the second edition of this book have been substantially revised and updated. The chapters on inclusive teaching, online courses, and teaching and learning gems are new. Many chapters are directly applicable to all law teachers, courses, and students, but six chapters focus primarily on doctrinal courses (Chapter 5—teaching the class, Chapter 6—online teaching, Chapter 8—experiential learning, Chapter 10—assessment, Chapter 11—teaching gems, and Chapter 12—troubleshooting).

While we were updating this edition, generative artificial intelligence (AI) exploded in use and continues to do so. Given the rapidly changing nature of AI and teachers' approaches to it, we have deemed it beyond the scope of this text. We recommend you consult other current sources for new ways to address students' and teachers' use of AI.

The Appendix provides examples of how we have implemented the principles discussed in the book. The Appendix is organized in the same way as the book. (*Note*: There are no appendices for Chapters 1, 6, 9, 11, and 12.) To keep the size of the book manageable, we put the Appendix online rather than at the end of the book. All material in the Appendix is available to be viewed and downloaded at caplaw.com/TLBD3e.

In writing this book, we are fortunate to benefit from the vast research on teaching and learning in higher education and studies of law students and legal education. The lists of resources that follow most chapters provide an entry to the literature on teaching and learning. We encourage you to explore that literature.

We wrote this book to share what we believe to be core principles of teaching and learning. The book also serves as a white paper for the "Context and Practice Casebook" series from Carolina Academic Press. The series is designed to apply the principles from this book to creating law school course materials.

We wish to thank the many people who made this book possible. We appreciate the support of our respective law schools and the patience of our families. We are grateful to our many students, who had no choice but to help us learn from our mistakes.

MICHAEL HUNTER SCHWARTZ
SOPHIE M. SPARROW
OLYMPIA DUHART
GERRY HESS

Teaching Law by Design

Chapter 1

What It Means to Be a Teacher

This chapter explores what we know about effective learning and effective teaching. In this short chapter, we cannot provide a graduate level exploration of either topic. Instead we are aiming for an only-what-you-need-to-know treatment of these topics. As a result, if you are familiar with the learning and teaching research, this chapter likely will not offer new, earth-shattering insights but might provide a useful review. If you have not encountered these ideas before, however, the discussion will provide necessary background. For both the teaching and learning theory novices and experts, we hope you will find the echoes of the ideas introduced in this chapter in our recommendations throughout the rest of the book.

What we know about effective learning

Educational psychologists and instructional designers have produced thousands of books, studies and papers addressing learning, and there is a growing cadre of authors from every other discipline, including law, who conduct their own, discipline-specific studies of student learning. Because the field is so vast, we cannot cover it all. Instead, we have chosen to focus on the three theories we believe are most salient for law teachers: cognitive learning theory informed by neuroscience, constructivist learning theory, and self-regulated learning theory.

Introduction

All learning theories assume a similar goal. Whether that goal is labeled "mastery" or "competency" or "transfer," the basic idea is the same. Students have learned something significant when they can apply what they have learned to solve a previously unseen problem. In the context of law school doctrinal classes, our students have developed competency when they are able to solve a legal problem by analyzing a hypothetical or real set of facts, articulating arguments competent lawyers would make, and predicting how courts would resolve the issue.

Illustration 1-1: A Model of Cognitive Processing

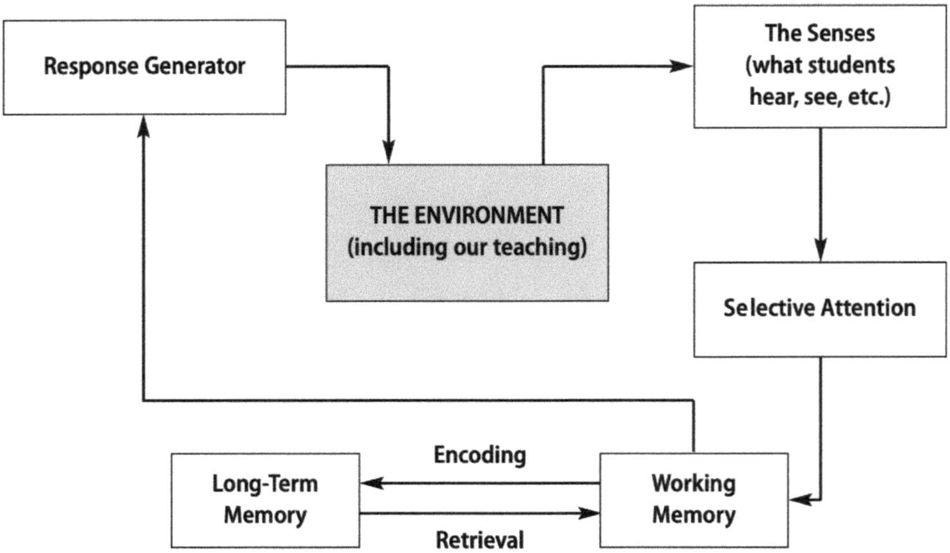

Cognitive Learning Theory and Neuroscience

Cognitive models aim to explain how our brains process, retain, and retrieve learning. Neuroscience, the scientific study of the brain, shows that for significant learning to occur neurons must create and strengthen connections with other neurons. To transfer learning, students must store their learning in an organized, meaningful and useable way. The processes of storing new learning and retrieving stored learning occur according to the sequence depicted above in Illustration 1-1. Although the sequence may appear linear, the process is much more fluid.

According to cognitive learning theory, hundreds of pieces of information reach our students' senses every moment. At any point during a class session, students hear what we and their peers say but also hear each other's clicks on their laptops or scratches on paper, see what's on their computer screens, feel how hard or soft their chairs are and how cold or hot the classroom is, and, perhaps, even smell each other's colognes and soaps. The information registers in our students' senses for a brief moment. Humans can attend, however, to only a few bits of information so our students must decide: which stimuli warrant attention? The process of choosing a focus is known as "selective attention." Thus, the learning process is over at the spigot if our students decide to pay attention to their e-mail, text messages, online purchases, social interactions, their breakfasts, the hardness of their chairs, or their doodling instead of attending to learning the skills and knowledge we are teaching. A common student response to our questions evidences such failures; they ask, "What was the question?"

If our students do pay attention, the lesson enters their working memory. Students' working memory can retain only a small amount of learning and only for a limited time. Most of us can remember a new phone number for only 10 or fewer seconds unless we do something to help us remember it, such as repeating it several times. When our students do something *active* to store their learning in a meaningful way, they are building and strengthening connections among neurons and the information becomes stored in their long-term memory, which has enormous capacity.

For this reason, cognitivists were the first to emphasize the crucial importance of engaging students in active learning. Active learning requires students to do something to mentally process the concepts we want them to learn. If students are writing about new concepts, discussing them with a peer, or figuring out how the concepts relate to each other, students are engaged in active learning.

The process of creating neural links and moving learning from the working memory to long-term memory is called "encoding." Over time, encoded learning can undergo "consolidation," a process in which neural connections are refined, strengthened, stabilized, and stored.

Many tools are available to facilitate encoding, consolidation, and deep learning, including:

- **Consciously connecting new material to what students already know.** For example, a student learning promissory estoppel might recognize the similarities between carelessness in actions (negligence) and carelessness in promising.
- **Retrieval practice**, such as self-testing with flashcards, quizzes, or practice exams.
- **Spaced practice**, by revisiting material repeatedly over days or weeks after initial learning rather than massed practice, such as cramming for an exam.
- **Interleaved practice**, by addressing a variety of concepts or skills in one learning session rather than focusing on a single skill or concept. For example, a problem set or simulation that incorporates several areas of the course.
- **Elaboration**, where students paraphrase difficult concepts, summarize the key ideas from a reading or lesson, explain the steps they took in addressing a problem, create a graphic representation of concepts such as a flow chart, or teach skills or concepts to peers.

The more deeply students think about what they are learning, the more likely they are to remember it. If students learn material so well that they can retrieve it with minimal attention, a process known as "overlearning," they have developed "automaticity." For example, most adults have developed automaticity with respect to reading; they can process the meaning of sentences and paragraphs without sounding out the words used and can often figure out unfamiliar words from context. Because adults can read so effectively, they can focus on learning the concepts the author is expressing. To be able to apply the high level intellectual skills we teach our law students, students need to have developed automatic knowledge of the rules of law, case holdings, and theory, and of the process involved in applying all three. This automaticity allows students to focus mental energy and effort on the more challenging skills involved in sifting facts and analyzing the complex combinations of issues students encounter on exams and lawyers encounter in law practice. Experts possess well-organized and deep wells of automatic knowledge.

The brain organizes long-term memories in hierarchical structures called "schemata," which hold together sets of neural links as students learn a subject. Schemata make it easier for students to integrate new learning into the preexisting structure. Think of a schema as being a little like the folder systems provided for users of computer operating systems. These hierarchical systems allow users to readily remember where they can find any document they need and where to store new documents. For example, Mike stores his contracts I course syllabus in a folder labeled "handouts." The "handouts" folder, as well as folders labeled "teaching notes," and "assessment," are in a folder labeled "contracts I." The "contracts I" folder is in a folder labeled "courses." If Mike creates slides for the course, a logical place to store them would be in a new folder labeled "slides" located in the "contracts 1" folder.

Based on this initial discussion, it is easy to develop a misperception that cognitive theory and neuroscience focus on acquiring and not on applying knowledge. Schemata, however, also are like entire computer programs in that the organized material includes structures that reflect how to perform skills. Thus, most adults who can play a musical instrument, such as the piano, have developed a schema for performing all the mental and physical steps involved. These steps include identifying each mark on the sheet of music, knowing what each mark means and understanding the relationships among: the marks, the black and white keys, their hands, the necessary fingering to reach all the keys, the pedals below the keys, and their feet. In addition, schemata are like theories in that they allow us to make predictions and to draw inferences.

But storing learned skills and knowledge in schemata isn't enough. To analyze a problem, students must recall ("retrieve") what they have learned and use that learning to interact with the environment in some way. In law school, this last step involves recalling cases, rules, and policies, and then generating an oral answer to a classroom hypothetical, writing a full analysis to a legal writing problem, or answering a timed essay test. In law practice, it includes interacting with a client, a judge, or another attorney, and drafting pleadings, briefs, contracts, wills, and other legal documents.

Constructivist Learning Theory

Constructivists focus less on the sequence of learning and more on the process required for new learning to become a more-or-less permanent part of who the students are. Three crucial learning principles derive from constructivist research.

First, students construct learning from their personal experiences. When students engage with materials in an active, effortful way and reflect on the process, they develop personal understandings. Those personal understandings, having been generated within the student's mind, stay with the student. Thus, significant law student learning only can happen if the teacher provides the students with opportunities to figure things out for themselves. Teachers in all fields (and many law teachers in our experience) complain that they can tell their students some things over and over again and yet their students don't recall those things on the day of their exam. Why don't the students remember? A constructivist would explain that merely "telling" the students did not allow them to develop a personal understanding. In other words, a teacher who wanted her students to understand the importance of personal jurisdiction might tell students they had to attend a pivotal hearing regarding their future at a distant, inconvenient location.

Second, constructivists emphasize the importance of real-world experiences, both in learning activities and assessment. Students learn when their opportunities to construct understandings are authentic, such as when their learning is anchored in a realistic context. Students should encounter complex, multifaceted, ill-defined problems that reflect real life. Thus, constructivists would advocate for students in clinical and externship courses to work on difficult, real-life problems. Likewise, law teachers who situate parts of their doctrinal courses in law practice problems, whether simulations or actual client issues, provide students the authenticity they need to construct meaningful understandings.

Third, constructivists emphasize the role of social interaction in learning. Students engage in crucial mental activity when they negotiate meaning and seek to synthesize their personal understandings. Hundreds of studies demonstrate the superiority of cooperative learning groups compared to all other teaching methods. These groups are so effective because they allow students to obtain access to multiple perspectives and thereby to develop the more complex approaches and understandings required to address complicated problems.

Of course, such results are the product of groups who know how to work together, how to subdue ego in service of the goal of obtaining the best results possible, how to develop "positive interdependence," where each member of the group invests in the success of every other member of the group, and how to develop "accountability," where each member of the group holds every other member of the group responsible for performing her or his share of the group work. Groups who do not develop these qualities may be dysfunctional and unproductive. When constructivists talk about the learning that comes from social negotiation, they are referring to effective groups.

Finally, a constructivist would encourage a law teacher to conceptualize law teaching more as coaching and less as lecturing. As the coach, the professor plans the sessions, organizes opportunities for practice, delivers explicit, corrective feedback, and encourages teammates to help each other improve.

Self-Regulated Learning Theory

Cognitive and constructivist learning theories implicitly assume students possess the skills, knowledge and values necessary to take control over their own learning. Many students, perhaps even most new law students, do not. Law school forces nearly all students to improve their self-regulated learning skills. Self-regulated learning, which is sometimes called "expert learning," is the process by which successful students manage their learning process.

> **Thinking exercise:** Think about the students you have most enjoyed teaching. What are they like? What do they do? List the characteristics of the students you most enjoy teaching.

We suspect many law teachers who list the qualities of the students they most enjoy teaching would include some of the following qualities commonly attributed to self-regulated learners:

- The student actively controls the student's behavior, motivation and thinking process when engaging in academic tasks;
- The student views academic learning as something the student does rather than as something that is done to or for the student;
- The student sets short-term and long-term learning goals;
- The student is interested in the subject matter, well-prepared for class, and ready with comments, questions, ideas, and insights;
- The student looks for problems and tries to solve them;
- The student seeks and creates opportunities for practice and feedback; and
- The student is unafraid to fail or to admit a lack of understanding, and the student is driven to rectify failure and to construct understanding.

Self-regulated learning is best understood as a cycle involving three phases: a planning phase, in which students decide how, what, when and where to study; an implementation phase, during which students execute their plans; and a reflection phase, during which students think back on their results and efforts, soberly evaluate their learning processes, and plan how they will learn even better the next time. Each of these phases involves several mental processes, all of which we explain below. Illustration 1-2 depicts the self-regulated learning cycle.

The Planning Phase. The planning phase consists of all the thinking the student does before engaging in a learning task. It is the preparation phase. Educational researchers have studied each of the activities involved in the planning phase and found that each independently improves a student's educational results.

As Illustration 1-2 reflects, the planning phase includes four principal activities: deciding what to learn, invoking self-efficacy and interest, setting mastery goals, and planning how, when, and where the student will study.

Deciding what to learn often begins with the course syllabus or website, which sets out the course assignments and assessments. Expert learners then identify the type of

Illustration 1-2: The Self-Regulated Learning Cycle

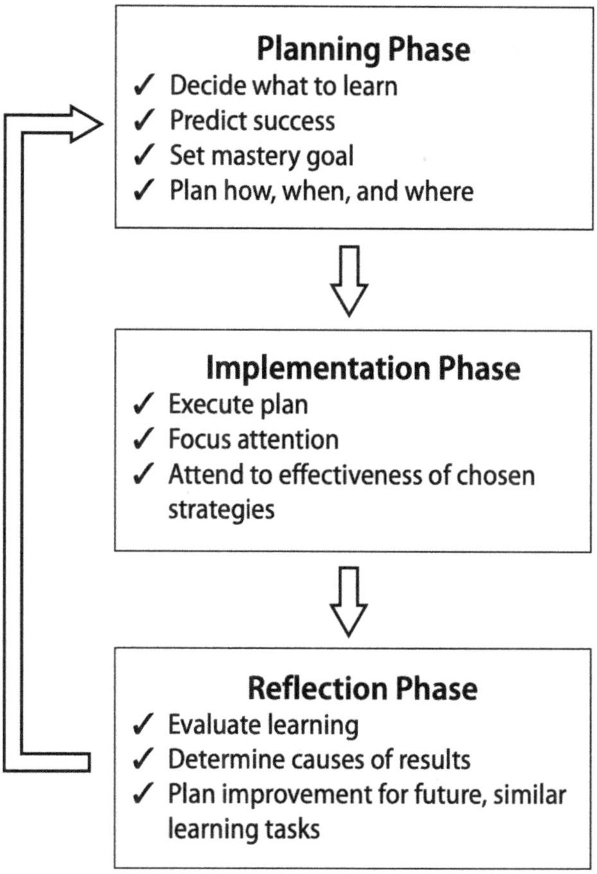

skills they will need to employ in order to successfully complete the learning task. Law school learning tasks typically fit in one of five categories: reading comprehension, research, synthesis, problem solving, and exam preparation. Classifying the learning task will help students choose appropriate learning strategies later in the self-regulation process.

Invoking self-efficacy and self-interest is a step many students skip. Yet thousands of studies show that students who believe they will succeed in learning (self-efficacy) and are interested in what they are learning (self-interest) outperform students who do not. Students may find the subject matter to be inherently interesting or they may be interested because the learning will help them achieve goals such as excelling in law school, passing a bar exam, and becoming a competent lawyer. The most successful students consciously invoke self-efficacy. Their belief that they can learn causes them to persist when they encounter difficulty, their persistence increases the likelihood of success, and those successes increase the students' self-efficacy. Thus, self-efficacy, itself, operates cyclically—high self-efficacy predicts persistence which predicts success which increases self-efficacy.

Self-regulated learners also set goals—specific desired outcomes—for each learning task. Effective learning goals are concrete, challenging, and achievable. Expert self-regulated learners set mastery learning goals that emphasize learning the material as well as possible. Students who set mastery goals earn higher grades than students who set grade goals, and students who set grade goals earn higher grades than students who set no goals or whose only goals are to complete assignments.

The crucial step of the planning process involves devising and tailoring a strategic approach to achieving the goal. The student identifies possible learning strategies most appropriate to the goal, reviews the student's own learning preferences, predicts outcomes based on the various options, and then chooses how to learn. Strategy selection also includes planning how the student will stay motivated and focused as well as where, when, with whom, and for how long the student will study.

The Implementation Phase. This phase is much simpler than the planning phase. Principally, the student just executes the plans the student made in the planning phase. One key to successful implementation is maintaining focused attention. Nearly all of us have experienced reading a book and an hour later discovering we cannot recall what we just read. The other key to successful implementation is called "self-monitoring." Successful students continually monitor whether they understand what they are supposed to be learning. When legal readers choose to re-read a paragraph of an opinion to make sure they understand the author's point, try to brainstorm a hypothetical that either proves the author wrong or confirms the author's assertion, or check their comprehension with the teacher or peers, they are engaging in self-monitoring.

The Reflection Phase. The reflection phase of the cycle guides the students' future learning endeavors. The students reflect on what they did and how effective it was and then consider the implications of their experience for future learning activities.

The students begins by evaluating how well and how efficiently they learned. Expert self-regulated learners accurately evaluate how they are doing and engage in this evaluation immediately after they have completed their learning activities. Thus, in a traditional, Socratic-style law school class, a self-regulated law student would evaluate how well the student would have been able to answer each of the professor's questions.

Having evaluated their performance, self-regulated learners develop attributions about the causes of their results. An attribution is an explanation for why the student performed well or poorly. Self-regulated learners are much more likely to attribute failures to correctable causes, such as insufficient effort or incorrect selection of learning techniques, and to attribute success to personal competence. These attributions lead self-regulated learners to try again and to try harder when they fail. In contrast, novice self-regulated learners are more likely to attribute their failures to ability and are more likely to give up.

Finally, the attributions influence students' future adaptations to their learning strategies. Having identified the correctable causes of any errors, the students brainstorm adjustments to their learning processes. In this way, self-regulated learners are more adaptive than their novice learner peers because they recognize both that learning difficult skills may require multiple practice cycles and that systematic variations in approaches will help them overcome learning difficulties.

What we know about effective teaching

What does it mean to be an "effective" teacher? What elements contribute to teaching excellence? How do teachers create healthy teaching and learning environments? Where do we find answers to these questions?

There is a vast literature on teaching effectiveness in higher education, including legal education, in books, web sites, and journal articles. Much of that literature is based on empirical studies of instruction and learning. Researchers approach the task of describing teaching excellence through several avenues—asking faculty members to assess their colleagues' teaching, reviewing student ratings of their teachers, directly observing teachers in their classrooms, analyzing student achievement in courses, and interviewing teachers about their educational philosophies and practices.

The first lesson we draw from the education literature is our definition of teaching effectiveness. For us, teaching excellence is measured by significant student learning. To what extent do students leave our courses with a deep understanding of legal doctrine and theory, competence in analytical and other lawyering skills, and internalization of appropriate professional values?

The second lesson is our synthesis of what faculty members can do to facilitate significant student learning. We have identified eleven elements for effective teaching. We recognize our list of elements is not exhaustive and teachers can help their students achieve significant learning in many different ways. These elements are the focus of the rest of Chapter 1.

Illustration 1-3: Eleven Elements of Effective Educators and Environments

1. **Subject matter expertise**
2. **Respect**
3. **Expectations**
4. **Support**
5. **Passion**
6. **Preparation and organization**
7. **Variety**
8. **Active learning**
9. **Cooperative learning**
10. **Clarity**
11. **Formative Feedback**

Subject matter expertise

An essential foundation of good teaching is subject matter expertise. To teach well, we need to know our subjects well. We should understand the subject's organizational scheme, the important details, the relationships among concepts, and the nuances. Subject matter expertise includes doctrine, theory, policy, practical application, thinking skills, performance skills, ethical issues, and professionalism. Each time we teach a course, we should strive to deepen and broaden our subject matter expertise. Our scholarship can play a vital role in enhancing our knowledge.

Subject matter expertise alone will not make an effective teacher. We could spend all of our professional time expanding our knowledge of our subjects. For example, Gerry taught environmental law courses and could have devoted every waking moment to learning more about that enormous, ever-changing topic. The same is true for most courses. Instead, to maximize our effectiveness as teachers, we must devote serious effort to the other ten elements of effective educators and environments.

Respect

Mutual respect among students and teachers is fundamental to a healthy teaching and learning environment. Respect should go in three directions: teacher to students, students to teacher, and students to students. Classrooms that feature humiliation, intimidation, or denigration lead many students to withdraw from participating and learning. In respectful environments, students and teachers feel free to explore ideas, solve problems creatively, make mistakes, and challenge one another to grow.

Although a precise definition of respect is difficult to articulate, most students and teachers know it when they see it and feel it. We can begin our courses by articulating the critical role that mutual respect will play in our classrooms. Then, students and teachers need to act in ways to maintain a respectful environment throughout the course. Here's a brief list of behaviors that foster respect.

- **Learn your students' names.** Call students by name in and out of the classroom. Do not allow students to go through your course anonymously. Is it hard to learn students' names in large classes? You bet. Seating charts, name tents, and pictures can help. The bottom line is that everyone from students to educational researchers tell us that it is well worth the effort. (See Chapter 11 for a detailed discussion of learning and using student names.)
- **Learn about your students' experiences and goals.** Have students introduce themselves by completing a short questionnaire in class or online. The information about students' education, work, goals, hobbies, and families allows us to appreciate and draw upon the tremendous human resources we have in our courses.
- **Value students' time.** Law students, like their teachers, lead busy lives. Time is at a premium. Start and end class on time. Be in your office during office hours. Keep appointments with students. Respond to students' messages.

- **Be inclusive.** Students come to law school with diverse backgrounds and perspectives. We motivate students when we make them feel welcome and when we try to tie their learning to their personal and professional interests. We can include diverse perspectives in our courses by choosing material that reflects a variety of viewpoints and by validating students who raise divergent views in the classroom. (Chapter 4 explores inclusive teaching in detail.)
- **Model respect.** Respect is more about what we do than what we say. It is how we treat students, colleagues, and staff on a daily basis. Many of the other elements of effective environments also demonstrate respect, including support for students and high expectations for each student.

Expectations

Teachers' expectations affect students' learning. High, realistic expectations lead to more student achievement; low expectations result in less student learning. Extensive research supports these simple statements. But implementing these principles is more complex.

> **Thinking exercise:** What expectations do you have for student preparation, behavior, and performance? How do you communicate your expectations to students at the beginning of the course? Throughout the course?

Five attributes of teacher expectations affect student motivation and learning: clarity, quality, achievability, uniformity, and credibility.

Clarity. Before a course begins, we need to think through our expectations for student preparation, participation, behavior, and performance. At the beginning of the course, we should clearly communicate those expectations and their rationale to students, orally and in writing. Throughout the course, we can continue to clarify our expectations through our actions; for example, giving specific directions for our assignments, articulating goals for each class, providing feedback on student performance in class and on written assignments. Lack of clarity in our expectations can occur because either we fail to communicate them to students or we act inconsistently with them.

Quality. The focus of our expectations for student learning should be on quality rather than quantity. Piling on more work, giving overly long reading assignments, and covering more content are unlikely to enhance students' motivation and learning. Instead, we can maximize student learning by focusing our students' attention and effort on the knowledge, skills, and values critical to the subjects we teach and to our students' professional lives after graduation.

Achievability. Our expectations should challenge students to stretch themselves and to do their best work. Expectations that are unrealistic and unachievable by even our best students are counterproductive. Our expectations for student preparation for class should be at a level that a diligent student can attain, day after day, in light of all the demands of the student's other courses. Our expectations for student performance in class, on assignments, and on exams, should be based on our students' current level of development and the requirements of professional practice after law school.

Uniformity. Effective teachers believe that every student can attain a high level of achievement. We communicate our expectation that every student can succeed by seeking participation from every student and by spreading difficult questions and assignments among all the students—men, women, and students with diverse backgrounds. However, individual students are at varying stages of professional development. We can challenge all students by building various levels of difficulty into our assignments, questions in class, and exams.

Credibility. Perhaps the best way for teachers to inspire students to excellence is through modeling. We should have high expectations for ourselves. Our high, realistic expectations for student preparation, participation, behavior, and performance are most credible when we demonstrate our commitment to meeting those expectations in our teaching. It does not mean we need to model perfection—that is unachievable for us and our students. Instead it means that we show, day after day, that we diligently seek continuous improvement in our professional practice.

Support

A supportive teaching and learning environment should accompany high expectations. We should show our commitment to helping each law student succeed. A supportive environment is built upon teachers' attitudes, availability, and trust.

One set of common descriptors of exemplary teachers focuses on their attitudes toward students—"helpful," "caring," "concerned," and "encouraging." Our attitudes have strong positive effects on students' motivation, level of engagement, willingness to take risks, and openness to new ideas and perspectives. Conversely, the quickest way to fail as a teacher is to communicate our lack of care about our students and their learning.

Another group of attributes of effective teachers is "available," "accessible," and "approachable." Student-faculty contact outside of formal class time is associated with students' motivation, satisfaction, and active involvement in their own education. We make ourselves available, approachable, and accessible in a variety of ways:

- arriving early and staying after class to talk with students;
- welcoming students when they come to our physical or virtual offices, rather than resenting the interruption;
- attending law school events;
- responding to student messages;
- sharing a meal with students; and
- holding conferences with students.

Most students trust us and respond positively to our trust in them. Personal attitudes tend to produce reciprocal attitudes in others. An operating assumption that reflects our trust is that "there is a good faith explanation for students' behavior."

Passion

Students regularly identify teachers' passion or enthusiasm as a critical ingredient of effective instruction. Our passion can inspire, energize, and motivate our students. Students take their cues from us. If we appear bored and disengaged, they will too. But when we convey our delight in teaching and love for our subject, many students will share our positive attitudes.

We communicate our enthusiasm for teaching and passion for our subjects by what we say, how we say it, and how we act. We should tell students directly what we love about teaching at this school, our joy in working with students, and our fascination with the subject matter. (If we do not feel passionate about any of those things, we should look for other jobs—many other people are eager to take our position as law teachers.)

Celebrate success in the classroom. Provide positive reinforcement when students produce insight, solid analysis, or creative thinking. Call attention to students who demonstrate professional skills and values. Congratulate students on significant personal and professional success (completing a half-marathon, engaging in significant *pro bono* activities, placing in a moot court competition).

Research has identified verbal and nonverbal behaviors that convey passion and enthusiasm. Verbal behavior includes speaking expressively, using humor, and not reading from notes. Teachers' nonverbal behaviors associated with enthusiasm include movement (away from the podium and out into the classroom), gestures, facial expressions, and smiling. These behaviors seem painfully obvious and simple, but together they reinforce our direct statements to students about our joy in teaching and passion for our subjects.

Preparation and organization

Thorough preparation and transparent organization contribute to teaching effectiveness and student learning. We believe this principle so strongly that we devoted several chapters of this book to those topics! Why? Because teachers and students benefit when they are clear about what should be learned, how that learning will take place, and how students will demonstrate their learning.

Course design. Comprehensive course preparation requires us to think through a series of design issues. Then we should inform students, through the syllabus and throughout the course, of our plan for the course. Course design issues (explored in detail in Chapter 2) include:

- Needs assessment—what strengths and weaknesses do students bring to the course, what aspects of the course do students learn readily, and with which skills, knowledge, and values do students struggle?

- Course goals—what should students know and be able to do at the end of the course?
- Policies—what are the expectations for student attendance, preparation, participation, and behavior?
- Teaching and learning activities—what methods, exercises, assignments will take place in and out of class?
- Materials—what print and electronic resources will support the teaching and learning activities?
- Pacing—what will happen on the first day of the course? The last day? In between?
- Feedback—how will students receive feedback throughout the course?
- Evaluation—how will student performance be assessed and graded?

Class design. A parallel set of issues inform our design of individual class sessions (addressed in Chapter 3):

- Where are students at this point in the course in terms of their understanding and skills?
- What are the two or three concepts, skills, or values that students should learn or practice in this class?
- What should students do outside of class to prepare (read, write, synthesize, etc.)?
- What will students do during the class (discuss, listen, write, collaborate, argue, perform)?
- How will the class begin? End?
- How will students and teachers get feedback about the class and the students' learning?

Preparation. A prerequisite to successful teaching, learning, and professional practice is thorough preparation. Successful teachers engage in two types of preparation for class. First, teachers need to understand at a deep level the concepts and skills that will be the focus of the class. Second, teachers should make conscious choices about all of the class design issues listed above. The first time we teach a course, much of our time is devoted to attaining an appropriate level of expertise in the subject and less time goes into design. As we become more comfortable with the subject, we should give more and more attention to class design and delivery. Finally, we should be thoughtful about how we can facilitate thorough student preparation for class . Planning need not lead to rigidity. In every course and many individual class sessions, opportunities present themselves to explore a concept in more depth, weave in professionalism, and build on students' insights and skills.

Variety

A characteristic that cuts across the design and delivery of courses and classes is variety. We can inject variety into many aspects of our teaching—objectives, teaching and learning methods, materials, and evaluation.

Course and class objectives should not be one-dimensional. Every subject can include goals for student learning of concepts, skills, and professional values. Teaching and learning activities in and out of the classroom can come from an extensive menu, including Socratic dialog, large group discussion, small group work, problem solving, lecture, simulation, experiential learning, electronic discussions, student presentations, writing, etc. Materials appropriate to support wide ranging teaching and learning activities include casebooks, statutory supplements, articles, computer programs (such as CALI), websites, pictures, podcasts and videos. Evaluating students can occur through exams, papers, and performances.

Variety is an important contributor to effective legal education for several reasons. First, different types of teaching methods and materials are appropriate to achieve different objectives. For example, a Socratic dialog dealing with appellate opinions may help students develop their case analysis skills, a contract drafting assignment may be a good vehicle for developing students' writing and strategic planning skills, and a simulation exercise may raise professionalism issues. Second, students have different strengths and weaknesses as learners. Throughout a course, a variety of teaching and learning methods, materials, and evaluation methods can maximize learning and give each student an opportunity to excel. Third, variety can keep students' interest and sustain their motivation throughout a course. Finally, different methods lead to different depths of learning. For example, students' learning of the law, policy, and strategy relating to filing a complaint in federal court will deepen as they read the relevant federal rules of civil procedure, brief a Supreme Court opinion on the sufficiency of a complaint, review sample complaints, and draft a complaint.

Active learning

Students learn from active and passive methods. Students learn passively when they listen to a presenter who organizes and conveys information. Active learning occurs when students engage in more than listening.

As shown in Illustration 1-4, student learning can be put on a continuum of increasing levels of activity.

Active learning is not "better" than passive learning. Effective teachers choose different methods to achieve various goals in their courses. Researchers agree, however, that active involvement by students enhances their learning. Active learning is particularly effective in achieving four types of core goals of legal education.

- **Thinking skills.** Active learning methods can foster critical thinking, such as making informed judgments about facts, law, and policy as well as higher-level cognitive skills like analysis and synthesis.

Illustration 1-4: Learning Methods Continuum

PASSIVE
Listen
Read
Take notes
Formulate questions
Answer questions
Organize and synthesize
Discuss
Write
Perform skills
Make presentations
Apply content and skills (simulation or real-life)
ACTIVE

- **Understanding concepts.** Active learning helps students learn content at a deep level. As students articulate their understanding and work with concepts in new settings, they are more likely to retain their knowledge and be able to apply it on an exam or in real life.
- **Lawyering skills.** Students learn skills such as interviewing and negotiation through experiential learning. Ideally, experiential methods allow students to have practical experiences, receive feedback, and refine their skills.
- **Professional values.** Complex, nuanced problems, simulations, and real-life experiences often raise professionalism issues. Student reflection, discussion, and writing about those issues can help students develop a healthy set of professional values.

Cooperative learning

A large body of research in higher education and legal education documents the effectiveness of students learning in small groups. In college education, cooperative learning fosters the following: (1) more student learning and better academic performance, especially when the task is complex and conceptual; (2) development of problem solving, reasoning, and critical thinking skills; (3) positive student attitudes toward the subject matter and course; (4) closer relationships among students and between students and teachers; and (5) students' willingness to consider diverse perspectives. Legal educators note additional benefits of cooperative learning. Cooperative learning enables students to learn to work in a team and develop collaborative approaches to negotiation and mediation. Moreover, cooperative learning helps students build community in and out of the classroom and to develop greater respect for one another.

Given the substantial benefits of cooperative learning, effective law teachers look for ways to incorporate small group learning in their courses. (Chapters 3 and 5 describe the design and delivery of small group exercises.)

Clarity

Clarity is an important aspect of our expectations, course design, and evaluation scheme. We need to think through and clearly communicate to students our expectations for student preparation, participation, behavior, and performance. Likewise, systematic course design leads to clarity through organization; for example, explicit course objectives, well-defined reading assignments, and focus questions guide students in preparing for class. Clarity in the evaluation scheme is especially important—students need to get our grading criteria in writing before the exam, paper, or performance (see Chapter 10 for more detail).

The present focus is on clarity in class sessions. Clarity is *not* about "spoon feeding" or "dumbing-down." Instead, it is about effectively communicating complex ideas, skills, and professional values. Several practices can help us communicate more clearly in class sessions.

- **Roadmap.** At the beginning of class, articulate the class objectives. Put concepts, skills, and values in the broader context of the course as a whole.
- **Closure.** At the end of a topic or unit, include an activity, problem, exercise, or brief lecture that provides synthesis and summary.
- **Examples.** Illustrate concepts, skills, and values with examples. We can find applicable, appealing examples from our own experience, from our students, from cases, and from current events.
- **Visuals.** Most students learn more when abstract ideas are supported with visuals. Handouts, slides, charts, and the whiteboard can foster organization and understanding. Pictures, videos, and documents such as contracts, complaints, and deeds can provide clarity that most of us cannot convey with words alone.
- **Questions.** Effective teachers consistently monitor student understanding. How? Pay attention to nonverbal cues during class. Ask for questions—and really mean it! Give students time to generate questions in class before moving on. Have students articulate questions in writing at the end of class, by email, or on the course web platform.

Formative feedback

Feedback is a critical, and often overlooked, element of teaching and learning. Law school challenges students to learn a complex set of doctrine, theory, professional values, and analytical and performance skills. Law school challenges teachers to strive to continuously improve their teaching effectiveness. Formative feedback helps law students and teachers meet those challenges.

Formative feedback is an essential part of the learning loop—students engage in learning activities, perform in writing or orally, and get feedback on how their learning and performance can be improved. Effective formative feedback has four characteristics: specific, corrective, positive, and timely. Feedback is most effective when teachers articulate specific criteria for student performance and give students feedback based on those criteria. Corrective feedback points out weaknesses in student work and provides strategies for improvement. Positive feedback identifies the strengths upon which students can build. Timely feedback comes relatively soon after student performance and gives students an opportunity to improve before their performance is evaluated. (Chapter 10 details types of formative feedback appropriate in law school.)

Formative feedback is essential for teachers' continued development as well. To make appropriate adjustments during a course, we need to get feedback from students about their learning. A variety of Classroom Assessment Techniques (discussed in Chapter 10) can give us that feedback. Further, for continuous improvement of our teaching practice, we can engage in self-reflection and gather input from students, consultants, and colleagues (the focus of Chapter 13).

What It Means to Be a Teacher—Resources

The first half of this chapter, "What we know about effective learning," is based largely on three books and an article:

- National Academies of Sciences, Engineering, and Medicine, How People Learn II: Learners, Context, and Culture (2018).
- Barbara Oakley, Beth Rogowsky & Terrence J. Sejnowski, Uncommon Sense Teaching: Practical Insights in Brain Science to Help Students Learn (2021).
- Michael Hunter Schwartz & Paula J. Manning, Expert Learning for Law Students (3d ed. 2018).
- Michael Hunter Schwartz, *Teaching Law By Design: How Learning Theory and Instructional Design Can Inform and Reform Law Teaching*, 38 San Diego L. Rev. 347 (2001).

The second half of this chapter, "What we know about effective teaching," is based largely on the Schwartz article above and two other sources:

- Michael Hunter Schwartz, Gerald F. Hess, Sophie M. Sparrow, What the Best Law Teachers do (2013).
- Gerald F. Hess, *Heads and Hearts: The Teaching and Learning Environment in Law* School, 52 J. Legal Educ. 75 (2002).

Chapter 2

Designing the Course

Introduction

This chapter and many of those that follow translates years of research on effective teaching into a set of concrete suggestions for planning your courses, for planning class sessions, for selecting among teaching methods, and for motivating and assessing students. Our goal for the remaining chapters is to provide concrete suggestions. However, if we were to provide examples of sufficient length to demonstrate how we have applied each of these principles, this book would be too long to be useful. Consequently, we explain the principles in the text and provide a few illustrative examples.

This chapter offers concrete ideas for designing courses. We see course design as a recursive process, as reflected in Illustration 2-1, in which you: (1) identify the skills, knowledge, and values you want your students to learn ("set course goals"); (2) evaluate your students' incoming knowledge, skills, and values ("assess the learners"); (3) decide how you will assess (a) whether students have attained the course goals and (b) whether your course design decisions are good ones, and then (c) design appropriate assessments ("plan assessment"); (4) select the texts ("select texts"); (5) design the course to help the students achieve the course goals by (a) constructing and synthesizing learning units, (b) writing the syllabus, and (c) designing a course web page ("design the course"); (6) implement the design ("implement design"); (7) evaluate the course design ("evaluate the design"); and, finally, (8) using the information you gained from evaluating the course, redesign the course according to the same process.

We have organized the rest of this chapter according to the timeline suggested by Illustration 2-1.

Initiating the design process: setting course goals

A goal is a statement of what students should be able to do by the end of your course. Although experts in education use a wide variety of terms for this concept, they all mean the same thing. The core idea is articulating what you want your students to learn from your course.

Illustration 2-1: The Recursive Course Design Process

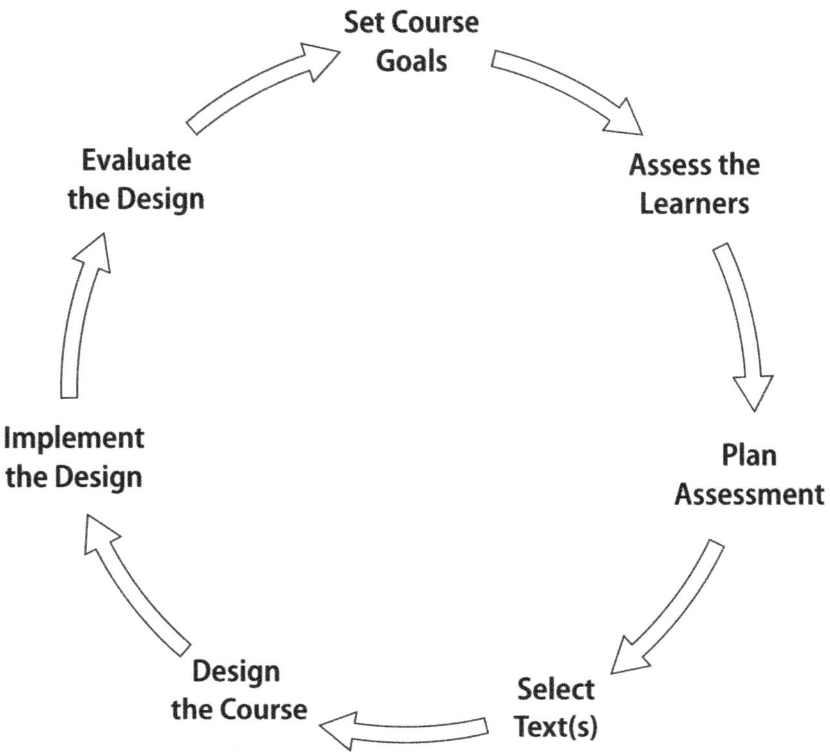

Goals influence which topics within the body of law to teach, your expectations for student class preparation, your design of your syllabus and class sessions, and your design of examinations and paper assignments. In most law school courses, your students' likely future use of what they learn in your course should drive your goals.

Thinking exercise: Think about a course you have taught recently. What skills, knowledge and values did you evaluate on your exam(s), paper(s) and other graded assignment(s)? What did you expect your students to do to prepare for class? What did you ask students to do in class?

All of these choices are the product of your beliefs as to what students should be learning in your class, i.e., your learning goals.

Consequently, a good place to start in identifying goals is by thinking about what tasks you can perform in this field *because* you are an expert. If it has been years since you practiced, you either can try to recall what you did or speak with a practitioner. (We have no doubt you have alumni who would appreciate a phone call or email asking for such information.) Another way to get at the question is to imagine your students a few years after they have taken your course. What do you hope the students have retained from the course?

We encourage you to be ambitious in describing your course goals—think beyond the limits of your assigned course label (clinic, contracts, legal writing, environmental law) and aspire to produce learning that transcends. We also encourage you to consider course goals that emphasize students' ability to learn and practice in your field, what we call self-regulated learning goals. Finally, consider whether you aspire to help students learn more about themselves or to develop particular values critical to our profession.

Limit yourself to three or four overarching learning goals per course, and focus not on what you know but, rather, what you are able to do. To be useful in course design, goal statements are most effective when they have three qualities:

- They focus on the student—not the teacher,
- They identify high-level intellectual activities or important values, not just knowledge, and
- They are concrete and not abstract.

A goal is student-focused when it describes what the students will be able to do or what value(s) they will adopt as their own and not what the teacher will do or say in the class.

A goal addresses high-level intellectual activities when it focuses on having students apply learning to new problems. All courses involve a mix of higher-level and lower-level thinking skills. In general, however, the higher-level skills require students to develop the lower-level skills. In the law school context, higher-level skills include: drafting law-related documents, analyzing and solving legal problems, evaluating cases, conducting client and witness interviews, etc. These higher-level skills implicate lower-level skills such as knowing and being able to explain the applicable law, being able to find a case or statute on point in a particular state, and generating policy justifications for the current state of the law or for changing the law.

A goal is concrete if you can measure its attainment. New goal writers tend to write goals that are so abstract that they provide little guidance in designing the course or assessing whether the students have attained those goals. Avoid goals that entail grasping ideas, e.g., "appreciating legal indeterminacy" or "understanding the complexity in legal decision-making." Neither phrase provides much useful guidance for designing a course. Instead, focus on how your students would show their appreciation and understanding, such as developing an original legal argument that is convincing yet runs counter to established doctrine or generating a statutory analysis that emphasizes the indeterminacy of a proposed statute to the types of problems that may arise.

Take a look at the example sets of course goals in Illustration 2-2. Why do these sets of objectives satisfy the above three criteria?

Once you have established your overarching course goals, you need to identify the subsidiary skills, knowledge, and values students need to achieve your course goals.

Illustration 2-2: An Excerpted Example Set of Course Goals for a Remedies Course

By the end of this course, given a legally-cognizable dispute, you will be able to

- Accurately identify the remedial options potentially available to the parties to that dispute.
- Anticipate and articulate the arguments lawyers representing all parties to the dispute would make in trying to secure and defend against the potentially-available remedial options.
- Correctly evaluate the likelihood that each of the parties would succeed in obtaining each of the remedial options potentially available to them.
- Effectively explain to a client the remedial alternatives potentially available, the arguments lawyers representing all parties to the dispute would make in trying to secure and defend against those remedies, and the likelihood that the parties would succeed in obtaining each of the remedial options potentially available to them.

In other words, what skills, knowledge and values would an expert need to perform each of the skills? For example, to analyze problems in a doctrinal field, practitioners would need either to know the relevant law or, at least, know enough of the law that they readily can recognize the doctrinal areas implicated by a problem and can find the law implicated by that problem. Likewise, a practitioner would need to be able to perform skills such as issue-spotting, evaluating evidence, distinguishing relevant and irrelevant facts, reading statutes and cases, applying rules to facts, and applying and distinguishing cases.

Educators label the process of identifying subsidiary skills, knowledge, and values *conducting a task analysis*. A task analysis allows you to generate a fairly long list of subsidiary goals, often called "learning objectives" or, more simply, "objectives." Together with the course goals, the learning objectives provide a tool you will find useful to make many of the decisions with which we law professors struggle: deciding doctrinal coverage, setting student expectations, creating assignments, assessing your students' learning, and using class time. At a minimum your course should address the learning objectives necessary to perform the tasks envisioned by your course goals.

You can do a task analysis on your own, but the ideal way to conduct a task analysis is to design a problem you would expect your students to solve by the end of your course and then ask two experts to speak aloud their thinking process as they analyze and resolve it. As they work on the problem, ask them how and why they made their various decisions. To elicit the information you need, use questions such as: Why did you immediately reject ________ as a possibility? How did you know you needed to do ________?

Once you have completed your task analysis, you are ready to write your learning objectives. Generally, learning objectives should conform to the criteria suggested above for course goals, but, you should not limit yourself to only stating high-level intellectual skills. Strive to include objectives across the full spectrum of intellectual skills. To assist you in that task, the comparison chart in Illustration 2-3 identifies one commonly-used taxonomy of skills and provides examples from law school learning.

We believe most law professors have intuited the hierarchy reflected in Illustration 2-3. If you ever have told a student that you do not want him to memorize the law but, instead, know how and when to apply it, you are suggesting this hierarchy. You are communicating that declarative knowledge is not enough; students must acquire principle learning and procedural learning so they can spot issues and apply the doctrine.

You may find it helpful, as you develop your learning objectives, to refer back to this chart.

One additional point about goals and objectives is worth noting: all of us expect our students to come to law school with some of the skills and knowledge they need to meet the course goals. Those of us who teach upper division courses also expect our students to have learned certain things in their prior law school courses. Many of us, however, have overestimated our students' entering skills, knowledge, and values. For this reason, in addition to establishing learning objectives, you also need to learn what your students *bring* to their engagement in your course.

Know your students: assessing the learners

While many of us have made the mistake of assuming, without any basis, what our students know and can do, the most common error committed by law professors is assuming their students are like them. In fact, recent studies suggest law professors are more like each other and much less like their students in terms of many of the characteristics that might influence how we should design our courses.

Those differences include the skills, knowledge, and values with which the students enter law school. In this sense, law professors are similar to their strongest students and quite different from a large percentage of the rest of the student body. Law professors typically were near the top of their law school classes and attended more exclusive law schools than those at which they teach, or, at least, attended law schools as exclusive as the law schools at which they teach. It's pretty much mathematically impossible that a significant number of your students are your equals in terms of entrance credentials, law school results, learning skills, time and workload management skills, writing skills, and knowledge of relevant concepts.

This difference between law professors and their students is exacerbated by the fact that law professors' law school experiences are several years in the past. As a result, some of us may inaccurately recall the knowledge and skill we possessed when we went to law school. We either may overestimate what we knew and what we think our students *should* know or be frustrated when our students do not live up to a somewhat distorted recollection of our past selves.

Illustration 2-3: Types of Learning

Intellectual Task	Description in the Law School Context	Example
Problem-Solving Learning	Given a legal problem, the student identifies the issues, applies the doctrine, cases and policy to the facts employing the kinds of arguments lawyers make, and predicts how a court might resolve those issues	The student interviews a witness to an alleged crime asking questions that reflect an understanding of the crimes implicated, the possible application of doctrine to the facts, and the kinds of arguments he would need to make
Cognitive Strategy Learning	The student adopts effective strategies for learning an aspect of doctrine the student has not previously encountered	Given a problem raising an issue of tort law the student has not yet learned (e.g., the intrusion upon seclusion form of invasion of privacy), the student effectively can teach herself the applicable law
Attitude Learning	The student adopts as his own a desired value, goal or ethic	The student plans to devote 5% of her future practice time to pro bono work
Principle Learning	The student applies individual rules and can apply and distinguish cases pertinent to a previously unseen problem	Given a potential lawsuit, the student can identify all jurisdictions that successfully could assert personal jurisdiction over the defendant
Procedure Learning	The student can follow all the steps involved in performing a lawyering skill	Given a problem raising a discrete legal issue, the student can follow the process of finding if there is a case or statute on point
Concept Learning	Given a legal problem, the student identifies the implicated legal issues	Given a contract, the student identifies contract language that could create an express condition
Declarative Knowledge Learning	The student accurately articulates a rule of law, case holding or public policy	Given a problem about an issue of adverse possession, the student can state the elements of adverse possession

Thinking exercise: Can you actually recall what you wrote in response to any of your law school exams? How deeply did you analyze the legal issues? How many original, creative arguments did you generate? How well did you integrate legal theory?

Law professors also often have different learning style preferences than their students. Many law professors enjoy learning on their own, whereas many law students are more extroverted than their professors, preferring to learn through collaboration with others. Similarly, while law professors tend to be comfortable learning from texts and by listening to lectures, many law students prefer visually-focused teaching and learning experiences or prefer learning experiences which are situated in authentic law practice contexts. More significantly, law students vary among themselves in their learning preferences; assuming that we should teach the way we liked to learn as law students is just wishful thinking.

You can discover your students' learning style preferences and whether they prefer working alone or in small groups through free, online versions of learning and personality style assessments available on the web, such as http://www.vark-learn.com/, http://www4.ncsu.edu/unity/lockers/users/f/felder/public/ILSpage.html, and http://www.humanmetrics.com/cgi-win/JTypes2.asp. None takes much time, and, by having your students self-report their results, you may learn something useful about them.

Assessing your students' entering knowledge may be more challenging and labor-intensive, but there are some shortcuts you could try. For example, you could develop a short survey and have students take the survey on the first day of class or create a multiple-choice, pre- and post-test of essential knowledge to discover what students know when they start your course and what they know by the end.

If you choose not to assess your learners, your students will benefit if you work from assumptions that (1) your students do not know everything you wish they knew and therefore will need instruction addressing skills and knowledge you think they already should possess, and (2) your students not only probably prefer to learn in different ways than you do but also vary greatly among themselves in terms of how they prefer to learn.

Determining who your students are, what they know, and how they prefer to learn is one form of assessment. The next step in your course design process will be to focus on other forms of assessment, including, among other things, how you will evaluate your students and how you will evaluate your course design.

Plan assessment: how will you know whether your students are learning?

Introduction

Our choice to make assessment the next topic is an intentional one. Thinking about assessment, even before you start designing your class sessions and syllabus, may seem counterintuitive to you. It is certainly counter to common law school teaching practice. You may even worry that, if you were to design assessment instruments before you designed your course, you could be accused of "teaching to the test." Educational experts, however, recognize that creating an assessment plan right after you have articulated your objectives ensures that your assessment instruments, class sessions, and syllabus are congruent with your goals. Congruence is essential to designing and teaching an effective course.

The process of designing the assessment should and often does influence your course goals and objectives. As you draft your assessment instruments—exams, law practice exercises, multiple choice questions, etc.—you may discover additional subsidiary goals and, in some instances, even reveal an additional course goal. You are even more likely to revise how you articulate your goals.

The process also will increase the likelihood that you include assessment items aimed at all thinking levels (from problem-solving to application to issue spotting to understanding). This variety of assessment items will, in turn, benefit both your students and you. It will assist your students in identifying at what level(s) they are struggling, and it will help you identify at what level(s) you need to improve the design of your course.

Even more significantly, designing your assessment instruments and revising your goals will (and should) influence how you design your course. Your assessment instruments should focus on assessing student learning of the skills you regard as most important, and you should be designing your course so that you and your students devote the greatest amount of time and effort to developing those skills.

By starting early, you also will create more and higher-quality assessment instruments and will have more opportunities to vet your instruments with colleagues. In an ideal world, you would write many more assessment items than you will need for any given offering of your course. By designing multiple sets of assessment instruments, you will gain greater insight into your objectives, increase the likelihood that your assessments are consistent over time, and generally feel less end-of-the-semester stress.

One final word about terminology to clarify our message. We have chosen to use the term "assessment instruments" and not "tests" or "tests and assignments" to communicate that we envision your assessment should expand beyond traditional pen-and-paper, timed, in-the-classroom tests. We use the term "assessment instrument" to broadly refer to any effort to determine the degree to which students are learning, and we envision you using your assessment results in at least three, very different ways.

The three uses of student assessment

The first use of assessment involves evaluating student performances on an aggregate level for the purpose of evaluating the effectiveness of your course. Your goal, in conducting this form of assessment, is to identify whether your students, on the whole, are learning what you want them to be learning. Generally speaking, educational experts have adopted Dr. Benjamin Bloom's 80-80 mastery learning standard as the hallmark of success: if 80% of your students have learned 80% of the skills, knowledge and values you have stated as your learning objectives, your course design is working. Chapter 10 provides a myriad of suggestions for conducting this type of assessment.

The second and third uses of student assessment are addressed in Chapters 7 and 10 and therefore only are touched on here. The second use of assessment is to help students learn more and learn better in your class and also learn to take control over their learning process, leading them to self-regulate their learning.

The third and final use of assessment is the one we regard as least significant in terms of its potential for improving the teaching and learning environment in your courses—evaluating student performances for the purpose of assigning grades. Because our goal is to help you become a more effective teacher, we are most interested in the two other uses of assessment.

Having decided what you want your students to learn, determined who your students are, and how you will determine whether your students are learning, you are now in a position to select a textbook. While it is possible to design your course and then select a textbook that will help you accomplish your design, we have found it helpful to select a textbook first. If you would feel more comfortable designing the course first, we encourage you to do so. There is no correct order with respect to these two tasks.

Finding the book of your dreams: sifting the morass to find the right textbooks for you

This discussion suggests some broad principles of textbook selection and provides a checklist you can use as you compare textbooks. We do not, however, recommend particular texts or a particular textbook series. Because we know what we are trying to accomplish in our classes, we have a very good idea as to what we need in a textbook, but we have no desire to impose our course goals on you.

Broad principles of textbook selection

No textbook will meet all of your needs. We certainly never have had that experience, and, together, we have used dozens of textbooks. In our experience, each book has strengths and weaknesses, and each will include cases or materials you love and omit cases and materials you wish had been included. Many law professors create supplemental materials. What you need is a book that you readily and easily can supplement.

Many law and other higher education teachers will suggest that you survey others who teach your subject or ask a colleague for textbook suggestions. We endorse that advice, but we do not endorse the idea of allowing those suggestions to make the decision for you. The fact that a book has been adopted by a colleague or by many law teachers says little about its efficacy as a tool for helping your students accomplish your course goals.

The core principle in selecting a textbook, therefore, is finding the book that best furthers as many of your course goals as possible. If, for example, one of your core goals is to have your students develop the ability to use the indeterminacy of doctrine and policy and develop creative and original legal arguments, your ideal textbook might pair cases that reach opposite results for conflicting factual and policy reasons and would include problems that allow students to use the cases to build arguments and other ideas for analyzing and resolving those problems.

Some points of textbook comparison we regard as significant

This short discussion is intended to provide you with tools for comparing your textbook alternatives. We start with a description of our ideal textbooks, and, then, to assist you in selecting from among the less-than-ideal choices available, we provide a casebook evaluation tool (Illustration 2-4) that you can use when you are comparing textbooks.

In general terms, an ideal textbook would:

- Be congruent with all of your course goals and learning objectives;
- Adopt cases that engage students, address significant issues, and are not unduly confusing;
- Have both large-scale law practice problems that require students to combine concepts and smaller-scale hypotheticals that allow students to practice applying the concepts as they are learning them;
- Introduce topics with overviews;
- Sequence concepts so that students don't start with the most difficult concepts;
- Include questions at all thinking levels;
- Include activities that engage students in adopting and reflecting on their adoption of learning strategies;
- Engage a wide variety of types of learners and not just the read-write learners;
- Provide a teacher's manual that facilitates all three types of assessment; and
- Provide a teacher's manual that suggests varied methods of instruction.

Illustration 2-4: Textbook Evaluation Tool

Author(s) Title Publisher	Congruence with Your Objectives	Case Selection and Sequencing	Quality and Quantity of Problems	Quality and Quantity of Questions	Teacher's Manual: Assessment Help	Teacher's Manual: Teaching Help
Text #1:						
Text #2:						
Text #3:						
Text #4:						
Text #5:						

Converting goals to results: designing the course to increase the likelihood students will learn what you want them to learn

Introduction

This discussion focuses broadly on what we see as the guiding principles for course design. Chapter 3 focuses on the design of individual class sessions. The current discussion focuses on designing individual learning units, e.g., personal jurisdiction, negligence, the parol evidence rule, and synthesizing those individual units into a comprehensive course design. The succeeding sections address how to effectively communicate your design in a syllabus and how to create an effective course webpage.

As you consider these suggestions in the light of your own course planning efforts, be sure to have your list of learning objectives and assessments by your side. The learning objectives and assessments will guide your course design decisions.

Designing learning units and synthesizing those units in an overall course design

To design your course at the level of the learning unit and then synthesize those units into a cohesive course, you need to start by dividing the subject area into at least five and as many as nine sub-categories, which we call "learning units." For doctrinal courses, nearly all of us divide our courses into learning units based solely on doctrinal categories. For example, in contracts, your learning units might be: formation, defenses, remedies, interpretation and the parol evidence rule, conditions and performance, and third party contract rights (third party beneficiaries, assignment and delegation).

We cannot encourage you enough to avoid over-prioritizing coverage. While we believe that coverage is important, we are convinced that law professors often sacrifice learning on the altar of coverage. Look over your list of teaching units. Try cutting all or a part of one or more units or consider giving students a choice of topics from which they can select.

In addition to developing a list of doctrinal categories, we encourage you to expand your learning units beyond doctrine. If your course goals include developing your students' ability to engage in problem-solving in your field, for example, if you expect your students to be able to analyze a problem in your field that implicates multiple sub-topics in that field, you need to reserve instructional time for problem-solving instruction. Likewise, you may want to include learning units that focus on other skill and professionalism goals you have for your students.

New learners in a field need learning experiences that allow them to practice applying each of the concepts and principles in isolation (more on this point in the section that immediately follows this introduction and in Chapter 3), *and* they need instruction in combining those concepts and principles and procedures to analyze complex problems that implicate multiple doctrinal areas. In an effort to save time or to cover as much doctrine as possible, you may be tempted to consider jettisoning either instruction focused on applying some of the concepts or problem-solving instruction. Both choices reflect a misunderstanding of what it means to be a novice law student.

Novices in a field experience each application of each concept as its own unique skill. When your students tell you that your course requires a vastly different form of analysis than one or more of your colleagues' courses, even though you know the differences are relatively minor, your students are communicating their struggle with transfer between your class and your colleagues' classes. In fact, students often struggle with transfer even within a single course. The fact that your students have learned to apply the law governing the intent requirement for intentional torts, for example, does not ensure they will know how to apply the actual malice standard to an alleged defamation of a public figure.

The problem-solving instruction is equally crucial. Law students struggle to see and understand the big picture. The essay answers of such students read as if the exam consisted of a series of one element mini-hypos, and the paragraphs in such students' essays are linked only by facile transitions such as "The first issue ...," "The next issue ...," etc. The students fail to demonstrate an understanding of the context in which each issue arises and the stakes of each issue, leaving the reader no sense that the student has been asked to analyze a single, complete problem.

Instruction specifically focused on building students' legal problem-solving skills *is* possible. Providing students with readings and other materials specifically directed to the problem-solving tasks in which they will be engaging (e.g., readings on conducting client interviews, analyzing law school hypotheticals, drafting pleadings, briefs, and contracts, etc.) gives them some guidance. Examples of how an expert would perform the skill, particularly in the form of a cognitive think-aloud (see Chapter 7), can be of enormous help, especially for students who prefer to learn through illustration. But creating multiple opportunities for practice and feedback in solving problems is most crucial. While we commend the practice, a single session, final exam "review" is insufficient, even if the professor engages in a discussion of the analysis of a problem or two. During their initial problem solving efforts, students need significant hints and cues. To maximize their skill development, you may need to point them in the right direction by, for example, suggesting the number of issues they should be identifying, by asking open-ended questions that help them develop difficult counter-arguments, and by suggesting combinations of cases they have read. As your students become more comfortable with the problem-solving process, however, you can gradually withdraw such support, a teaching tactic colorfully referred to as "fading the cue."

Designing each learning unit. In this section, we focus on general principles for organizing your students' work in your courses. This section discusses the relationship between in-class learning activities and students' out-of-class preparation, the kinds of class preparation activities you should be creating, and the types of learning activities for which your presence, as a live teacher, is essential.

We all have a basic sense that students' out-of-class work should consist of reviewing what they learned in the previous class session, synthesizing the new learning with what they learned in prior class sessions, and preparing for the next class session. Most of us, however, only explicitly develop assignments relating to preparing for subsequent class sessions. Moreover, most such requirements focus exclusively on textbook reading tasks.

In terms of class preparation assignments, the research strongly suggests that students learn more and learn it better when they read cases for the purpose of solving a problem. Students are more likely to give skills reading assignments the required attention if those assignments are situated in a simulated law practice problem. Consider how a practicing lawyer would use the principles and skills you seek to teach in each of your learning units and introduce each topic with an appropriate problem the students should be able to solve by the time they complete the unit. Your students will engage themselves in the reading because they will be looking for ideas they can use to solve the problem.

The research also suggests law students, like practicing lawyers, learn more from cases when they possess relevant prior knowledge *before* they begin reading specific cases. Consider providing or assigning introductions from secondary sources, for example, to each of your learning units. These introductions provide students with a schema for organizing what they learn from the assigned cases. If you do so, you will enhance your students' ability to remember the concepts and facilitate their development of issue spotting skills.

Moreover, students learn more when they engage in deep processing of the materials. By expanding your conception of the term "assignments" and therefore explicitly assigning tasks in addition to reading a list of assigned cases and statutes, you can engage your students in a wide spectrum of intellectually-challenging processing activities, including:

- developing a theory that explains the need for the doctrine;
- synthesizing the reading assignments with past assignments in this and other courses by creating a graphic organizer or by analyzing a multi-subject problem;
- comparing a case or series of cases to an existing or proposed statute;
- developing examples and non-examples of a concept addressed in their readings (an example has all essential features of a concept, such as all the elements of a battery, whereas a non-example is identical in all trivial respects, such as the parties, location of the incident, but lacks an essential feature of the concept, such as the touching element);
- analyzing hypotheticals that require the students to apply the new concepts;
- generating their own hypothetical problems;
- drafting a pleading or contract clause designed to address the problem; or
- drafting a proposed statute to address a problem raised by a line of cases.

Consequently, merely assigning a list of cases (or a range of page numbers from a casebook) is aiming too low. Illustration 2-5 suggests the relationships between these types of assignments and the higher level intellectual goals discussed in the section on course goals and learning objectives. It also provides examples of each of the types of processing assignments and explains the relationship between the assignment and the objective. Please note: because each of the assignments engages students in using a cognitive strategy to process what they are learning, you should also consider each of the activities as directed at developing students' learning skills. You can make such an exercise even more explicitly a learning strategy exercise by also asking students to compare the usefulness of engaging in one activity to the usefulness of other assigned activities and reflecting on why in light of what they know about their learning processes and preferences.

> **Thinking exercise:** As you look over Illustration 2-5, try to imagine what a similar assignment in one of your courses might look like.

To maximize your students' learning experience, consider creating learning experiences that engage students in a wide variety of the activities described and exemplified in Illustration 2-5. This approach will help you better address the variety of learning styles represented by your student population.

Illustration 2-5: Deep Processing Activities and Higher Level Intellectual Learning Objectives

Learning Activity	Example	Type of Learning Objective
Required Theory Development	Be prepared to explain the policy trade-offs implicit in granting or denying relief for unilateral mistake.	Principle learning (because students are constructing an understanding as to the whys underlying the rules which will help them be able to apply the rules)
Synthesizing new cases with prior cases and other courses by creating a graphic organizer	Create a mind map depicting how negligence per se fits within the larger body of negligence doctrine.	Concept learning (because students are developing an understanding of how concepts fit together, which will help them be able to spot issues)
Comparing cases and statutes	Evaluate whether a proposed criminal code section solves the problem addressed in the assigned case.	Principle learning (because students are applying the proposed rule to the problem)
Developing examples and non-examples	Generate two original examples of common law burglaries and two non-examples (the non-examples should have facts identical to the examples in all non-critical respects).	Principle learning (because students must understand how to apply the principle to be able to generate examples and non-examples)
Analyzing practice hypos	Prepare a written analysis of the following adverse possession hypos.	Principle learning (because the students are practicing applying the principle but not in the context of analyzing any related issues)
Generating debatable hypotheticals	Create a hypothetical for which the application of intentional infliction of emotional distress doctrine would be unclear.	Principle learning (because students must really understand the application of the principle to generate a debatable hypo)
Drafting pleadings or contract terms	Create a contract clause that unquestionably making getting a home loan an express condition of purchasing a home.	Problem solving (because the student is engaged in using what she has learned to solve a practice-oriented problem)
Drafting a proposed statute to resolve a doctrinal problem	Revise section ____ of the ____ code to eliminate the defendant's argument in the _____ case.	Problem solving (because the student is engaged in using what she has learned to solve a practice-oriented problem)

If you choose to have your students engage in any class preparation activities, whether those assignments include activities similar to those described in Illustration 2-5 or just ask your students to read cases and statutes, your classroom activities should be linked to and depend on students' preparation efforts. Thus, if your students prepare for class by drafting a proposed statute, their classroom experience should engage them in discussing and evaluating such solutions in light of the principles they learned by reading other assigned materials.

Thinking through the kinds of activities in which you want your students to engage is crucial because you want to be sure that you maximize your classroom time with students. Educational experts frequently talk in terms of selecting the best medium for delivering a particular aspect of students' learning. Available instructional media include: texts, live teachers, computer programs—such as CALI exercises—and websites, video and podcasts, and small group experiences. Live teachers are, by far, the most expensive medium of instruction. In comparison to computer programs and websites, live teachers are less able to individualize instruction for each student in each single moment. They also are generally less consistent in terms of how they present information and teach skills. However, live teachers, in comparison to all alternative media of instruction, are uniquely flexible and adaptable and uniquely possess empathy. Live teachers can be the best instructional medium for inspiring learners and possess the unique ability to teach by functioning as role models.

Consequently, you need to be making conscious decisions about the aspects of your teaching that require your physical presence and the aspects you can move to another instructional medium. You should consider, among other possibilities, whether you can transmit some information by video or podcast. For example, if you were to decide your students need to know things about the construction contracting process to understand some of the major contract law cases or information about banking for a payment systems course, you could save classroom time by presenting this instruction via a podcast and offering it to students on your course webpage. This approach has the extra benefit of respecting the fact that some of your students will know this knowledge based on their life experiences and past jobs.

You may also consider whether the time you spend on announcements, assignments and syllabus adjustments is an optimal use of your extremely limited time with students. Announcements, assignments and syllabus revisions easily can be delivered via e-mail or using the announcements function on your course webpage. You may choose to create an FAQ (frequently asked questions) page of your course webpage and to use e-mail messages to address common areas of student confusion.

Finally, you may be able to move some assessment activities outside the classroom. Consider asking students to take quizzes online or at home and to submit classroom assessment responses by email.

Thinking exercise: What aspects of a course you currently teach require your live presence? What aspects of your teaching can you move outside the classroom? How will you deliver such outside-the-classroom instruction?

Synthesizing the learning units in a course design. Having decided how you will structure each individual learning unit, consider how you will combine the units to create a course design. There are a number of considerations that warrant attention as you begin this synthesis process.

First, consider how best to sequence your learning units and, within each learning unit, consider how best to sequence students' progress through that unit. It may be tempting to adopt the sequence used by the author of the casebook you have selected. Don't assume the author of your casebook knows best. Students prosper most when their learning experiences are challenging but not overwhelming. In particular, strive for a progression from relatively easier learning units to relatively harder learning units and, within each unit, from easier topics to more challenging topics. By designing your course with a goal of getting your students to experience success right from the beginning, you increase the likelihood students will have the self-efficacy they need to persist when they encounter the more difficult concepts.

We are not suggesting that you alter some of the learning units in your course to make them easier than they are. In fact, even students' first learning unit in your course should be challenging. We are suggesting you account for the fact that novices are encouraged by early successes and can be discouraged by early failures. For example, if you teach civil procedure as a first semester course, it is worth considering whether you should start with personal jurisdiction and, within personal jurisdiction, it is worth considering whether to start with a case as challenging as *Pennoyer v. Neff*, 95 U.S. 714 (1877).

It is equally important to gradually increase the difficulty of the intellectual challenge in your course. Give students a sense of progression and growth. If your students perceive the material as too easy or repetitive, they are likely to disengage. For example, if you are teaching statutory construction skills, the statutes with which your students work at the end of the semester should be the most challenging statutes. By the end of the semester, students should be interpreting the statutes on their own and for a purpose analogous to one that would be assigned a practicing attorney.

Sequencing also is a matter of prioritizing. Many law professors ignore the issue of prioritizing and teach their courses as if the most important topics are the ones with which their courses start and the least important are those with which they end their courses. For generations, law students—and other higher education students—have complained about the end-of-the-semester rush; the professor abandons all semblance of active learning, uses lecture format exclusively, and moves through the materials like a tank going through wet paper. On the one hand, using this teaching method suggests the materials are relatively unimportant; on the other hand, the desperate nature of this choice suggests the students are receiving essential instruction without which they cannot survive as lawyers.

Second, consider the burden you are imposing on the students, their competing obligations in their other courses, and the importance of school-life balance for your students.

Third, make sure you consciously sequence your course for variety. As we explained in Chapter 1, variety allows us to retain our students' attention, and their attention is a foundational prerequisite to their learning. The law practice problems should engage students in the wide spectrum of activities in which lawyers engage, including arguing, evaluating, reading, drafting, re-writing, negotiating, communicating with others (clients, colleagues, other lawyers, judges), interviewing, planning, and presenting. Your expectations for class participation also should have variety in terms of both the intellectual skills the assignments implicate and in terms of the type of activity. Students' experiences within any given class session should vary (see Chapter 3), as should their experiences between classes.

Finally, carefully plan how you will begin and end your course. At the beginning of a course, students are most eager to learn your expectations (see "Writing your syllabus" below). They also hope you will provide a few other things: (1) context—how what they learn in your course fits in with what they already have learned and what they will learn in other courses and the relationship between what they will learn in your course and their future practice of law; (2) inspiration—what is exciting about your course topic; and (3) reassurance—you know what you are doing, want them to learn, and are trustworthy. You can provide context by showing them the kinds of problems they will be able to solve by the end of your course and helping them to identify how they will use what they have learned in your course in practice. For example, in Mike's second semester contracts class, he gives students a contract on the first day of class and explains his goal that the students develop the ability to review such a contract, recognize and understand the implications of the various types of contract clauses the students will study (e.g., liquidated damages clauses, express and constructive conditions, merger clauses, time is of the essence clauses, force majeure clauses), and identify potential ambiguities.

You can share what is exciting about your course by introducing students to the big questions and big problems in your field. For example, in a torts class, you can start the course with a hypothetical involving a person who became distraught after hearing a nasty insult and use the discussion of whether to grant relief as a springboard for introducing the goals and policy trade-offs in the torts field. In a civil procedure class, you might start with a professionalism problem raising the conflicts among what you legally can do, a client's professed strategic goals, the high cost of litigation, especially for non-corporate actors, and the lawyer's role as an officer of the court.

You can convince students you know what you are doing by your level of preparation, by your organization of the course, by your explanation of the relationship between your course goals and your syllabus, and by the overall clarity of your syllabus. By adopting recurring practices, such as having a rolling outline on a whiteboard, chalkboard, or slide, you can communicate the overarching structure of the course and give students a constant sense of where in the course they are, where they are headed, and your plans for making sure they get from where they are to where they need to be.

A well-designed course ending provides students with opportunities to recall and reflect on how much they have learned, guides students to consider how they will use what they have learned in the future, and solicits ideas for improving the course in the future.

Writing your syllabus

Introduction

Your syllabus can be a list of assignments. But it also can be culture-making. In many instances, our first interaction with our students occurs via the course syllabus. These pages have the potential to engage students, to inspire their confidence and interest in you and your subject, to communicate your investment in their success, to display your professionalism as a teacher, to demonstrate your skill in planning the course, and to establish high expectations in terms of the effort you want them to put into your course, and their likelihood of succeeding in learning what you want them to learn. Your syllabus also can leave students cold or, worse yet, discouraged, disinterested, disengaged, anxious, confused, and hostile. In other words, your syllabus likely will influence whether your new students anticipate that your class will be a healthy and productive learning environment.

Syllabus construction is mostly a matter of science and careful decision-making, but it is not completely artless. It is a matter of science because there are certain topics you should address in your syllabus, and there are some best practices for addressing those topics. At the same time, your syllabus communicates a lot about you: based on your syllabus, your students will draw inferences about who you are and how you will teach. They will look for clues as to whether you are, among other things, professional, flexible, creative, open-minded, demanding, passionate, organized, funny, caring, and accessible.

This discussion has two sections. The first section explores the topics you should address in your syllabus and articulates our views on trade-offs in establishing course policies. We do not provide "model policies" because we see the proper resolution of the trade-offs as indeterminate. The second section focuses on what we see as the more important goals of syllabus construction: communicating a tone of excitement, engagement, and passion; conveying high expectations; establishing your view of student learning; and giving students a role in structuring their own learning process.

What topics should be addressed in your syllabus?

Your syllabus serves as a contract between you and the students. It defines your relationship, establishes your respective rights, and creates your respective responsibilities. As with any contract, problems arise if the obligations it describes are expressed ambiguously or if either party asserts rules or expectations not articulated in the document. Consequently, make sure you have a colleague read your syllabus before you distribute it to your students.

Syllabi should provide the basic information students need and should address all the issues that reasonably might arise in the class, including:

- the name of and contact information for the teacher;
- policies about office hours, appointments, and e-mails;
- the name of the course, the required texts, and a description of the course;
- attendance and timely arrival for class;
- course goals, your teaching philosophy, and teaching methods;
- expectations for class preparation and other classroom conduct;
- schedule of class meetings, readings, projects, and other assignments;
- grading, late assignments, and failures to complete assigned projects;
- name and pronoun identifiers;
- campus resources for basic needs; and
- plagiarism, artificial intelligence policies, and/or any other forms of academic misconduct that may arise in your class.

If you have a course webpage, your syllabus should provide information about accessing it and your policies for using it.

Many institutions mandate the inclusion of certain additional information in syllabi, such as the institution's mission statement, information about disability accommodations, general information about academic misconduct, and other such matters. Check with your institution.

At the outset it is useful to consider the degree to which you wish to give yourself leeway to modify policies stated in your syllabus. For example, you may decide to devote an extra class session to a topic because the students are struggling, or you may choose to modify the form or content of your final examination. If you wish to retain the ability to modify your course policies, be sure your syllabus communicates you can do so, e.g., "The format of the final exam is subject to change."

You should also consider the degree to which you adopt strict rules and retain the discretion to modify their application to extraordinary circumstances or adopt less onerous rules and have to get tough if students take advantage. The former approach, which many have likened to defensive driving, protects you against later challenges by outlier students who are unprofessional or disrespectful. It allows you to resort to objective principles and helps you avoid claims of bias. The latter approach communicates confidence in your ability to manage the class and to address outlier problems by directly confronting such students about their behavior.

A few less critical points are worth considering. First, if you were to adopt all of the suggestions below, your syllabus would be quite long and daunting. You make an important trade-off if you choose completeness. Some students may be less likely to read significant portions of a very long syllabus; others may draw the inference that you must be a particularly officious professor. Second, there are some things you can do to offset these effects. Some experts recommend splitting off the assignments from the rest of the syllabus. Others try to create an incentive for students to study their syllabi by including a few questions regarding course policies on students' first quiz and disclosing their plans to do so in advance.

The remainder of this discussion addresses our suggestions for each of the topics listed above.

The name of and contact information for the teacher, and policies about office hours, appointments and emails. Generally, the contact information includes the teacher's name, office hours, office location, telephone number and email address. Many law teachers choose to include a statement about the frequency with which the teacher will check email and respond to student messages and expectations for student responsiveness to emails from the teacher.

This section of the syllabus also should identify the instructor's preferred method of contact, should communicate office hours (if the teacher holds office hours), and should explain what students need to do if they wish to make an appointment with the teacher.

The name of the course, the required texts and a description of the course. Include the name of the course, the titles and the required editions of texts. It is also common to include a description of the course. Some teachers lift the description right from their law school's catalog. We suggest you instead try to capture what you find exciting about the course. Consider describing how the course relates to students' future law practice and to their current lives. This approach is more likely to bring the course to life for students whereas a lifted catalog description adds little value.

Course goals, statement of your teaching philosophy and teaching and learning methods. Although students consider a section on course goals an important syllabus component, professors tend to underestimate the value of this information. The course goals section allows students to self-evaluate their progress in your course. Moreover, making those goals explicit communicates that students have an important role in meeting those goals. You may want to explicitly communicate your belief that attaining the course goals is a collaborative student-teacher venture.

The description of your teaching philosophy and the teaching and learning methods, along with your assignments, lets students know how they will achieve the course goals. We think it's helpful to use the label "learning philosophy" or "teaching and learning philosophy," and to emphasize that you regard teaching methods as effective only if they produce learning. We also emphasize the central role of active learning.

The link among the goals, the assignments (see below), your teaching and learning philosophy, and your teaching methods should be transparent, allowing students to recognize the connection between what you are asking of your students and what the students should be learning. This link gives students a sense that you know what you are doing, believe in yourself, and believe in them.

Attendance and timely arrival for class. We think it's valuable that you address both issues in your syllabus, but we have no opinion as to a right set of policies. We have found that inspiring students to want to be on time for class and to attend class is the most effective way to achieve both goals. Chapters 3–8 describe our ideas about engaging students. That said, stating policies that limit absenteeism and tardiness will minimize your time on these issues and make it simpler to deal with students who refuse to attend your class or to show up on time.

Expectations for class preparation and other classroom conduct. As a preliminary matter, we find it useful to communicate expectations of ourselves as well as expectations for our students. This approach combats the top-down, excessively and obsessively hierarchical law professor-law student dynamic and communicates your commitment to doing right by your students.

It also is helpful to frame your class preparation expectations in terms that make explicit that your expectations are no different than those of legal employers. We also find it useful to address what students should do if, for some reason, they are unable to be prepared for class; we suggest you analogize the students' obligations in such circumstances to what lawyers must do when they are unable to complete a law practice task on time.

Finally, even though most law schools' honor codes include statements about non-discrimination and many address issues of tolerance and respect, you may find it useful to communicate those policies and to directly address respect for others' ideas and differences, not only differences in terms of culture, life experiences, race and ethnicity but differences in terms of learning style preferences. Some students, particularly extroverts, believe they learn best by wholly engaging themselves in class discussions; at some law schools, such students are labeled "gunners" and are thereby discouraged from learning according to their preferred method.

Schedule of assignments. Students want specific details about when and how the teacher expects them to fulfill their scholastic duties. Your schedule should include all assignments and projects, the dates they are due, and the dates of any exams. Organize these elements by topic rather than by chapter or page numbers. In other words, slot reading assignments addressing promissory estoppel under a heading labeled "promissory estoppel." Doing so helps reinforce the connection between the assignment and the course goals and provides useful context for students' efforts to understand the cases, statutes, and other course materials.

Of course, your schedule is only useful to students if it is reliable. At the same time, both students and teachers prefer the teacher retain some discretion to modify the assignments after the semester begins. An easy way to retain this flexibility is by including a disclaimer at the beginning of this section of your syllabus that states "To maximize student learning in this class, I may need to adjust the assignments. I promise to give you at least one week's notice before implementing any such change." Requiring one week's notice prior to a change respects students' need to manage their coursework and maintains students' overall sense that your schedule is reliable without restricting your flexibility. Another approach is to give out assignments for three-to-four weeks at a time. This approach gives you even greater flexibility.

Grading system. For many law students, the grading section of the syllabus is the most important section. The combination of their past educational successes and the mythology and fact of law school grading practices leaves students very concerned about how they will be graded. Students want to know what weight will be placed on the various graded activities in the course and whether other factors such as class participation and course webpage contributions will be factored into their grades. It is particularly useful to provide students with guidance about the standards by which you will be evaluating their work. Such grading rubrics (see Chapter 10 for additional information) help eliminate confusion and concerns over the accuracy or fairness of grading. You can alternatively or additionally distribute your rubrics when you distribute your assignments. If your students will be handing in work, make sure you also communicate policies addressing what happens if students hand in assignments late or not at all.

Tone, high expectations, communicating your attitude about student learning, giving students a role in constructing your syllabus

As important as each of the above suggestions is, none trumps the suggestions in this section. In fact, if you successfully implement the recommendations discussed below, your students will be very likely to forgive any errors you make in omitting information they want or in being overly inclusive and creating a treatise of a syllabus.

Before you start writing any of the above sections, think carefully about the overarching messages you wish to communicate to your students. Whether you want them to do so or not, students will draw inferences about who you are, what you value, what you think of your students, and how you will teach based solely on what you say in your syllabus and the tone with which you say it. Carefully consider what message(s) you wish to communicate in your syllabus.

> **Thinking exercise:** What do you want your students to know about you and your course from reading your syllabus?

At the most general level, your tone sends messages about who you are and how you will teach the class. Note, for example, our suggested language for communicating the possibility of changes to the schedule of assignments, "To maximize student learning in this class, I may need to adjust the assignments. I promise to give you at least one week's notice before implementing any such change." This language communicates that teachers treat student learning as the highest ethic in the class, see themselves as part of a community to which they owe obligations, and have respect for the impact of his decisions on their students. You also may find it helpful to express humility and to include some self-deprecating humor in your syllabus. For example, in explaining your class preparation requirements, you might state, "I do not treat incorrect responses to my questions or problems as irrefutable evidence of a lack of preparation. Smart, effective, well-prepared lawyers err, and I certainly will make errors in teaching this class."

The research on teacher expectations suggests the most effective teachers demand a lot from their students, communicate confidence in their ability to teach, and express confidence in their students' ability to learn. Thus, your section on teaching methods might communicate your knowledge of the various teaching techniques you plan to deploy and explain that you are doing so to meet the learning needs of a wide variety of learners. Likewise, consider writing your section on course goals as if you have no doubt the students will learn. Finally, your schedule of assignments can manifest your confidence in students' learning by making explicit the relationship between the assignments, the classroom activities and the course goals; referring to the goals in shorthand next to class sessions in which the students will be introduced to the skills, practice the skills, or demonstrate mastery sends the right message. Explicit references to your sequencing choices also can help communicate your confidence in yourself and the students.

Studies of effective teachers also suggest that teacher enthusiasm plays an important role in student learning. Show your enthusiasm for your subject in your syllabus. Your enthusiasm is probably best communicated by how you describe the course. Consider showing that enthusiasm by expressing excitement about the area of law, about the importance of the policy questions the class will be unpacking, about how the students will use what they are learning in your class, or about the cases they will be reading.

Your explanation about your teaching philosophy can offer particular insights into how you will teach your class. Be explicit about why you do what you do. If you place great emphasis on authentic, law practice problems, explain that you believe students learn better and retain their learning more when their teachers ask them to use what they have learned to solve the kinds of problems lawyers in the field must be able to solve. If it's important to you that your students become independent, self-directed learners, tell them so.

Because law students are adult learners (for the most part), one of the best things you can do to enhance their learning experience is to *share* your power to establish course policies. By ceding some power to students, you convey important messages about your sense of the students' competence, autonomy, and abilities. You also show that you have faith in and respect for them and that you have confidence in your own ability to synthesize their needs and the course goals.

With first-semester students, who know very little about the law school learning process, sharing power may involve no more than just letting the students know why you have designed the course the way you have designed it. For example, if you choose to provide multiple assessments and other opportunities for feedback, you may quickly discover that many of your colleagues do not. Your syllabus can explain that you have done so because you are passionate about and committed to their development as lawyers and concerned about making your grading as fair and accurate as possible. Similarly, if you choose to supplement traditional law school Socratic-style teaching with other teaching methods, explain that you are doing so to meet the widest possible variety of student learning style preferences and because you believe active learning experiences produce deeper learning than passive (lecture) or vicarious (law school semi-Socratic) teaching methods.

In later semesters, consider ways you can engage your students in making decisions about course policies and assignments. The easiest facet of your syllabus for sharing control is course coverage. Most law teachers find it impossible to cover all possible topics within a subject area. We emphasize deep learning of the topics we do cover rather than covering all topics within the subjects we teach. If you are inclined to do so, select those topics you regard as essential and then let your students select from among the remaining topics. All of us also have found it easy to allow students to articulate their expectations of us as teachers and to suggest teaching methods they would like us to include in our repertoire. Because we hold variety as an ethic in our teaching and therefore use a wide variety of teaching methods and have very high expectations for ourselves, the students have yet to suggest expectations or teaching methods we were not already planning to use.

You can also ask students to develop or contribute to your list of student expectations and for input into your grading scheme. Because we also greatly value multiple assessments and criterion-referenced grading (see Chapter 10), we do not leave the grading scheme entirely to the students but instead communicate that the scheme must incorporate the best practices because we see them as essential.

If you are inclined to give your students input into your syllabus construction process, we suggest you start small. For some professors, the uncertainty of jumping off this particular bridge proves too uncomfortable, and they regret ceding so much control.

Course web page design

We use course web pages. The particular medium, the learning management system you use, such as Canvas, Blackboard, TWEN, or your law school's own designated platform, is not the key to success. A webpage is useful or useless to students based on the quality of its content.

At the simplest level, course webpages provide a mechanism for an easy and environmentally-conscious transmittal of information. Most simply, the ability to easily contact an entire class of students by email improves communication. The course webpage can be the portal through which students access electronic versions of course materials such as cases, statutes, articles, handouts, video lectures, and podcasts.

Course webpages, however, also provide a mechanism for transmitting student learning tools. For example, a course webpage is a good tool for communicating lesson-by-lesson learning objectives, answers to frequently-asked questions, and studying suggestions. All these tools have the potential to benefit some students (and to be ignored by others). Many will look at these resources only if and when they are struggling in your course.

Your course webpage can also make it easy for you to provide other supplemental learning tools. Uploading partially-completed outlines and graphic organizers, including mindmaps, hierarchy charts, and flowcharts, to your course webpage also can benefit your students. Of course, requiring, encouraging, or even rewarding students who develop and post their own outlines and graphic organizers to your course webpage is an even better practice. These tools help students develop their schemata for retaining their new learning and help students attempt and evaluate these powerful learning strategies.

You also can use your course webpage to facilitate your efforts to implement the cooperative learning ideas addressed in Chapter 6 of this book. For example, you can create separate discussion boards for each of the groups you have created for your class. These discussion boards can make it easier for your students to collaborate, particularly those who commute to your law school or who work.

The testing functions available on most course webpages are particularly powerful learning tools. Many law professors provide students with few opportunities to practice the skills they are expected to display on their examinations or to obtain corrective feedback on their practice efforts. In fact, for many law students, the only concrete feedback they receive is their final exam, when it is too late for the students to learn from their mistakes. Efforts to solve this problem, however, are often burdensome on instructors; many law professors regard the task of evaluating and commenting on 120 students' practice examinations even twice over the course of a semester as prohibitively burdensome. Course webpages provide possible solutions.

While multiple choice and short answer practice questions may not address the high level intellectual skills implicated on many law school examinations, such questions do provide students with useful signposts along the way and can supplement your efforts to evaluate your students for the purpose of assigning grades. Weekly 10-question multiple choice quizzes usefully can supplement the teaching and learning process. In fact, well-drafted multiple choice questions can test not only knowledge but also a wider range of legal analysis skills, including issue spotting skills, argument evaluation skills, and legal reasoning skills.

The testing software's feedback function allows you to direct students' efforts at re-learning the material if they answer a question incorrectly. You can suggest cases the students may want to re-read, additional cases exploring the issues, and excerpts from law review articles.

Most importantly, student results on such quizzes can serve as a tool for you to evaluate the effectiveness of your teaching and course design. You can discover what your students have learned and have not learned and develop new learning experiences aimed at remediating unanticipated gaps in your students' understanding.

Course webpages also can allow you to offer students opportunities to write practice essays without dramatically overburdening yourself. In addition to the cooperative learning group practice exam experience described below, you can ask small groups of students to post their analyses of hypos and ask other peers to comment on the essays. You can chime in if the students' peer commenting is insufficient. This approach benefits the authors of the answers, the commenting students, and the rest of the class. The authors get the benefit of practice and feedback, and the rest of the class, especially those that try to answer the hypos themselves, get vicarious feedback. But the peer commentators, who need to understand the problem well enough to provide productive feedback, often develop even the deepest understandings, and, by being forced to identify flaws in their peers' papers, they become better able to see similar errors in their own work.

Perhaps the most powerful tools made available by course webpages are the discussion boards. Discussion boards allow students freely to ask questions, provide help, explore ideas, and discuss their learning experiences with each other. This tool allows you to move instruction outside the classroom and, thereby, free up classroom time for activities for which your physical presence is essential. Such discussions also allow you to identify those students who are able to generate wonderful and useful insights in writing but for whom the large classroom experience is anathema. In fact, some experts hypothesize that students who are members of traditionally-disenfranchised groups may be especially well-represented among those who shine on a course webpage.

Finally, course webpages also provide a mechanism for providing students with links to helpful learning resources, such as links to CALI exercises, to law school learning resources, and to helpful cases and law review articles.

Evaluate the design and plan for the future

Having designed the course, created a syllabus and set up a course webpage, the next logical step, of course, would be to teach the course. If you have adopted the recommendations of this book, your course design has embedded multiple assessments throughout so that, during the semester, you are gathering data about how well your students are learning and, where possible, making appropriate adjustments in the design of your course.

Ideally, the goal in course evaluation and redesign is to be systematic, reflective, and continuous. Your approach is systematic to the extent that the information you strive to develop from your efforts at assessing your students' learning covers the breadth and depth of skills, knowledge, and values you teach and evaluates student learning up and down the hierarchy of learning objectives. No one in legal education has managed to be perfectly systematic. Strive for the best approximation, and use all of the information available to you. After you have finished reviewing your students' exams for the purpose of assigning grades, look at them for the purpose of identifying patterns of error. Consider adding just 2–3 multiple choice questions each class offering and keep track of your students' aggregate results.

Your evaluation process is reflective if you devote time and effort to reflecting in some written fashion, such as a teaching journal, on each class session after it ends and reflect on the results of your efforts at assessment. Even five minutes of writing can serve as a crucial resource when you go back and consider how you can improve the design of your course. Teaching journals are described in detail in Chapter 13.

Finally, the word "continuous" conveys that your efforts should continue throughout the semester and each time you teach your course. The idea is analogous to the continuous improvement model in business planning or the self-regulated learning cycle described in Chapter 1. In both contexts, data is used to inform future planning, and each implementation is treated as an opportunity to improve.

Checklist for course design process

Illustration 2-6 is a checklist you can use as you work through the course design process.

Illustration 2-6: Course Design Checklist

- ❑ **Determine what you want students to know, value, and be able to do**
- ❑ **Figure out who your students are**
- ❑ **Decide how you will assess students and draft assessments**
- ❑ **Choose texts**
- ❑ **Design each part of the course**
- ❑ **Design the course as a whole**
- ❑ **Create a syllabus that**
    - ❑ Provides the basic information students need and addresses all the issues that reasonably might arise in the class;
    - ❑ Engages students;
    - ❑ Communicates high expectations;
    - ❑ Includes challenging and appropriate reading and problem-solving assignments;
    - ❑ Paces the course carefully to make sure the course has an engaging opening and an effective closing and avoids the end-of-semester rush; and
    - ❑ Devotes instructional time to problem-solving instruction and experiences.
- ❑ **Create a course webpage (if you have decided to have one)**
- ❑ **Implement your design**
- ❑ **Evaluate your design**

Designing the Course—Resources

These two books contain extensive treatments of instructional design principles appropriate for all levels of education, from elementary school to graduate school and beyond.

- Patricia L. Smith & Tillman J. Ragan, Instructional Design (3d. ed. 2005).
- Walter Dick, Lou Carey, James O. Carey, The Systematic Design of Instruction (6th ed. 2005).

These two articles address the application of instructional design to law teaching.

- Michael Hunter Schwartz, *Teaching Law by Design: How Learning Theory and Instructional Design Can Inform and Reform Legal Education*, 38 San Diego L. Rev. 347 (2001).
- Gerald F. Hess. *Value of Variety: An Organizing Principle to Enhance Teaching and Learning*, 3 Elon L. Rev 65 (2011).

Chapter 3

Designing Each Class Session

Planning an individual class session is pretty straightforward for many law teachers. They decide how many pages in the casebook they will try to "cover" in the class session. The cases and problems in the text, along with a statutory supplement perhaps, make up the primary materials for the class. The class will begin with a brief lecture to remind students where they are in the course. The rest of the class typically consists of Socratic-style questions and answers and large group discussions on the assigned cases and problems. The teacher may decide to provide visual aids by writing on the board or projecting slides. The class will conclude with final comments from the teacher about the material covered that day and a reminder of the assignment for the next class, and, sometimes, unfortunately from our perspective, the teacher looks up, sees the class time has expired, and simply dismisses the class.

We believe that law school class sessions can lead to more significant student learning, and teacher satisfaction too, through a more intentional approach to class design. We recommend a five-step class design process, reflected in Illustration 3-1. The remainder of this chapter will explore each element in detail. However, a few preliminary comments may be helpful.

We recognize that our five-step process to class design is more elaborate than the class planning most law teachers currently do. But we intend our process to be useful, not intimidating or overwhelming. Many law teachers implicitly engage in some or all of the elements of our process. This chapter can help those teachers be a bit more intentional in their planning. In addition, our proposed process is not an all-or-nothing deal. Even if the entire five-step process is not for you, we believe that you can improve your teaching and your students' learning by expanding your class design efforts in any of the elements described below. Finally, we believe that our class design process applies to all forms of classes—face-to-face, on line synchronous and asynchronous, and blended (a combination of on line and face-to-face or a combination of synchronous and asynchronous online classes).

Illustration 3-1

Context

Although each class session can be a singular event for design purposes, it does not take place in isolation. Instead, each class occurs in a larger context, which includes important background aspects of the course, the students, and the teacher.

Course context

The nature of the course affects class design. Is the course required or elective? Law schools may mandate that certain concepts or skills be taught in required courses to prepare students for subsequent courses, the bar exam, or practice, and new ABA standards seem to require such coordination. Elective courses may provide faculty members with more options in choosing learning objectives, appropriate instructional activities, and accompanying materials.

Time and scheduling matter in class planning as well. Is the class in the day or evening? How many times does it meet each week? How long is the class? The number of learning objectives, the types of instructional activities, and the nature of the material may differ substantially in a class that meets during the day for 50 minutes, three times per week, compared to an evening class that occurs three hours once per week.

The class format affects design decisions as well. Will the class be face-to-face in a classroom, synchronous online, asynchronous online, or some combination of those formats? The instructional activities, materials, and feedback may vary significantly if the class takes place online asynchronously rather than face-to-face in a classroom.

The course classroom plays a role in class planning. Does the room configuration and seating lend itself to particular methods? For example, small group discussions are easier in flat classrooms with movable chairs. The room affects the choice of visual aid materials. Does the room contain a computer? White-, black-, or smart-board? Document projector? It may be necessary to move to a different room to accomplish particular goals and activities for a class session. For example, an oral argument exercise may be more effective in the moot courtroom.

Where the class fits in the life of the course has a significant influence on class design. Will the class be toward the beginning, middle, or end of the course? At the beginning or end of a unit? Will the class introduce new concepts or skills? Or will the class be designed to reinforce earlier learning or deepen analysis? What instructional activities did you use in the prior couple of classes? Is it time for variety in methods for the next class?

Student context

The needs and motivation of our students change as they progress through law school. For example, many first-semester, first-year students are interested in their courses and eager to learn, but most lack basic legal analysis skills and are uncertain about what they should be learning. Those characteristics of first-year students may lead us to design a class session with an objective that focuses explicitly on analytical skills (such as an element of case or statutory analysis), an exercise to practice the skill, and feedback to students on their progress in learning the skill. On the other hand, second-semester, third-year law students may display less interest in their courses but are eager to graduate, pass the bar exam, and begin their careers. Those attributes could lead us to design a class with an objective addressing content and skills that are directly relevant to law practice such as drafting a valid will or creating a discovery plan, and feedback designed to refine the skill.

Our students' prior learning can affect our design decisions. Have all of the students encountered a concept or skill in a prerequisite course? If so, we may decide to briefly refresh that learning and then move to more sophisticated aspects of the content or skill. Or, if some students are encountering the content for the first time, we may decide to incorporate background reading, a CALI exercise, or pre-class video lecture to bring them up to speed.

We know that our students learn in a variety of ways, such as through reading and individual reflection, discussion, hands-on experience, or collaboration with a small group of peers. Consequently, as we design class sessions, we can maximize student learning by incorporating a variety of methods. Even in a 50-minute class session, student engagement and attention will benefit from using more than one learning activity, and students will appreciate the effort.

As we plan our class sessions, we should be cognizant of other academic and life challenges our students are facing. If our students have a major assignment or exam immediately before our class, we can build a session with that reality in mind. For example, introducing complex new material through lecture or Socratic questioning may not be effective that day while a problem set that reinforces and deepens prior learning may succeed. Likewise, if we know that an individual student is struggling with a significant life event, we may decide not to call on that student for that day.

A final student context factor is the number of students in the course. We believe strongly that a variety of active learning methods and feedback are essential elements of successful class sessions regardless of the size of the class. Nevertheless, enrollment affects the types of objectives, instructional activities, material, and feedback that we select for a class. For example, in a small class, individual drafting assignments including individual feedback from the teacher are preferable, while in a large class, it may be best to have the same assignment completed by small groups of students.

Teacher context

The third context element is our own professional and personal situation. We all have strengths and weaknesses as teachers. We are more comfortable with some methods than others. Our level of understanding of content and competence with skills varies. And at different times during the course, we are overwhelmed with challenges in other aspects of our professional and personal lives. Classes that address content and skills with which we are comfortable may be appropriate for us to experiment with new learning and feedback activities. On the other hand, on days when we are on shakier ground or are struggling with other matters, we may choose to stick with the tried and true.

The course, students, and teacher are all important elements of the context in which we design classes. However, analyzing the context should consume very little of the teacher's planning time. All we need to do is spend a few minutes thinking about the context as we move along the rest of the class design process.

Class objectives

In Chapter 2, we showed how course goals and learning objectives should drive course design. Similarly, objectives are the foundation on which each class should be built. The objectives for each class share the three basic characteristics of course goals and learning objectives:

- Learner, rather than teacher, centered;
- Encompassing a broad range of professional knowledge, skills, and values; and
- Clear and concrete.

We discuss each of those characteristics below, after we address the question, "How many objectives are appropriate for a single class session?" The answer is, of course, "It depends." On what? All of the context issues we discussed above. In general, we favor depth over breadth, significant learning versus coverage. Consequently, one to three class objectives are generally appropriate for a one-hour class session.

Learner-centered

Articulating learner-centered goals represents a subtle, but fundamental, shift for many faculty members. For some teachers the objective for the class is to get through 20 pages of material, or to cover three cases, or to discuss four problems. Other teachers may say that their objective is to present an analytical framework for an aspect of the course or to demonstrate a skill, such as interviewing. All those objectives are teacher centered—they describe what the teacher hopes to accomplish in class.

Learner-centered objectives focus on what students will learn, rather than what will be covered or what the teacher will do in class. To shift the focus to student learning, we begin class objectives with the phrase "As a result of this class, students will be able to." Then, we complete each objective with the knowledge, skills, or values that students should learn in the class session. For example, "As a result of this class, students will be able to define the concept of 'specific jurisdiction' and each element of the applicable 'minimum contacts' analysis." Or, "After this class, students will be able to use six tools of statutory interpretation to analyze problems involving statutes and regulations."

Professional knowledge, skills, and values

Success as a legal professional rests on a set of knowledge, skills, and values. Consequently, our course goals and class objectives should focus on students learning and practicing knowledge, skills, and values related to the course. In three years of law school, we cannot effectively teach everything a lawyer needs to thrive in the profession. We must make choices. So, as we design a class session, we should focus on the critical knowledge, skills, or values for that day. The process of articulating class objectives helps discipline us to make those choices intentionally.

For most law school courses, knowledge includes legal doctrine, policy, and theory. An individual class session will focus on a small subset of the relevant knowledge for the course; for example, a course objective might state that students will be able to articulate the analytical framework for the Seventh Amendment right to a jury trial and the role that civil juries play in a democracy.

Most law teachers strive to teach thinking skills in their courses, such as case analysis, statutory analysis, problem solving, or critical thinking. Thinking skills are hierarchical. In the 1950s, Dr. Benjamin Bloom developed a taxonomy of educational objectives, which was revised in 2001 to improve its pedagogical accuracy. Illustration 3-2 summarizes the revised taxonomy and applies it to legal education.

The important point here is not to fit our objectives into boxes but to recognize that thinking skills applicable to law school and law practice vary in sophistication. Not every class session will include objectives at all levels of thinking. Students need to understand concepts before they can apply or evaluate them. Over the span of a course, however, we should include objectives in some class sessions that reach the most complex levels of thinking.

In most courses, relevant skills should go beyond thinking skills to include other skills lawyers need to succeed in practice. For example, the MacCrate Report lists ten "Fundamental Lawyering Skills": problem solving, legal analysis and reasoning, legal research, fact investigation, oral and written communication, counseling, negotiation, litigation and alternative dispute resolution, organization and management of legal work, and recognizing and resolving ethical dilemmas.

A sophisticated class objective in a pretrial litigation course could be "As a result of this class, students will be able to create a cost effective fact investigation plan for a hypothetical lawsuit using the formal discovery devices under the Federal Rules of Civil Procedure and informal investigation methods."

Professional attributes and values are perhaps the most overlooked aspect of traditional legal education. Yet lawyers consistently identify a number of aspects of professionalism as among the most important to success in law practice, including honesty, integrity, reliability, responsibility, judgment, diligence, grit, perseverance, tolerance, self-motivation, empathy, and respect for clients, lawyers, judges, and staff. We should look for opportunities to include values in our class objectives. For example, a trial advocacy course could include an objective that "Students will be able to give five examples of respectful and disrespectful behavior toward opposing counsel in a trial."

Illustration 3-2: Levels of Thinking Skills

Level of thinking	Taxonomy for teaching and learning	Law school application
Higher level	6. ***Create***—reorganize elements or ideas to create a new pattern or structure	Students make arguments for the extension or reversal of existing law
	5. ***Evaluate***—judge based on a set of criteria	Students use the IRAC method to respond to an essay question; students evaluate the relative strengths of different causes of action
	4. ***Analyze***—break ideas into component parts to understand organizational scheme	Students outline the law and policy of perfecting security interests
	3. ***Apply***—use new learning to solve problems or complete tasks	Students use electronic research to find authority relevant to a hypothetical
	2. ***Understand***—explain concepts in own words	Students are able to define proximate cause or give examples of illusory promises
Lower level	1. ***Remember***—retrieve knowledge from long-term memory	Students can identify the elements of negligence or the defenses to first-degree murder

Thinking exercise: In the context of a course that you teach, identify one item that would be appropriate to address in a class session or sessions for each of the following categories:

- Legal doctrine
- Legal theory
- Low-level thinking skill
- High-level thinking skill
- Lawyering skill other than legal analysis or problem solving
- Professional value.

Illustration 3-3: Action Verbs for Concrete Class Objectives

Remember	Understand	Apply	Analyze	Evaluate	Create
choose	associate	apply	analyze	appraise	assemble
define	convert	complete	arrange	assess	compose
describe	defend	compute	break down	compare	construct
identify	discuss	demonstrate	categorize	conclude	create
label	distinguish	discover	classify	contrast	design
list	estimate	divide	develop	criticize	generate
match	explain	examine	diagram	critique	improve
quote	extend	interpret	differentiate	evaluate	invent
recall	extrapolate	modify	discriminate	grade	plan
recognize	generalize	operate	illustrate	interpret	predict
repeat	give examples	prepare	relate	judge	prepare
reproduce	infer	produce	research	justify	revise
select	paraphrase	solve	separate	measure	show
state	summarize	use	use	rank	write

Clear and concrete

The key to clear and concrete class objectives is to focus on observable student behavior. We can't observe students "understanding" a concept or "appreciating" a value. We can observe students' ability to set out the analytical framework for an area of law, students' identification of legal issues in a fact pattern, or students' demonstration of respect for other students in the classroom. To help you generate concrete objectives, Illustration 3-3 contains a list of action verbs applicable to various levels of thinking according to Bloom's taxonomy of educational objectives.

There is nothing magic about this list of verbs. Other verbs may more accurately capture the type of student learning that you seek. And many of the verbs could fit in more than one category. Although we believe deeply in the importance of articulating class objectives, we are not dogmatic about their precise form. The critical point is that for each class we ask ourselves "What are the essentials in terms of knowledge, skills, or values that the students should have when they leave this class session?" The answers to that question are the heart of our class objectives for the class. And those answers should drive our design of instructional activities, feedback, and materials.

Instructional activities

We chose to label this aspect of class design "instructional activities" rather than "teaching methods" or "learning activities" because effective class planning requires attention to both what we will do during the class and what our students will do. For design purposes, we divide the class into three parts: (1) opening—the first one to five minutes; (2) body—the bulk of the class period; and (3) closing—the final one to five minutes.

Opening

The first few minutes of a class can be the most valuable. Our opening can grab attention, motivate, communicate objectives, and build a bridge to previous learning. We may not attempt to accomplish all those items in the first few minutes, but each is worthy of our consideration in class planning.

Thinking exercise: Reflect on the last several class sessions you have taught. What happened in the first few minutes of those classes? Keep track of what happens in the first few minutes of the next several classes you teach. How can you maximize the effectiveness of your openings?

Students won't learn much if they are not paying attention. We can plan to gain students' attention in many different ways—a projected image relevant to the subject for that day, a mental challenge represented by an overarching question for the lesson, a news story, a personal anecdote, or by celebrating student success, such as excellent performance in a trial or competition.

Once we have students' attention, we should provide motivation for them to maintain their focus throughout the class. We can motivate students by communicating our own passion for the class and our excitement to be in the classroom with them exploring interesting ideas. Show students how the concepts or skills for the class will be relevant and valuable to them in the future—in their personal lives, on the bar exam, or in practice.

Share the class objectives with the students. The process of articulating class objectives helps us focus our teaching. Likewise, objectives focus student learning. When students know what content, skills, and values matter for that day's class, they can devote their effort to learning the essentials, rather than tangential matters. We can inform students of the class objectives orally, on the board, in a handout, or on a slide.

Plan the transition from previous classes. We should put the day's class in the larger context of the course. Many students have difficulty seeing the big picture. A chart or diagram can help students fit the lesson into the broader context. Further, we should prompt student recall of relevant prior learning—the concepts, skills, and values learned earlier in the course that apply to the class at hand.

Body

The primary design decision for the body of the class is the selection of teaching and learning methods. Many types of methods are appropriate for legal education, including Socratic questioning, lecture, discussion, reading, problem solving, writing, role play, simulations, and experiential exercises (Chapter 8 addresses experiential learning). For example, we could plan a class session to include small group problem solving, followed by Socratic questioning, culminating in a large group discussion. Our selection of teaching and learning methods should be guided by several considerations: congruence, variety, and grouping strategies.

Congruence

The most important consideration in choosing teaching and learning methods is congruence—choose methods to maximize student learning of the objectives for the class. Teaching and learning methods do not have inherent value, or lack thereof. Socratic dialogue, lecture, or simulations are not "good" or "bad" methods. They are tools to facilitate student learning. The appropriateness of methods varies according to class objectives. For example, if our objective is that students will accurately articulate the elements of a doctrine, we may choose to lecture or conduct a Socratic dialogue regarding a case that explores the elements. If our goal is for students to develop interviewing skills, we may do a demonstration or show a video followed by students interviewing one another in pairs. Likewise, if we want students to develop healthy professional values, we could have them interview experienced lawyers and write a reflection paper on the key values the lawyer articulated.

Variety

There is great value in variety. Our students learn in many different ways. Consequently, we should plan to use more than one method for each class session and should incorporate many methods throughout the course. For example, Fleming and Mills' sensory-based learning model identifies four learning modalities but presumes that most students (and their teachers) rely on more than one modality. Illustration 3-4 identifies four modalities and examples of teaching learning methods directed at each .

Empirical research supports the learning benefits of multiple-sense, multiple-method instruction. In general, students learn more when instruction accesses multiple senses—seeing, hearing, speaking, doing.

In every course, some content and skills are more important than others. We should design instructional activities that involve multiple senses and methods for the most important aspects of the course. For example, if a significant learning objective is for students to have deep understanding of the law, policy, and strategy involved in creating security agreements, we may ask students to read applicable sections of the Uniform

Illustration 3-4: Sensory Based Learning Modalities

Learning Modalities	Teaching/Learning Methods
Digital • Learn via reading and writing • Logical, deductive reasoning • Abstract thinkers • Find patterns and organization	• Read to prepare for class • Brief cases • Write responses to problems • Outline course • Lecture—listen and take notes
Auditory • Learn via hearing and speaking • Process and store information chronologically • Memory aided by mnemonic devices	• Socratic dialogue • Large group discussion • Small group problem solving • Debate • Listen to stories, cases, hypotheticals
Visual • Learn via sight • Organize concepts through spatial relationships • Store ideas graphically	• Visual tools of all types—whiteboard, pictures, videos, handouts, slides • Diagrams, flow charts, graphs, concept maps
Kinesthetic • Learn by doing • Store knowledge as experience • Attend to physical and emotional manifestation of concepts	• Simulations and role plays • Authentic law practice experiences, including service learning, clinical, and externship experiences • Real documents—pleadings, contracts, deeds

Commercial Code, discuss cases or problems applying those sections, review a sample security agreement, and draft a security agreement for a hypothetical or real client.

Using a variety of teaching and learning methods enhances student attention and motivation. We have observed dozens of law school class sessions. In general, student attention wanes the longer we use any particular method. Each time the teacher changes methods, student attention revives. In addition, active learning methods and authentic experiences where students are acting like lawyers enhance interest and motivation for most students because it helps students connect their learning to their career goals. Finally, when students see their professor making an effort to vary methodologies in service of their learning, they often both appreciate the effort and feel inspired to devote more effort themselves.

Grouping Strategies

Intertwined with our planning decisions about teaching and learning methods are our grouping choices. We have three basic options—individual, large group, and small group. For example, if we plan to have students analyze a problem that we will present in class, we could have students generate an individual response, ask students to work with a partner or in a small group, or conduct a large group discussion or Socratic dialog exploring the problem.

Most student class preparation activities are done individually, such as reading, viewing a video, listening to a podcast, responding to problems, drafting, or completing a computer-based exercise. In traditional legal education, large group activities make up the bulk of the class—Socratic dialogue, discussion, or lecture. Individual activities in class are common as well—responding to a question, making a comment, or taking notes. We can create additional individual engagement opportunities in a class session by administering quizzes and short, in-class writing exercises, such as generating a written response to a hypothetical projected on a screen or in a handout. Our most significant grouping choice, however, is the use of small groups.

More research on small group learning exists than on any other instructional method. Hundreds of studies have established the benefits of collaborative learning in higher education. When compared with individual or competitive structures, collaborative small group learning arrangements result in increased student motivation, higher achievement, more high level thinking, better solutions to problems, more innovative ideas, greater respect for peer differences, and greater transfer of learning to new situations.

Our experience using small groups in law school classes is that many students identify it as the teaching/learning method that most enhances their learning. However, some students are frustrated by small group activities, especially when the small group activity lacks sufficient direction and structure. Small group experiences can be dysfunctional if the professor has not adequately designed the activity. Effective use of small groups in class requires thoughtful planning. Small group design issues include the group type, size, membership, and assignment.

Small groups can be informal or formal. Informal groups are formed quickly and work together for a brief period of time. The group may discuss an issue, analyze a problem, or brainstorm ideas. Formal groups work together to reach a more complex goal, such as developing an argument or drafting a document. Formal groups may be together for several class periods or even a whole semester.

Optimum group size depends on the nature of the group, the physical setting, and the assignment. For informal groups, pairs or triads work well because they maximize the involvement of each student and can be formed easily in almost any classroom configuration. Formal groups may have from two to seven members. Groups of seven have more human resources than groups of three, but the larger size is harder for the group to manage and individual members may have little involvement.

Group membership can be determined in three ways. First, students can choose their fellow group members. Student choice is common in informal groups when students simply turn to a neighbor and in formal groups when students sign up to work

Illustration 3-5: Small Group Assignment

Climate Change—Briefing Document

As a class we will create a "briefing document" on climate change science and law. The document should be designed for interested, intelligent members of the public and press. The purpose is to summarize the current science and law of climate change in approximately 6 pages. The document will have 6 sections. Each section should be about one page, single-spaced, 12 point font. It can be in paragraph form, bullet list, or any other format that would be effective.

Each group is responsible for one section. Email the section to me at the end of class today.

Group 1. Greenhouse Gases, Significant Sources, Sinks

Group 2. Projected Major Impacts of Climate Change

Group 3. Mitigation and Adaptation Strategies

Group 4. United Nations Framework Convention on Climate Change

Group 5. Kyoto Protocol

Group 6. Paris Climate Agreement

on a project with one or more other students. Second, groups can be formed randomly. Students can count off in class, receive a playing card at the beginning of the class, or be assigned to groups via web conferencing software. Third, the teacher can choose the members, which is a common way to form formal groups. This method allows the teacher to shape the characteristics of the group to achieve balance in terms of gender, ethnicity, experience, expertise, etc.

To maximize the effectiveness of small group activities and to minimize students' frustration, it is critical that the assignment be clear. The instructions should be in writing, either on the board, a slide, or a handout. The instructions should include the time allotted to the activity, the task the group is to perform, and the product the group is to generate. For example, instructions for an informal group activity could be: "You and your partner should generate an argument on behalf of the plaintiff that includes relevant law, policy, and facts. You have five minutes to construct the argument. Be prepared to give a 30 second summary of your argument." Illustration 3-5 is an example of instructions provided on a handout for a formal small group activity, for which the teacher chose the group membership to balance gender and expertise.

Closing

The last few minutes of class can be a time of significant learning if designed well. When we do not plan a closing, our classes often end with students looking at the clock as we try to cover one more point. Instead, we can plan the last few minutes of class to review, summarize, transfer learning, and re-motivate students.

Students need to consolidate new learning. We have many options to solidify student understanding at the end of class. We can review and comment briefly on the class objectives or articulate the few essential concepts, skills, or values students should have grasped in the class. With a graphic projected on a screen or with a handout, we could demonstrate how the doctrine, theory, or skills fit in the larger scheme or analytical framework. Students can play an active role in the closing by voicing the key concepts they learned in that class. We could ask students to complete a diagram or chart that draws together the learning for that day.

Transfer of learning and re-motivation can be easily melded in the closing. Students need to use the knowledge, skills, and values learned during a class session in the future—in the course, on the bar exam, or in the profession after graduation. We can facilitate transfer by showing students how the learning from the class will be valuable in the future or by asking students to brainstorm about that.

The closing of class can be used effectively for feedback and classroom assessment activities as well. These topics are discussed in the next section of this chapter and in Chapter 10.

Thinking exercise: Reflect on the last several class sessions you have taught. What happened in the last few minutes of those classes? Keep track of what happens in the last few minutes of the next several classes you teach. How can you maximize the effectiveness of your closings?

Feedback

Research clearly establishes the central role that feedback plays in effective teaching and learning. We cannot overstate how firmly we believe that feedback should be a part of our course design, class planning, and the teaching/learning activities we use with our students. Nevertheless, we each struggle with the challenge of turning those beliefs into reality in our teaching.

To help you and ourselves meet the challenge, we have addressed feedback in several chapters of this book. Chapter 7 explores means to encourage students to give themselves feedback through reflection on their learning. Chapter 9 explores the role of formative feedback in fostering deep, lasting learning. Chapter 10 discusses Classroom Assessment techniques, designed to give students and teachers feedback on student learning. Chapter 10 also explains the use of rubrics, quizzes, and practice exams as learning tools and feedback devices. Chapter 13 focuses on formative feedback to teachers through self reflection and information gathered from students, colleagues, and consultants.

Our emphasis here is on the design of class sessions to include feedback on student learning. Our major point is that as we design class sessions, we should look for ways to incorporate formative feedback. By the end of the course, feedback should have been part of many class sessions.

We can design feedback to occur at various points in a class session.

- **Opening.** A feedback activity is an excellent way to gain students' attention and to build a bridge to prior learning. Class could begin with a short multiple-choice quiz that addresses key concepts from prior classes and important aspects of the current class. The quiz could be on a handout, a slide, or via an electronic response or "clicker" system. Immediate feedback should follow the quiz.
- **Body.** During the bulk of the class period, feedback can vary from simple to elaborate. For example, when a student performs a skill well, we can call attention to it briefly—"Leila just synthesized a line of cases by ..." or "Fran drafted an excellent set of interrogatories that...." Or we could spend half of a class period going over the rubric for a practice exam and involving students in assessing their exam performance.
- **Closing.** By reviewing the class objectives or summarizing the major points for the class (done either by the teacher or students), the students get feedback on the critical content, skills, and values they *should* have learned that day. Or the class could end with a problem that integrates the learning for that day—feedback on the appropriate analysis could be immediate, happen via the course web page, or be part of the opening of the next class.
- **After class.** Feedback on assessments such as quizzes, problems, hypotheticals, outlines, can take place in a discussion on the course web page, via an applicable computer exercise, or one-on-one in the teacher's office. We can facilitate this type of feedback by initiating the web-based discussion, recommending an applicable computer exercise, or announcing our willingness to meet with students to review their efforts.

We can design feedback to come from a variety of sources. We believe that a primary obligation of effective teachers is to take the lead in providing feedback to students. Sometimes that obligation means that we will provide the feedback directly: giving clear feedback to students' oral responses in class; drafting a practice exam and a score sheet or rubric; composing a hypothetical and going over the appropriate analysis in class; critiquing student performance of an interview; meeting with students outside of class to review a portion of a student outline; or commenting on drafts of papers. Other times we can fulfill our obligation by facilitating feedback from other sources: creating a detailed rubric that students can use to assess their own performance; drafting a form that students can use to provide feedback on one another's oral arguments or presentations; creating an online discussion in which students comment on each other's analysis of a hypothetical; or calling students' attention to computer exercises and exam books that students can use for practice and as sources of feedback.

Materials

In the context of class session design, materials include both print and electronic resources that students will use outside of class or that students and teachers will use during class. Examples include readings, websites, pictures, videos, podcasts, computer exercises, handouts, slides, objects, and items written on the board or a flip chart.

We can choose and design materials to perform four basic functions:

Achieve class objectives. Just as class objectives drive our choice of instructional activities and feedback, they inform our selection of materials. The primary function of materials is to facilitate student learning of the content, skills, and values that are the focus of the class session.

Guide student preparation. Much of the material we choose is designed to be used by students outside of class to prepare them to participate in a meaningful way during the class session.

Support instructional activities. Once we decide what instructional activities will take place in the class opening, body, and closing, we are ready to select material to support our teaching of each portion of the class.

Facilitate feedback. Except for feedback that happens spontaneously during class, feedback depends on material—quizzes and rubrics for example.

The four functions of materials provide guidance on the types of materials we should select for each class. Several additional considerations apply regardless of the type of material. Effective materials are selective, variable, focused, and interactive.

Selective. For virtually any topic we address in class, we could find hundreds of pages of text (cases, statutes, articles) along with websites, pictures, and videos. Consequently, for every class session, we are choosing a tiny slice of the available material. What should guide those choices? First, we should select the material that is most relevant to our class objectives. Perhaps the cases, statutes, problems, and articles selected by the casebook authors will be relevant—and perhaps not. Second, we should limit the material we assign to students to a reasonable amount. We believe that the traditional guideline of two hours of student preparation for each hour of class is reasonable. If we expect students to read, brief cases, and generate responses to problems, a sixty-page assignment is not reasonable for a one-hour class. Instead, we can require the most relevant twenty pages and alert students to supplemental material that they can explore if they want to broaden or deepen their understanding. If you struggle to cut a case, consider making it a hypothetical.

Selectivity applies to our use of materials during class as well. Research shows that students will copy verbatim anything we write on the board or project on a screen. The words or diagrams we write and project go directly into our students' notes. So we should be thoughtful about those words and images. Less is more. A few key phrases or a clear, simple flow chart will aid student learning more than a board covered with our writing or slides jammed with text.

Variable. Variety in materials is a virtue for several reasons. In modern life, we get information from both print and electronic sources. Our class materials should reflect that reality. We miss opportunities to enhance our teaching and our students' learning if we march through the casebook without incorporating relevant stories, documents, and images. Further, variety makes our classes more interesting. Each time we shift material in the classroom, we grab attention. When we distribute a handout, project a picture, show an object, run a short video, most students are alert and on task. However, most students' attention will wane if we proceed through a dozen slides or show a forty-minute video. In addition, different students will respond more favorably to different types of materials. Some students hone in while reading and briefing cases. For other students, a picture really is worth a thousand words. Some need to work with real documents (contracts, wills, pleadings). To focus students' attention, use text boxes, bullets, numbering, bold and underline font, symbols, and color in course materials.

Focused. One way to facilitate student preparation for class is to provide, before class, questions about the material. These questions allow students to focus their preparation, just as a lawyer prepares for the issues that will be central to a motion hearing. We ask many other questions in class, just as judges ask lawyers questions in court. We can provide the advance questions to students in writing via a supplement, webpage, email, or a handout. Illustration 3-6 contains focus questions that address doctrine, skills, and values.

Interactive. Much of the material we assign to students is designed for students to read, such as cases, statutes, and articles. Likewise, materials we use in class are often intended for students to read or view, including slides, handouts, pictures, and diagrams. This type of material is valuable for presenting doctrine, policy, analytical frameworks, and theory to students. To maximize the effectiveness of material in achieving class objectives, we should look for ways to make materials interactive as well.

Simple techniques can add interactive features to many types of materials.

- **Readings.** The most passive use of readings is to simply assign pages. We can encourage more active reading by giving students focus questions (discussed above) or by asking students to do something with the reading—brief a case, apply a statute to a problem, or synthesize the law and policy from the material for the previous several classes.
- **Videos.** Short video clips relevant to the class objectives can be powerful teaching and learning tools. We can record our own short videos or find video clips online. Books such as *Reel Justice* describe portions of movies that illustrate doctrine, skills, and values. We can make the clips even more effective by providing students with questions or problems to focus their attention.
- **Slides.** Presentation software allows us to produce slides that transmit information and images to students. These visual aids are helpful to many students. On the other hand, if we use slides extensively and the slides do no more than present information, many students will become passive receivers. We can change

Illustration 3-6: Focus Questions

Doctrine Questions—Case

Parklane:

1. Define offensive issue preclusion.
2. What incentives does offensive issue preclusion give plaintiffs?
3. What test does the Court adopt for offensive issue preclusion?
4. Should the Court have decided to prohibit offensive issue preclusion in all cases?

Doctrine Questions—Statute

Clean Air Act sections 108 and 109:

1. What are National Ambient Air Quality Standards (NAAQS)?
2. What factors is EPA required to consider when setting NAAQS?
3. Why did Congress prohibit EPA from considering cost when setting NAAQS?
4. Should the CAA be amended to allow EPA to consider costs when setting NAAQS?

Skills Questions—Analysis

Identify five elements of statutory analysis that the Supreme Court employs in *Sweet Home*. Apply the elements of analysis to the problem following *Sweet Home*.

Skills Questions—Fact Investigation

Tomorrow in class you will depose Ms. Dominguez. Read the material on conducting and defending depositions at pages 33–35 in the supplement. Prepare at least five questions you would like to ask Ms. Dominguez.

Values Questions

Identify at least three ethical issues you see in *A Civil Action*. Assess the professionalism of Schlictmann, Facher, Cheeseman, and Skinner.

this dynamic by including interactive slides, that is, slides with questions, problems, quizzes, and hypotheticals designed to facilitate active student engagement in the classroom.

- **Boards, flip charts, and projectors.** These basic tools excel at supporting discussions. We can easily capture student contributions to class discussions on the white-, black- or smartboard, a chart, or a document projector.
- **Word processing software.** We can accomplish the interactive aspects of presentation software and whiteboards by projecting a document on a screen in word processing software. The document can include questions, problems, quizzes, and hypotheticals. We can capture student contributions during class discussion and send the document to students after class if we desire.
- **Diagrams, flow charts, and tables.** These tools, which education experts refer to as graphic organizers, can be excellent devices to organize concepts and illus-

Illustration 3-7: Case Synthesis Chart

	Case 1	Case 2
Issue		
Holding		
Defendant's contacts		
Reasoning		
Distinction between cases		

trate the interrelationships among ideas. Better yet, we can provide students with partially completed or blank diagrams and tables, and have them complete them before or during class. For example, Illustration 3-7 is a simple blank chart that helps students synthesize two cases.

- **Handouts.** We can accomplish many of the functions of materials with handouts, distributed in either paper or electronic form. Handouts can include readings, pictures, questions, problems, hypotheticals, quizzes, rubrics, flow charts, and diagrams. The interactivity of a handout we design for use during class depends in part on how we incorporate white space. Illustration 3-8 contains portions of a handout designed to support a fifteen-minute lecture/large group discussion on three United Nations organizations. Students reported that their active engagement, in terms of taking notes and making comments, was lowest in Section 1, higher in Section 2, and highest in Section 3. This result is consistent with studies that have compared the learning results of (1) students given the professor's notes, (2) students given a bare-bones outline into which they can take notes, and (3) students given nothing. The students in group (2) learned more than the students in groups (1) and (3), and the students in group (1) and (3) learned at about the same level.

Evaluate and Revise

In Chapter 2 we extolled the virtues of a systematic, reflective, continuous process for evaluating and revising our course designs. We urge you to engage in a similar process for your class design decisions.

The evaluation and revision process can be quite simple. After class, spend five minutes reflecting. Were the class objectives achieved? How effective were the open-

Illustration 3-8: Handouts and White Space

1. Commission on Sustainable Development.
Origin—Rio Conference
Program areas
    Agenda 21 implementation
    Reports on the sustainable development efforts of each country
    Technology transfer
Successes
    Information and Monitoring—e.g., Annual foreign aid target of .7GDP
    Forum for nations to discuss sustainable development
www.un.org/esa/sustdev National Sustainable Development Strategies

2. United Nations Development Program (UNDP)

www.undp.org Millennium Goals

3. United Nations Environmental Programme (UNEP)
Origin ____________________
Headquarters ____________________
Funding/Budget ____________________
Successes
    Environmental Law ____________________
    Clearinghouse ____________________
    IEL agenda ____________________
www.unep.org Thematic Areas

ing and closing? The teaching and learning activities? Would other grouping strategies have worked better? Did you provide feedback to students? Were the materials appropriate and effective? Memorialize your reflections in writing and keep them someplace that you will not lose them, such as with your notes for the class or in a teaching journal.

The next time you teach the class, begin your preparation by reviewing your reflections. Then, after considering the new context that will apply the next time you teach the class, make appropriate revisions in the class objectives, instructional activities, feedback devices, and materials.

We believe that there is no such thing as a perfect class session. We do not seek perfection in our classes. Instead, we strive to make incremental improvements in our classes over time. The five-step class design process helps us, and can help you, improve teaching and enhance students' learning class-by-class.

Sample class designs

Illustrations 3-9 and 3-10 are examples of class plans that incorporate the five design elements discussed in this chapter.

Illustration 3-9: Civil Procedure Class Design—Discovery Obligations and Sanctions

Context

Civil Procedure is a two semester, first year, required course with an enrollment of 70 students. This 50-minute class session takes place in the last week of class during the first semester.

Class Objectives

As a result of this class students will be able to:

- Define the obligations the Federal Rules of Civil Procedure place on attorneys when they respond to discovery requests;
- Identify the policies supporting the Federal Rules of Civil Procedure sanction provisions for discovery abuse;
- Evaluate attorneys' discovery behavior and justifications based on the obligations imposed by the Federal Rules of Civil Procedure; and
- Articulate their views of the effects of discovery behavior on professional reputation and responsibility.

Instructional Activities

- Before class. To prepare for class, students read a case and a Federal Rules of Civil Procedure in light of focus questions about the case and rule.
- Opening. Share objectives with students, brief review of discovery sanction law explored in previous classes, describe the substantial national influence of the case.
- Body. Address ten questions about discovery obligations, policy, strategy, and ethics. Divide class into ten small groups—each group addresses one question. Then each group reports to the class their response to the question. Large group discussion of issues raised.
- Closing. Two minute writing exercise in response to the prompt: "The lesson of the *Fisons* case for me as a lawyer is...."

Feedback

- During small group activity, teacher interacts with groups to keep them on track.
- After class, teacher compiles themes from student responses to the writing exercise, posts the document on course web page, and begins next class with teacher and student comments on the themes.

Materials

- Reading—ten-page case from casebook, one-page rule from statutory supplement, and five focus questions from course supplement drafted by teacher.
- Handout with ten questions and writing exercise prompt in a text box
- Word document projected on screen to memorialize student responses to questions
- Document compiling themes from writing exercise posted on course web page

Illustration 3-10: International Environmental Law Class Design—Drafting Fundamental Principles

Context

International Environmental Law (IEL) is an upper-level, elective course with an enrollment of twenty-four. This 50-minute class takes place in the first third of the course. It is the first class of a three-class simulation to draft and negotiate a world environmental charter.

Class Objectives

As a result of this class, students will be able to:

- Define four principles of IEL;
- Develop a negotiation position based on research about a country other than the US; and
- Draft four world charter principles from the perspective of a country other than the US.

Instructional Activities

- Before class. Students are assigned a country to research on the US State Department web site. Students read text about fundamental principles of IEL.
- Opening. Teacher presents overview of the three-class simulation—drafting, bi-lateral negotiations, multi-lateral negotiations. Teacher shares class objectives with students.
- Body. Students work in groups of four, chosen by the teacher to achieve identity-based balance. Each group drafts four world charter principles from the perspective of their assigned country.
- Closing. Large group discussion debriefing drafting exercise. Teacher previews the next class.

Feedback

- While students are drafting principles, teacher circulates among the groups commenting on draft principles.
- When all groups finish drafting, large group discussion on the challenges of drafting charter principles.

Materials

- Reading. Twelve pages from the IEL text.
- Web research. US State Department website country profiles.
- Handout explaining the details of the three-class, world charter simulation.

Checklist for class design process

Illustration 3-11 is a checklist you can use as you work through the class design process.

Illustration 3-11: Class Design Checklist

- ❑ **Consider the context of the class:**
  - ❑ Course context
  - ❑ Student context
  - ❑ Teacher context
- ❑ **Draft learner-centered, clear, concrete class objectives:**
  - ❑ Knowledge (doctrine, theory)
  - ❑ Professional skills (thinking, performance)
  - ❑ Professional values
- ❑ **Choose instructional activities to achieve class goals:**
  - ❑ Opening
  - ❑ Body (teaching/learning activities, groupings)
  - ❑ Closing
- ❑ **Provide feedback to students**
- ❑ **Select materials:**
  - ❑ Use outside class (readings, CALI, Internet)
  - ❑ Use in class (slides, whiteboard, videos, diagrams, handouts)
- ❑ **Evaluate your design**

Designing Each Class Session—Resources

These two books contain extensive treatments of instructional design principles appropriate for all levels of education, from elementary school to graduate school and beyond.

- Patricia L. Smith & Tillman J. Ragan, Instructional Design (3d. ed. 2005).
- Walter Dick, Lou Carey, James O. Carey, The Systematic Design of Instruction (6th ed. 2005).

These two articles apply instructional design principles to legal education.

- Michael Hunter Schwartz, *Teaching Law by Design: How Learning Theory and Instructional Design Can Inform and Reform Legal Education*, 38 San Diego L. Rev. 347 (2001).
- Gerald F. Hess. *Value of Variety: An Organizing Principle to Enhance Teaching and Learning*, 3 Elon L. Rev 65 (2011).

Chapter 4

Inclusive Teaching

Make it real.

Those three words should drive the law teacher eager to create a more inclusive classroom that values diversity. Like every other hallmark of excellent law teaching, inclusive teaching practices should be intentional and aimed at supporting student success. They must also be authentic.

This chapter offers a framework for creating an inclusive classroom environment rooted in respect and authenticity. It starts with an explanation of inclusive teaching and the rationale for creating an inclusive classroom, offers teaching and curriculum practices that can help create an inclusive classroom, and concludes by addressing common concerns for teachers working to create inclusive classrooms.

Principles for inclusive teaching: what it is and why it matters

Inclusive teaching is grounded in equity—allowing all students to reach their potential and feel a sense of belonging. Law teachers who employ inclusive teaching practices recognize—rather than ignore—differences among students. Further, the classroom and teaching practices designed with inclusion in mind can help close the learning gap between students. These practices can also foster self-efficacy, a learning trait essential for any lawyer and even more important for minoritized students.

An intentional course design must include careful plans to build an inclusive classroom that is thoughtful about the intersections of law teaching and race, socioeconomic status, gender, ethnicity, LGBTQ+ status, religion, neurodivergence, various levels of physical and intellectual abilities, and diverse viewpoints. These issues have always been important. They take on special significance as the American Bar Association ("ABA") Standards and Rules of Procedure for Approval of Law School now requires law schools to "provide education to law students on bias, cross-cultural competency, and racism."

The interpretation of ABA standard § 303(c), adopted in 2022, specifically calls for law schools to integrate training on the professional and ethical responsibility for lawyers to eliminate bias, discrimination, and racism.

> **Interpretation 303-5**
>
> Professional identity focuses on what it means to be a lawyer and the special obligations lawyers have to their clients and society. The development of professional identity should involve an intentional exploration of the values, guiding principles, and well-being practices considered foundational to successful legal practice. Because developing a professional identity requires reflection and growth over time, students should have frequent opportunities for such development during each year of law school and in a variety of courses and co-curricular and professional development activities.
>
> **Interpretation 303-6**
>
> With respect to 303(a)(1), the importance of cross-cultural competency to professionally responsible representation and the obligation of lawyers to promote a justice system that provides equal access and eliminates bias, discrimination, and racism in the law should be among the values and responsibilities of the legal profession to which students are introduced.

The relatively new ABA mandate to introduce law students to these critically important goals reifies a more robust embrace of inclusive teaching methods. Introducing law students to this competency must be centered in a classroom setting that reinforces these learning goals.

Inclusive teaching practices are not just an effective tool to prepare lawyers to combat systemic bias. They are an essential element of effective learning. Deep, lasting learning—examined more concretely in Chapter 9—is built on an effective teaching and learning environment. The essential foundation for an effective teaching environment is one that is challenging, supportive, and collaborative. This environment is only possible when there is mutual respect between students and teachers. Inclusive teaching practices promote respect. That respect fuels both community and collaboration. It also sets students up for success and prepares them to meet the challenges of a rigorous learning environment.

> **Thinking exercise:** How can you convey respect to your students? How can you encourage them to show respect to each other and you?

Researchers who study inclusive teaching practices argue that teachers make their inclusive practices explicit, rather than implicit. For some teachers, this practice may seem counterintuitive. They may worry that explicitly signaling their efforts to create an inclusive classroom might feel stigmatizing to their minoritized students. However, if the teacher carefully grounds the practices in messages about creating a culture of caring, students will feel empowered by the acknowledgment of the real difference that students confront—whether rooted in racism, sexism, ableism, classism, transphobia or homophobia, or some other bias. Such messaging must be matched by equally consistent messaging about the students' ability to succeed. "Equity acknowledges the differences between learners, their diversity, and the types of learning environments that help diverse students succeed" (Addy et al., p. 4).

In *How Learning Works*, researchers recommend fostering a course climate where instructors "convey their confidence in the abilities of all students in the course to meet their challenges" (p. 179). As discussed later in this chapter, creating an inclusive, supportive classroom environment is not antithetical to creating a rigorous environment that supports and challenges all students. Rather, fostering a sense of belonging in the classroom sets students up for success. "Fitting into one's environment influences our ability to succeed in it, as theories of student retention and success have noted" (p. 169).

Emotion and cognition are closely connected in education. There is no doubt that activated emotions have a clear impact on cognitive capacity. As illustrated in Illustration 4-1, emotions specifically impact "aspects of cognition that are recruited most heavily in education, including learning, attention, memory, decision making, motivation and social functioning" (Eyler, p. 122). Helping students experience a sense of belonging, then, helps them learn. Conversely, failing to design an inclusive classroom environment that promotes belonging can create obstacles to the learning process and thwart student success.

Thinking exercise: Can you recall an experience where you did not feel like you belonged? Were you able to thrive in that community? Are there any other experiences you have had where your emotional state impacted your ability to learn?

Illustration 4-1: Aspects of Cognition Used in Education

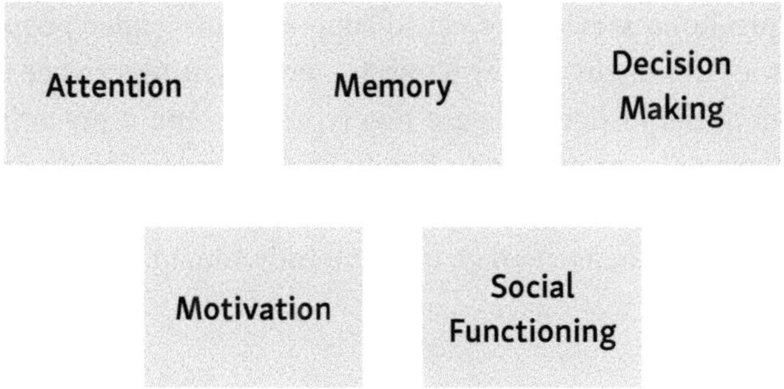

Practical strategies: toward a more inclusive course design

As a practical matter, creating a more inclusive course design should be reflected in both small and large-scale teaching methods. Everything from the micro strategies (including pronouns on your own signature block) to macro strategies (including an explicit Gender & the Law component in a course) can help you move toward a more inclusive course design.

The strategies listed here are aimed at giving you a solid toolkit of inclusive teaching strategies. Importantly, like most of the recommendations in this book, they are manageable changes that can be realistically implemented by a busy teacher confronted with all the competing time demands. The principle of small, accessible improvements certainly applies to integrating more inclusive teaching methods into an existing course. The following section focuses on these types of practical strategies. Small but powerful adjustments can have a huge impact on student learning.

While this book focuses on what teachers can do in their classes, we also believe it is important to pursue more expansive efforts to bolster inclusive curricula. Such efforts would include creating new courses exploring the intersection of law and race, socioeconomic status, gender, ethnicity, LGBTQ+ status, religion, neurodivergence, various levels of physical and intellectual abilities, and diverse viewpoints. These more robust efforts should also include creating curricular threads focused on structural inequities throughout the justice system, perhaps even a concentration, and clinical and experiential opportunities that support marginalized populations.

Such expansive changes require a more comprehensive examination of curricular needs and institutional approval. All these strategies must be thoughtfully approached and reflect the teacher's authentic values. Belonging and inclusion for all groups should also be cultivated in the broader law school, university, and even local communities. For example, a pro bono service project to support transgender people who need a name change or a Dr. Martin Luther King, Jr., letter-writing project to raise awareness on a current social justice issue are two types of community activities that law schools can support or even require to highlight differences and diversity. These are very important improvements to make to the curriculum and law school culture, but this chapter is primarily focused on changes an individual teacher can make in core law school classes.

Setting the tone

Even before school starts, teachers can convey their commitment to an inclusive classroom by setting the tone in multiple ways. By taking small actions, teachers can set the groundwork for a healthy learning environment; such steps relay to students that they have a support network led by their teachers.

You can establish your commitment to diversity, equity, and inclusion in your syllabus and other introductory materials. You can also draft a "Day One Memo" to help orient students and emphasize your teaching ethos, especially your interest in fostering an inclusive community of learners. Your syllabus, as detailed in Chapter 2, can communicate your commitment and begin to establish your culture. It is also helpful to learn as much as you can about your students with a pre-class survey, or by consulting with student services. If you find that you have a student in a wheelchair before class starts, for instance, you can ensure that your room is set up in a way that promotes accessibility.

Inviting students to introduce themselves before class with a photo or short video is another easy way to start to build community and emphasize the diversity in the classroom. Students also feel safer sharing a little about themselves when teachers create a short video or slide show about themselves. One colleague created a video that relays her interest in kayaking, love of poodles, and pride as a first-generation college graduate. Such subtle messaging in a personal narrative creates a greater sense of community and helps build trust with students. Other ways to signal an inclusive environment include listing your pronouns on your signature block or syllabus and being explicit about the need for classroom respect in your syllabus or Day One Memo. Illustration 4-2 is a sample of such language from a Current Constitutional Law Issues Seminar.

Highlighting the need to respect diverse viewpoints as a "Classroom Expectation" in the course syllabus centers the need for respect in the classroom environment. If only mentioned tangentially in a welcome at the start of class, such respect is likely to be lost. To reinforce the expectation for listening and respect, one teacher explicitly incorporates "respect and listening" into the participation rubric for courses. This rubric should be distributed before the first day of class for signaling and tone-setting. Another teacher has students co-create expectations for civil disagreement. This approach sends a message of trust, even if, during the discussion, the teacher may need to suggest key facets of this expectation.

One additional way to help set the tone for an inclusive classroom environment is to host a panel of experts on the first or second day of class. The panel should offer former students the opportunity to offer "expert advice" to the new students. This example of near-peer mentoring works best when it also reflects the community diversity. Therefore, teachers should be intentional about picking students from diverse backgrounds

Illustration 4-2: Classroom Expectations—Respect

> Our learning community is enhanced by the frank, earnest participation of all class members. Therefore, it is essential that students show respect for differing viewpoints and seek to learn from a healthy (sometimes challenging) classroom debate. To ensure that everyone will feel comfortable sharing their ideas, we will all listen and respond respectfully. That is a non-negotiable expectation for everyone in this class.

for the panel. Even if these students do not talk explicitly about race, sexual orientation, or gender, for example, they can serve as powerful examples for new students if they reflect people from these different communities.

Thinking exercise: Think of two ways you can telegraph to your students before the first day of class that you recognize and embrace diversity in your class?

Teaching materials and strategies

There are unlimited possibilities for a teacher committed to making the law school classroom more inclusive for students. In the past few years, there has been a much greater emphasis on the need to create an inclusive classroom that embraces differences and welcomes students from all backgrounds. In turn, the list of resources for promoting inclusive teaching materials has grown dramatically. Professor Teri McMurtry-Chubb has published a free resource for teachers who want to integrate diversity, equity and inclusion assignments into their law school curriculum. The book features many excellent lesson plans, learning outcomes, rubrics, and course planning templates for several core law school classes. There are also several excellent law review articles—some featured in this text—that also highlight pedagogically sound advice and techniques for integrating more inclusive teaching practices into the law school classroom.

It is also helpful to speak to your student services office, office of disability services, or campus learning center to get more information about how to make your class and assignments more accessible to all learners. For instance, changing accessibility settings on Zoom can offer students live transcriptions and increase post-meeting functionality. PowerPoint and other slide-making tools include accessibility checkers that can suggest steps you can take to make your slides more accessible to people with different auditory or visual abilities. Attendance and assignment policies should also factor in the disparate burden on students with religious observances and the extra time needed to secure any accommodations.

Creating an inclusive classroom stretches beyond race, gender, and physical and intellectual abilities. Teachers should also think about the socioeconomic spectrum, which can create unintended barriers for students in class. According to a note written by Taifha N. Baker: "Some statistics have shown that at some TLS [traditional law schools], 60% of the incoming students come from the top 10% of the economic spectrum, while only 5% of incoming students come from the bottom half" (p. 129). This spectrum should inform the challenges that may emerge from a well-intentioned teacher who creates tort hypothetical questions set on a golf course, rather than at a grocery store.

Law teachers are also more aware of the role they must play to help first-generation law students succeed. Professor Paula Lustbader makes this issue clear:

> For first-generation law students, much of the new information shared in law school classes does not reflect, or is irrelevant to, the first-generation students' lives. Professors can explicitly relate new information to students' prior knowledge or experience so the students can assimilate new ideas and properly characterize them (p. 844).

For the law teacher working to ensure a more inclusive classroom, this work includes deliberately designing a curriculum that is accessible to students from various socio-economic backgrounds. It also includes creating learning opportunities for students for whom English is a second language, considering the experiences of first generation law students, and accommodating other less traditional law students.

Teachers should brainstorm with their peers and with teaching assistants to identify ways to ensure that the law school class and curriculum reflect the community it serves.

Teachers who take an intentional approach will have several different ways to incorporate inclusive teaching strategies and exercises into the law school classroom. To help launch your own list of ideas for your courses, here are some strategies to consider, most of which are recommended elsewhere in this book:

- Assigning reading material that reflect culturally relevant issues
- Including diverse scholars in reading materials
- Including diverse perspectives in reading materials
- Engaging in legal discourse on how race, gender, sexual orientation or poverty impact case outcomes
- Drafting Legal Research & Writing memos based on hypotheticals that explore the rights of minoritized communities. (For example, examining Constitutional access to gender- affirming care for individuals dependent on state medical care.)
- Teaching in multiple modalities
- Assessing in different methods (see the "Alternative Assessment" discussed Chapter 11)
- Sharing technology tools and resources to help neurodivergent students and students with intellectual disabilities
- Examining legislative history of statutes to examine issues of race, class, gender, and sexuality in public policy discussions
- Acknowledging—not ignoring—the social climate and pressures that students confront. (While every class doesn't have to address every issue in the news; it is harmful to students to simply ignore the lived realities for students in crisis. Even a moment of silence or reminder of law school resources can help.)
- Creating discussion posts that address recent articles, cases, and statutes examining issues related to transphobia, racism, sexism, or poverty
- Offering guided reading reflections that explicitly call for a consideration of status

- Providing conspicuous syllabus placement of university resources and accommodation procedures
- Providing frequent reminders about law school mental health services and highlighting counseling services on your course's learning management system (i.e., TWEN or Canvas)
- Reviewing accessibility settings on electronic learning platforms, recordings, and slides
- Using cognitive protocols to build self-efficacy and responsibility among students
- Seeking feedback during the course, not just at the end of the course, regarding your efforts to create an inclusive classroom
- Making class recordings and PowerPoints readily available after class
- Being explicit about teaching methodologies, assessment techniques, and challenging coverage areas
- Modifying instruction based on student feedback
- Ensuring that videos, slide images, and other visuals reflect students from diverse backgrounds
- Ensuring that names used in hypotheticals reflect names from various cultural backgrounds
- Learning student names or asking all students to use name tents so you can call on students equitably. If using name tents, providing a name tent for yourself.
- Learning how to properly pronounce the names of your students
- Drafting learning outcomes that address cultural competency
- Utilizing low-risk and no-risk formative assessment
- Hosting a panel of experts featuring students from diverse backgrounds
- Hiring Teaching Assistants from diverse backgrounds
- Ensuring the guest lectures from practicing attorneys and judges are from diverse backgrounds
- Adding structure to small group discussion so that everyone is able to lead, speak and learn
- Allowing anonymous participation through online platforms such as Padlet so that introverts or students with a minority viewpoint feel more comfortable participating
- Sharing *some* of who you are as a person; a picture of a pet in your office, a quick reference to a favorite movie, or an occasional funny story about your Aunt Ivory helps humanize you
- Teaching students to use inclusive language when speaking with clients in clinics and field placements

- Fostering micro-inclusions—making a deliberate effort to make every student feel welcome and valued (not just directing support to the students who have the most in common with you)

> **Thinking Exercise:** Review your most recent syllabus for a course. Can you identify any areas where you can integrate learning activities that promote an inclusive stance to material?

Sustaining an inclusive classroom culture

Even if you have adopted the most welcoming efforts and devoted extraordinary attention to inclusive teaching materials, you will need to regularly revisit the tone of your classroom to make sure it is inclusive. It takes work to make sure that the welcoming, belonging stance you articulate at the start of the class isn't lost later in the semester. Design a course that includes multiple opportunities to model and re-affirm your inclusive teaching ethos.

It is critically important to interrogate the inherent privilege that law teachers have in the classroom and the world. The classroom power imbalance means that students—especially students from minoritized communities—may be sensitive to real or perceived harms from faculty. If you have harmed a student with an insensitive comment or another student has done so, use your position to acknowledge the harm and apologize. As the teacher in the room, it is our responsibility to restore and maintain a positive learning environment—no matter the cause. Again, this is a best practice for any effective teacher.

Even when external circumstances such as current events or campus activities violate the inclusive environment you have sought to create in your classroom, help students by acknowledging these challenges and sharing tools they may need to cope. (This may be as simple as reminding them of campus mental health resources, teaching them grounding techniques, or sharing a free app on meditation.) Legal education must remain the focus of your classroom. However, ignoring the harsh realities some of your students are navigating will make their learning more difficult and may mean that you fail to equip them with the lawyering skills needed for self-care.

A few more points to consider

Creating an inclusive law school classroom is not a goal with a defined finish line. Instead, learning how we advance justice and inclusion in both our classes and campuses is truly a lifelong labor.

And while the work to build an inclusive classroom is recursive, there are some "evergreen" caveats that should be noted. Importantly, even teachers with the best intentions who are working hard to implement inclusive teaching strategies should carefully guard against two common pitfalls: tokenism and their own biases.

Tokenism

Among the most common complaints by historically underrepresented students, particularly students of color, is the threat of being tokenized by teachers and classmates. Sometimes, teachers who are attempting to bring alternative voices to the table on important matters concerning diversity turn to the underrepresented students in the room for feedback. Examples include calling on the one Black student in a Criminal Law class to discuss policing practices in communities of color, calling on an LGBTQ student to discuss *Obergefell* and marriage equality in Constitutional Law, calling on a woman to discuss reproductive autonomy, or asking a Latino student to comment on a new immigration policy.

If these students from diverse backgrounds volunteer to discuss any of these issues because they want to engage in the discourse, calling on them is appropriate, even a good practice. But teachers should not assume that the underrepresented student in the class should be prepared to speak on such topics. One student referred to this practice as being "exoticized."

Students have also complained that teachers sometimes suggest that the student is speaking as a representative for their entire community. Of course, no single community is monolithic. It is unfair and unacceptable to ask a student from a particular community to speak on behalf of an entire community with diverse views. Historically underrepresented students should be pushed in class like their peers, but they should be pushed on the same subjects and skills as their peers are pushed. Again, being intentional about an approach to material may help avoid this particular pitfall.

Teacher bias

We each bring our own biases and assumptions to the classroom. That simple fact—coupled with the imperative to bring authenticity to an inclusive approach to teaching—creates inherent tension. The result is that teacher bias can infect a classroom. Learning to interrupt bias can help mitigate this threat. It requires constant awareness, self-reflection, and audits. As Jessamyn Neuhaus relays in *Picture a Professor: Interrupting Biases About Faculty and Increasing Student Learning*, inclusive teachers "are aware of their own biases and mitigate their impacts." (p. 23).

Though the research is limited on the impact of bias interruption, acknowledging your own bias and making a conscious effort to mitigate bias through structure and practices are important first steps. The National Center for Cultural Competency at Georgetown University also promotes self-reflection and self-assessment as important tools to interrupt bias. There are several useful tools online to assess implicit bias. Being aware of our own blind spots is an important step in mitigating the harm we unintentionally do to others.

Illustration 4-3: Inclusive Teaching Principles, Strategies & Pitfalls Checklist

This checklist summarizes the importance of creating a more inclusive classroom and highlights key points in building a more inclusive classroom that supports all students.

The Basics

- Inclusive teaching must be intentional, authentic, and rooted in respect.
- Aims to promote student success, belonging, and self-efficacy, especially for minoritized students.

Why Inclusive Teaching Matters

- Grounded in equity: Recognizes student differences and aims to close learning gaps.
- Supports ABA Standard 303(c): Requires education on bias, cross-cultural competency, and racism.
- Promotes professional identity and ethical responsibility in law students.
- Backed by research: Inclusive classrooms improve learning, engagement, and retention.
- Emotions and cognition are intertwined—belonging boosts learning.

Principles of Inclusive Teaching

- Be challenging, supportive, and collaborative.
- Encourage respect, mutual trust, and belonging.
- Use explicit inclusivity (e.g., acknowledging race/gender/class realities).
- Convey belief in student capability and potential.

Sample Inclusive Teaching Strategies

- Syllabus statements, Day One Memos, pre-class surveys.
- Personal videos or stories to build rapport and trust.
- Name pronunciation, pronouns, and diverse student panels.
- Diverse authors, culturally relevant readings, multimodal teaching.
- Diverse hypotheticals, assessments, and case discussions.
- Legal memos involving marginalized communities.
- Guided reflections and mental health resources.
- Anonymous participation tools (e.g., Padlet).
- Guest speakers and TAs from diverse backgrounds.
- Structured group work and inclusive visuals/materials.

Sustaining Inclusivity

- Reaffirm inclusivity throughout the semester, do not just highlight at the start.
- Acknowledge harm when it occurs; maintain a safe environment.
- Share tools/resources for mental health and coping during societal crises.

Pitfalls to Avoid

- Tokenism: Do not single out students from underrepresented groups to speak for their communities.
- Teacher bias: Recognize and interrupt personal biases through self-reflection and external resources (e.g., implicit bias assessments).

Take Aways

- Inclusive teaching is lifelong work—there's no finish line.
- Root your practices in authenticity, self-awareness, and student-centered design.
- An inclusive classroom enhances learning, community, and the future of the legal profession.

With thoughtfulness and careful planning, teachers should work toward an inclusive classroom. A student-centered approach rooted in authenticity and respect provides a solid foundation to implement some of these strategies. An inclusive classroom creates a more welcoming learning environment; further, it helps students learn.

Thinking Exercise: How do you think inclusive teaching strategies boost student learning?

Inclusive Teaching—Resources

This chapter is based largely on the following resources. In addition to literature on legal education, the resources also include higher education literature on teaching and learning, as well as the ABA Standards impacting curricular goals.

- AM. BAR ASS'N , SECTION LEGAL EDUC. & ADMISSIONS TO BAR, *Standards and Rules of Procedure for Approval of Law Schools* § 303(c), at 20 (2024–2025), http://www.americanbar.org/content/dam/aba/administrative/legal_education_and_admissions_to_the_bar/standards/2024-2025/2024-2025-standards-and-rules-for-approval-of-law-schools.pdf.
- TRACIE MARCELLA ADDY, DEREK DUBE, KHADIJAH A. MITCHELL & MALLORY E. SORELLE, WHAT INCLUSIVE INSTRUCTORS DO: PRINCIPLES AND PRACTICES FOR EXCELLENCE IN COLLEGE TEACHING 4 (2021).
- MARSHA C. LOVETT, MICHAEL W. BRIDGES, MICHELE DIPIETRO, SUSAN A. AMBROSE & MARIE K. NORMAN, HOW LEARNING WORKS: 8 RESEARCH-BASED PRINCIPLES FOR SMART TEACHING 179 (2d ed. 2023).
- JOSHUA R. EYLER, HOW HUMANS LEARN: THE SCIENCE AND STORIES BEHIND EFFECTIVE COLLEGE TEACHING 122 (2018) (citing MARY HELEN IMMORDINO-YANG, EMOTIONS, LEARNING AND THE BRAIN: EXPLORING THE EDUCATIONAL IMPLICATIONS OF AFFECTIVE NEUROSCIENCE 37 (2016)).
- JAMES LANG, SMALL TEACHING: EVERYDAY LESSONS FROM THE SCIENCE OF TEACHING (2d ed. 2021).
- Olympia Duhart, *Better Together: Building Community in the LRW Classroom*, 68 ST. LOUIS U.L.J. 459, 467 (2024).
- TERI MCMURTRY-CHUBB, STRATEGIES AND TECHNIQUES FOR INTEGRATING DIVERSITY, EQUITY, AND INCLUSION INTO THE CORE LAW CURRICULUM: A COMPREHENSIVE GUIDE TO DEI PEDAGOGY COURSE PLANNING AND CLASSROOM PRACTICE (2022); *see also* Alena M. Allen, *Equity and Inclusion as Unifying Principles*, 29 ROGER WILLIAMS U.L. REV. 49, 50 (2023) ("Diversity is concerned with representation, whereas equity is concerned with access.").

- Taifha N. Baker, Note, *How Top Law Schools Can Resuscitate an Inclusive Climate for Minority and Low-Income Law Students*, 9 GEO. J.L. & MOD. CRITICAL RACE PERSP. 123, 129 (citing Daniel Fisher, *Poor Students Are the Real Victims of College Discrimination*, FORBES) http://www.forbes.com/sites/danielfisher/2012/05/02/poor-students-are-the-real-victims-of-college-discrimination/ (May 9, 2012, 12:12 AM).
- Paula Lustbader, *From Dreams to Reality: The Emerging Role of Law School Academic Support Programs*, 31 U.S.F.L. REV. 839, 844 (1997).
- Rachel Croskery-Roberts, Alison Mikkor, Sara Berman & Olympia Duhart, *Demystifying the Lawyering Skills Classroom for First Generation Students*, *in* FOSTERING FIRST GEN SUCCESS AND INCLUSION: A GUIDE FOR LAW SCHOOLS (Brittany L. Raposa ed. forthcoming April 2026).
- PICTURE A PROFESSOR: INTERRUPTING BIASES ABOUT FACULTY AND INCREASING STUDENT LEARNING 23 (Jessamyn Neuhaus ed. 2022).
- Jon Garon, *To Be Seen But Not Heard: How the Internet's Negative Impact on Minors' Constitutional Right to Privacy, Speech, and Autonomy Creates a Need for Empathy-By-Design*, MERCER L. REV. Vol. 73: No. 2, Article 5 (2022).
- *Six Interventions to Tackle Unconscious or Implicit Bias*, NAT'L CTR. FOR CULTURAL COMPETENCE, http://nccc.georgetown.edu/bias/module-4/2.php (last visited June 11, 2025).

Chapter 5

Teaching the Class

This chapter focuses on in-person and synchronous online teaching. Some preliminary points:

1. you can teach effectively in many different ways;
2. effective teaching is science *and* art;
3. planning, thinking about your students, and using a variety of teaching techniques contribute to effective learning;
4. regardless of our best efforts and expertise, we all have good days and bad; and
5. our perceptions of "good" and "bad" classes can vary widely from our students'.

Immerse yourself in the process and learn as you go. (Chapter 13 has great ideas for using a "teaching journal"—one of the most effective ways to learn from your teaching experiences.)

Keep one fundamental question in mind as you teach your students:

"Who in the room is acting like a lawyer?"

In most law school classes, the teacher and a handful of students are: students who are called upon and those who volunteer. Many and maybe most students in any given class session are not acting like lawyers. We hope they are all vicariously engaging in the Socratic dialogue between the teacher and an individual student; the research does not support that hope.

If you keep this fundamental question in mind as you teach your class—***who in the room is acting like a lawyer?***—you will be more likely to stay focused on your learning goals and maximize students' experience. When students act like lawyers, they are likely to remember and develop higher-level cognitive skills. The more students are *engaged in acting like lawyers—speaking and doing—the more they are likely to learn.*

A related question about live teaching is,

"Who is doing most of the talking in class?"

Many people believe teaching is about *what the teachers do* in the classroom. They focus on what teachers say and how they present information or ask questions. We suggest a different perspective: *Teaching is creating a space where students learn.* Creating such a space means teaching is less about what teachers do and more about what students are doing and learning.

From Chapters 2 and 3, you know dividing the course into units and sequencing classes within those units will help students learn. During individual classes the most effective approach is focusing on one to three learning objectives per class. This chapter suggests ways you can engage students effectively in achieving those objectives.

Create a positive learning environment where students feel they belong and can safely take risks

We suggest you start by focusing on the "art" side of live teaching, the ineffable "feel" of the class. As noted earlier, creating a positive learning environment is critical to student learning and self-efficacy. Across all domains, one of the key components of effective learning is being "community-centered." Having a positive classroom affect takes more than teaching technique and subject matter expertise. Creating and sustaining a place in which students learn means we need to consider the values, attitudes, and nonverbal cues we send students about our social and emotional engagement in the class. Below are some suggestions for building a positive classroom environment.

Know and use students' names

Commit to learning students' names, pronouns, and the correct pronunciations of their names. Some teachers learn all their students' names by the first day of class. If you have a harder time learning names, practice for a few minutes a day with flash cards, make a video of students talking about their interests, or use other devices. Regular practice and using name cards (see Illustration 5-1) enables most teachers to learn students' names within a few weeks, even in classes of over 100 students. If learning students' names is not feasible, use name cards throughout the term so that you can say students' names during the class.

Be conscious of the messages you send

In the classroom, be aware of what your body language may convey to students. Eye contact, listening attentively, and projecting confidence and openness are as important as any specific teaching technique.

Sometimes we unintentionally transmit negative emotions. If we are annoyed, angry, or frustrated, we may send that message through eye contact, tone of voice, or gestures. Students notice these messages. Even if you are annoyed or frustrated, we encourage you to act *as if* you were happy to be in the classroom. Research shows when we act *as if* we are positive and happy, our ever-flexible brains rewire our emotional systems so we become more positive and happy.

Find an image of students that helps you visualize them positively. Think of them as your guests at a dinner party, siblings, offspring, or young relatives (how would I respond if my favorite niece asked that question?). Consider students future professional law colleagues.

Illustration 5-1: Name Cards

Using Name Cards

Have students make or bring "table tents" or "UN Name Cards" to class. These name cards have students' names printed in large font on the front and back. With the names on both sides, students can also learn each other's names.

Cards printed on heavy card stock paper can last weeks or months, depending on student use. If your school has the resources, an administrative assistant can print these from your rosters. On the first day of class, distribute the name cards and have a heavy black marker available to those who want to modify their name.

Alternatively, bring in photocopy paper, ask students to fold the paper twice in half lengthwise, and write their names in ALL CAPS on both sides, using a heavy black marker.

Encourage students to bring the name cards to class until you know all their names—even better, wait until all students know each other's names. The name cards help you and the students connect names to faces starting on the first day of class.

Be enthusiastic

Even though you may be nervous, your students appreciate your projecting confidence and enthusiasm. If we act like we don't care to be in the class, students wonder why they should; if we act excited to be there, students are more likely to want to know why we love teaching the course so much. You can always find something to be enthusiastic about in teaching, such as loving the subject matter, appreciating being a law teacher, or enjoying seeing students' "aha!" moments. You don't need to be ragingly enthusiastic about a particular doctrine if you are enthusiastic about students and their learning. You can show enthusiasm with small gestures: starting the class with a smile and "Good afternoon!" makes a difference.

Experts tell us that moods are catching and have serious health consequences. Being around positive, empowered, and cheerful people builds confidence and self-efficacy. Being around grumpy, anxious people does the opposite. We're not suggesting you slap a fake smile on your face and keep it there; we do recommend you focus on something you like about teaching. Having observed many classes at many different law schools, we know the power of teachers who clearly enjoy students and teaching.

Model taking risks and acknowledging weaknesses and errors

It's ok to say, "Great question. I never thought of that. I'll think about it and get back to you." Students greatly respect and appreciate teachers who are self-confident and excited enough about student learning to acknowledge students who come up with a new insight or question. Or you could say, "I'm going out on a limb here. I am not sure if this exercise will work, but I am going to ask you to engage in a different kind of learning exercise today."

If you made a mistake, as we all have, tell the students. "Last class I gave you some misinformation. Let me try to clarify." It helps students to know you struggle. Let them know that you, too, must work at writing complex prose, speaking in public, and teaching effectively. Apologize when you err. Apologies are not a sign of weakness. Admitting your errors and asking for students' pardon treats students with respect.

Envision yourself less as the "sage on the stage" and more of a "learning coach"

Actively engaging most students in the class may be more work than teaching traditionally, but if it helps our students learn more effectively, the extra work is worthwhile. In an effective live classroom, teachers are coaches, managers, directors, conductors, and choreographers. We have the expertise, but our main role is to help students learn, not show how much we know. One educational expert uses the image of a teacher as a white water rafting guide. A guide must safely navigate a boat through treacherous white water rapids but the guide alone can't do the job; the others on the raft must paddle hard.

As the coach, tell students you have high expectations for them, both because you believe they can meet your expectations and because you will coach them to get there. These statements show students you have confidence in them and help them develop intrinsic motivation to learn.

Be transparent

Tell students what you are doing and why. Even if students want a concrete answer to an unresolved issue, explain why the answer is "it depends" and what it depends on. When you use different instructional activities, explain why, at least the first few times you use them. Be honest. You may say \there is no right answer, but you mean there is no *one* single right answer. Instead, there are a handful of right answers and a larger group of wrong ones.

Be authentic

As the well-known education scholar Parker Palmer says, "We teach who we are." If you tend to be self-deprecating and you are good at telling jokes, do so. But don't try to be someone you are not. Experienced teachers often say it takes three years to develop your teaching persona. Pay attention to what feels right for you in helping students learn.

> **Thinking exercise:** Consider a few recent classes. Who in the room was acting like a lawyer?

The nuts and bolts

We've broken this part of the chapter into the following four main sections:

- Pre-class—the fifteen minutes before class starts
- Openings—the first five minutes
- Body—the heart of the class session (Instructional activities)
    - Active learning exercises
    - Lectures
    - Questioning techniques
    - Discovery sequence instruction
    - Visuals
    - Timing
- Closings—the last five minutes

In the opening, tell the students what you want them to learn; during the body of class, engage them in instructional activities to help them learn; and for the closing, summarize what you want them to learn.

Pre-class: the ten-to-fifteen minutes before class starts

First, arrive early.

We recommend you arrive at least 10 minutes before class. If this is the very first class of the course or you are new to the room, try to check out the room in advance. Plan how to use the room. Practice using the technology, including chalk or markers, before you go live. Consider how to arrange small groups, and whether anything impedes students' views of the board or projection.

During those pre-class minutes, check the room. If you are lucky, all systems are working, chairs are in place, and you can calmly set out any materials, project first slides, or write your objectives on the board. In the remaining minutes, you can casually chat with students who have arrived early, review your notes, take a deep breath, and focus on your learning goals. If you have already learned the students' names and faces, greet them by name; your effort will delight them.

You may be less fortunate. We've arrived in classrooms to hear jackhammers blasting, experienced 95-degree heat, found computers and screens not working and, sometimes, discovered fruit flies buzzing around the trash can. Most of us experience these kinds of problems as stressful. Arriving early doesn't eliminate any problems but showing up early allows you to learn about any problems and try to fix them before class. Even if you can't solve the problems, you have at least a few minutes to figure out how to work with or around them.

Entering the classroom early is not always possible. Some classrooms are scheduled with only a few minutes between classes. In that case, you can arrive early and chat with students in the hall. Your efforts show you are interested in the students and committed to their learning, factors that help engage the students and keep them motivated.

Openings: the first five minutes of class

You make a powerful first impression at the beginning of class. Recall the elements of effective teaching and learning from Chapter 1:

Good teachers:

- Show respect for students;
- Have high expectations;
- Support and coach students to reach high expectations;
- Are enthusiastic and passionate; and
- Are prepared and organized

To focus on students' learning, in those first five minutes, give students a roadmap for the class, identify the class learning objectives, and show your enthusiasm.

Because most students benefit from having information in more than one medium, it helps to provide a "roadmap" or outline of the class learning objectives visually *and* verbally. Visually, you can provide the roadmap on a slide, a handout, or on a board. Verbally, you can flesh out the objectives and provide context, explaining how this class session fits within the learning unit and the course as a whole:

> *In the last few classes, we were looking at a range of crimes, ending with murder. We looked at what a prosecutor would need to prove to charge a defendant with negligent homicide, manslaughter, felony murder, and first- and second-degree murder. In groups you made arguments applying the elements of those felonies to different factual situations.*
>
> *Today we are moving from those crimes to conspiracy. Specifically, today we are considering prosecution and defense arguments for conspiracy and attempted conspiracy. We will build upon the same skills—articulating the law, facts and policy—in making and responding to arguments.*

You can further explain what will be happening in the body of the class:

> *Today you will be working with one partner to compare and analyze your individual responses to Problem 7-A, using cases A, B, and C.*

It also helps to acknowledge when cases, concepts, or learning objectives are intellectually or emotionally challenging to many students. Students who have struggled and feel anxious may feel less stressed, and those who mastered the materials will feel empowered.

At the beginning of class, you may also want to use a few minutes to see if students have questions.

> *Any questions or clarifications you would like at this point?*

Pause. Practice being quiet. Mentally count to five to allow students time to gather their thoughts. If you don't want to or don't have time to respond to any questions, avoid asking for them.

If many students have questions and you lack time to answer them, you can answer a few and then encourage students to email you, talk to you after class, come to office hours, or post questions to a course webpage.

Alternatively, as suggested in Chapter 3, to assess whether the students are ready to move on, you could administer a short quiz or pose a series of questions before moving on.

> *I am handing out a quiz/problem/hypothetical scenario. Read the facts and jot down your answer. When you have completed your answer, turn to two classmates sitting next to you. Compare your answers and discuss why you arrived at your conclusions.*

You can then ask for responses or give students an answer to the problem. Clickers or other multiple-choice response tools available on most students' phones are another great way to assess how much students have retained from previous class or classes.

Special classes—first day of the course; other significant classes.

On the first day of the course, your opening may be longer. You may want to lay out more of the course landscape, or tell a story about the course, the students, law practice, or yourself. It helps to recognize and honor that you are at the beginning of a course. You may feel like you are just teaching another property course; for your students, your course is likely the students' only such course.

Explain any policies for attendance, seating, and using names. Some teachers like to be called "Professor X"; others are comfortable with a range of names. One of our colleagues introduces themself by saying something like:

> *My name is Logan Diaz. You can call me Logan or Professor Diaz. I'll call you by whatever name you prefer. Today I will go through the roster; let me know if I have mispronounced your name or if you would like to use a different name.*

If your course differs from the culture of other courses at your school because you have students work in teams, or involve them in course design, let students know why you use a different approach. As Chapter 2 suggests, it's also helpful to put this information in your syllabus. Use time the first day to reinforce major points.

> *One of the course goals is having fun. This is because learning experts have found people learn better when they have fun. Humor, it turns out, lubricates the learning process. Sometimes students assume having fun means the class is easy. I have high expectations for your performance, but I'll do my best to see that we have fun learning. Let's not take ourselves seriously, but let's be serious about learning.*

You can further explain your views on teaching and ask for students' patience:

> *We'll be using a variety of teaching and learning strategies in this class. I will lecture, ask you to do group work, complete in-class and team-based exercises, and ask you to practice other lawyering skills. You all have different learning preferences and not all techniques may suit you. I ask for your forbearance when we use an approach that works for others, but not for you.*

If your students have experienced a crisis, such as flooding, violent conflicts in the local community, or other matters that affect the students as a group, you may want to delay the formal opening to allow time for reflection, silence, and a chance to discuss. Instead, you could acknowledge the crisis and provide some quiet time.

> *As most of you have heard, last night terrible storms attacked the west coast. I know many of you have been concerned about family and friends in the area and whom you have had a hard time contacting. Let's take two minutes to sit silently or write. At the end of that time, anyone who wants to can share thoughts about this tragedy.*

If this is uncomfortable, you could acknowledge the event and move on. Be authentic and remember students crave to connect with our humanity.

> *I heard about the shooting in City X yesterday and am very sorry for all those involved. If any of you would like to talk to me about it outside of class, I would be happy to do so.*

While not exactly at the same level, when students are facing significant challenges, it helps to acknowledge them. We've noticed many students appear strained in November and March. As they face the pressure of final exams and their need to put together months of material, many students become tired and stressed. You could say something like:

> *I realize many of you are in the middle of moot court arguments / interviews / extracurricular events / journal applications / midterms / writing assignments—let's take a poll. Raise your hand if you are feeling overwhelmed.*

Students frequently come to class with many other things on their minds. Acknowledging their challenges and inviting them to focus on class helps them engage in their learning.

> *OK, so many of you are preoccupied. For now, I am going to ask you to set those concerns aside for the next 55 minutes and practice being corporate lawyers.*

The beginning of class sets the tone and provides a map for the rest of the class. Use it to prepare your students to learn.

Body—the heart of the class

The body of a class is where you will spend most of the class, focusing on your core learning objectives. Take the total class time and subtract about ten minutes—five minutes for the opening and five for the closing. Having a visual of your learning objectives is helpful; if your learning objectives are on a handout, slide or board, you will be more likely to honor your implied promise to help students achieve those objectives.

For a one-hour class session, focus on one to three learning objectives. As explained earlier, once you have identified concrete learning objectives for each class, work backwards to design effective classes. For example, if you want students to outline the steps involved in registering a new trademark, identify what students need to do and how you will know whether they have correctly outlined the steps. Estimate how much time you want students to work on each class objective. Remember students are more likely to retain a deep understanding of the material if they are actively engaged.

Most law teachers spend the body of the class lecturing, having a class discussion, or both. For example, in a trademark course, the teacher lectures students about the registration requirements for a new trademark, delivering a lot of content and information, and then asks individual students to verbally outline the steps for registering a different kind of trademark. Teachers also ask students about assigned legal authorities, "Why in *Case B* did the court deny the registration after the lower court held. . . ." Working through a series of authorities through questioning, teachers might ask about the rules, principles, or policies students gleaned from the authorities. Under both these approaches, students would have been exposed to the material, and some students will have actively engaged in talking about it. Some students, however, become disengaged during lectures or during the teacher's questioning of the students' classmates.

Instead, you could start the main portion of class with a question encompassing your objectives. "How can a party obtain injunctive relief?" Tied to your learning objectives, one or more key questions can provide a unifying theme to the class. Like a musical refrain, the repetition of key points and concepts can keep students aware of what you want them to learn. Use most of the class time to engage as many students as possible in a variety of instructional activities. During these activities, repeat and flesh out your main question to keep students focused on the main learning objective. Summarize and repeat important points as you go; effective teachers frequently repeat anything they really want students to know and remember.

Active learning exercises

Use active learning exercises to engage students in acting like lawyers.

Students are engaged when they are:

- Writing
- Talking and listening
- Reading
- Reflecting
- Demonstrating

Illustration 5-2 lists five active learning exercises you can use in the body of your class. Each of these exercises is described briefly below. When they are engaged in these exercises, the students, not just the teacher, are "doing the work"—acting like lawyers by actively solving problems, thinking, talking, listening, taking notes, reading, and writing. When you use these techniques, the energy, volume, and activity in the class usually soar. Chapter 8 has more information about using experiential learning techniques—real-world experiences and simulations.

Illustration 5-2: Instructional Activities: Active Learning Selections

- **Think-write-pair-share**
- **Small group discussion**
- **Student-to-student group discussion**
- **Small group role-playing**
- **Point/counterpoint**

You don't need to be an expert in these exercises to be an effective teacher. You can include many simple, quick techniques in law school classes. Multiple sources list a range of techniques and how to use them. Start simple, start small, and give yourself time to work these into your classes and learn from experience. As we have suggested, ask yourself, "Who in this room is acting like a lawyer?" *and* "Who in this room is talking?" *Choose one or two new exercises a semester. Don't give up just because they didn't work as well as you hoped the first time, or some students didn't like them.*

Ideally, use three or more different exercises per class. Variety is key to student engagement and learning; it keeps the class interesting, engages students in different levels of thinking, and addresses different learning preferences. When we recommend colleagues try different exercises, we often hear, "OK, but I already did that activity last month." The implication is that any approach other than the traditional Socratic-style questioning is a gimmick and should be used sparingly. We suggest that you consider Socratic-style questioning as one teaching tool you use (more about how to use Socratic-style questioning effectively below) and combine it with a variety of other instructional techniques.

Here are five active learning techniques to try.

Think-write-pair-share

This technique is one of the quickest, easiest, and most versatile. Pose a question verbally, in writing, or both. Ask students to think about the question for one minute and then note their responses. Once students have completed their responses—one to three minutes depending on the complexity of the question—ask students to exchange their ideas with a neighbor, discussing their answers and reasoning—another one to three minutes.

Call on a few students to respond or ask one or two students to volunteer a neighbor's response. Note responses on the board, enter and project them, or verbally reinforce them. When students talk to each other, they often learn that their classmates found the question difficult, the material confusing, or they hear a different perspective. Following a think-pair-share, a much greater range of students volunteer and are comfortable being called on.

Small-group discussion

Pose a question or problem students must work together to solve. Students can collectively discuss and answer questions at different levels of thinking, e.g., *What are the elements of the statute? Which element is at issue in this client's case? How would you describe federal preemption to a layperson? What are the differences among courts' tests for issuing preliminary injunctions?*

As the groups work, you may circulate among the groups, be available as a resource, sit in and listen to a few groups, or let the groups work on their own. If you circulate, you can address common areas of confusion and get a sense of how the groups are functioning. If the groups work on their own, some students may be more likely to take risks. Once groups have discussed their responses, call on a couple of different students—ideally those who have previously not contributed to the large group discussion—to talk about their group's response. When you have one response, invite other students to contribute different responses or elaborate on the first response.

As noted in Chapter 3, to have effective small group discussions, group assignments must have clear directions. Specify how long groups should collaborate, allowing less time than you think students will need. During the exercise, add more minutes if students are still focused and more time would help them attain the learning goals. Gauge how things are going by asking the class as a whole or circulating and asking different groups whether they would like another couple of minutes. At the end of the exercise, if all the groups are working on the same problem, avoid doing a "report back" where each group gives a presentation on the same topic. (The report-back group responses get tiresome and most students disengage after a few minutes.) Instead, call on different groups or individuals within groups.

Student-to-student group discussion

Ask students to lead the discussion by calling on each other. For example, after posing a question about a rule, factual analysis, or other learning objective, tell students the goal of the next few minutes is for them to achieve that objective by talking to and calling on each other without your involvement. You can start the discussion by asking a student, perhaps one who has previously not spoken, to respond to the question you have posed. After the student has contributed, each subsequent student must call on the next one to further the discussion. While students talk and refine their understanding, you or another student can serve as a scribe and note responses on the board.

Small group role-playing and simulations

Divide the class into sections and assign a role to each. For example, in an employment law class, you might assign groups to represent employees and other groups to represent employers, in-house counsel, and legislators. In small groups, ask the students to collaboratively outline their positions, using notes or bullet points. Ask them to think about the big picture, not particular words, and explain they may want to start in the middle or end and bounce around as they work. One or two groups from each section could write their outline on chart paper, overheads, board or laptop, and show their analysis to the whole class. (For more ideas about simulations and experiential learning, see Chapter 8.)

Point/counterpoint

From different sides of the room, ask students to take turns making arguments. In this part of class, ask a student on one side of the room to make a statement advocating a position, and then identify someone on the opposite side of the room to argue the opposite. Continue for a few minutes as both sides of the room explore the analysis. At the end of this exercise, ask students to vote on the strongest arguments using a response system or raising their hands.

Additional points about active learning instructional activities.

Keep track of time. Active learning instructional activities can take on a life of their own. Help keep students on task and focused on the learning objectives. On the other hand, as a hedge against an individual or group of students finishing an activity early, plan additional instructional activities you can assign.

Close the loop. After students have engaged in active learning activities, explain what they have done and reinforce the learning you have observed. Summarize main points, engage in a whole-class discussion, invite students to share what they learned from the activity, or clarify questions the exercise precipitated.

Common misperceptions about active learning instructional exercises

Many teachers hesitate to use the techniques above. We didn't experience these techniques as law students, and, if we did, were not always aware of what was going on. Instead, we tend to default to the teaching techniques we were exposed to. Before we discuss other instructional activities, we want to address some negative perceptions about active learning activities.

Active learning takes too much time in class. A related concern is that we will cover less material if we engage students in active learning. Well-designed active learning exercises have been shown to maximize students' deep learning of knowledge and skills, and many law professors do not believe they are sacrificing coverage by engaging their students in active learning. Use active learning activities for the most important learning objectives.

Active learning is touchy-feely. As with any role, we must be authentic to be effective. Some active learning techniques ask students to reveal more of themselves than they do in many other classes, such as when students write reflective journals or work closely with others. This classroom work is related to law practice, where reflecting and cooperating are critical skills for success and satisfaction.

Active learning requires a degree in advanced psychology or education. Asking students to work together to solve a problem does not require extensive knowledge of group dynamics or learning theory. If you are explicit about directions and expectations, your lack of expertise will not be an issue.

Active learning means losing control in the classroom. Creating situations where students are engaged may mean the classroom "looks messy." Students are gesticulating, the noise level is high, and the teacher appears to be doing nothing. In fact, active learning requires more advance planning and allows exercises to proceed in a controlled fashion.

Reconvening the whole class once students have engaged in active learning can be challenging. Try flicking ceiling lights, calling students' attention to the class, giving students a warning about how many minutes they have left, and using their names "I see that Masha's, and Carlos's groups are ready to discuss their responses with the class.... Others?"

Lectures

Lectures can lead to significant student learning by clarifying concepts; providing examples; organizing, summarizing, and synthesizing important information; and modeling legal analytical thinking. Teachers lecture effectively when they:

- Limit lectures to ten minutes;
- Add valuable content;
- Surround lectures with other active learning activities;
- Use supporting media; and
- Speak expressively at around 100 words a minute

Use micro-lectures

Students have short attention spans. Studies show within ten minutes, students' attention considerably drops off. And no matter how dynamic we are, few people retain more than a small portion of any lecture. Make your lectures mini-lectures: limit them to ten or a maximum of fifteen minutes.

Teachers' mini-lectures are highly effective when they address students' misconceptions about a concept, give students feedback, show connections between concepts, provide real-world examples, model a skill, or summarize part of the class. Many teachers like to give students a mini-lecture followed by questions or problems for students to solve. Instead, mini-lectures can be more effective when you give them *after* students have done some preparation and have tried to engage in problem-solving. Then, students are primed to pay attention; they realize where they need information and guidance.

Add valuable content

Avoid lecturing about content you can deliver in print—unless it will help students learn. Instead, use mini-lectures to build upon what you have assigned students to prepare in advance or highlight important points missing from the written material or needing emphasis.

Surround mini-lectures with other activities

Before and after mini-lectures, pause, ask a question, give a mini-quiz, pose a problem, engage students in a small group discussion, or use other activities that actively engage your students. Include pauses between main points to let students catch up on notes, review, and consolidate their thinking. Even a one-to-three-minute pause or other learning activity between each ten minutes of lecturing helps students refocus, re-engage, and increase their ability to retain information.

Include other media

Use sound, pictures, graphics, videos, props, and other material to reinforce important points. With material available online, you can easily find enhancements for your mini-lectures. Providing students with a bare-bones outline or chart into which they can take notes, an activity known as "guided note-taking," also requires them to pay attention and use mental effort while listening.

Deliver mini-lectures effectively

Follow the basics of effective public speaking. Use a voice audible from the back of the room. Vary your phrasing and allow for pauses. Modulate your voice. Move around. Make eye contact with students. Periodically include students' names, "So if Marcella was deciding to file a Section 1983 claim, she would ..." Tell students which points are especially important and encourage them to write them down. Repeat main points. Speak at a rate of about 100 words per minute.

> **Thinking exercise:** Think about a course you taught recently. How many different teaching techniques did you use during a regular class?

Questioning techniques

Most law teachers think law teaching is about "Socratic" dialogue, and posing effective questions can be an effective way to engage students in achieving all levels of critical thinking. (We're not discussing the different kinds of "Socratic" dialogue, such as questioning the way Socrates did it vs. any other modification; we're referring to the law school questioning process as Socratic-style questioning.)

Like any other technique, Socratic-style questioning's effectiveness depends on its execution. One of the greatest weaknesses of traditional law school Socratic-style discussion is that most students are not engaged. The questioned student is actively engaged in the conversation with the teacher and receives feedback on her learning process. For all other students, however, the learning process is vicarious at best. We may want each student to mentally compare their answers to the questioned student's answers, and evaluate, based on their peers' and the professor's reactions, whether their ideas and the selected student's ideas reflect insight, confusion, or something in-between.

Unfortunately, many students are shopping online, e-mailing colleagues, or sending texts about something entirely different. Even in classes taught by masterful practitioners of Socratic-style teaching, we've observed students disengage, especially if they know they will not be called on. You can enhance Socratic-style questioning's effectiveness when you:

- Prepare students in advance;
- Ask clear questions;
- Ask one question at a time;
- Ask a range of questions;
- Elicit different levels of thinking;
- Allow sufficient wait-time (three seconds or more);
- Encourage and promote effective responses;
- Respond appropriately to ineffective answers; and
- Use discovery sequence instruction

Preparing students for your questions

From handouts, web pages, syllabi, or other resources, give students enough information in advance so they are prepared to respond to the questions. (See Chapters 3 and 7.) Particularly for more complex thinking skills, giving students advance notice of the kind of thinking you want them to show will help them target their out-of-class studying. Not all questions need to be given in advance, but giving students core questions before class will help them focus and deepen the level of class discussion.

Model the kinds of responses you seek. For example, if you want students to analyze and evaluate a defendant's response to a negligence claim, first show them how you would do it. For example, you can present students with a problem and model your steps to solve the problem, talking through each step, and admitting where you're uncertain. Pause as you go, letting students catch up and take notes.

> *Ok, I've got these facts. I'm considering what arguments I might make and which are strongest. I'll address the arguments in the order of the elements of negligence: duty, breach, causation, and harm. Right now, because I haven't fully analyzed*

> *the scenario, I don't yet know if my client has a good defense. So I don't know whether it would be better to fight this claim or settle it. I also don't know the plaintiff's damages, which would affect any recommendation for how to proceed.*
>
> *First, I'm going to start with duty. As the driver of the car, the defendant definitely owed a duty of due care to the pedestrian he injured. Nothing in the facts suggests otherwise, so I am going to concede this element and move onto the next element*
>
> *Second, it looks like the defendant breached the duty of care. He was trying to find music and failed to look completely to the right as he pulled out of the parking lot. There may be an argument the defendant acted reasonably, but I don't see it yet; I'll come back to this one....*
>
> *Now coming to the element of proximate cause or scope of liability. Hmmm. Let me see. I think the defendant has a potentially strong defense here....*

This technique, called a "cognitive think-aloud," stems from the research on expert performance. Because experts tend to skip steps and quickly make and discard hypotheses, be vigilant about your thinking process. Having a colleague in the room, who can ask you questions about skipped steps and discarded hypotheses, adds richness and subtlety.

Ask clear questions

Asking good, clear questions is hard. As the questioners, we know what we are looking for. The students, some terrified of "getting it wrong" in front of their peers, may stumble and have no idea what we are really asking. Writing the questions in advance and ensuring they align with your class learning objectives will improve the clarity of the questions you ask and help you determine what types of thinking you are looking for. Projecting your questions on a slide or writing them on a board will help students more easily process and focus on answering the question. Avoid questions that suggest you are really asking, "What am I thinking?" If you have a definite point you want a student to make, you may be more effective in stating the proposition and asking students whether and why they agree.

Some educators advocate asking no question to which you know the answer, as those are inauthentic questions that stifle rather than stimulate dialogue. But part of our job as law teachers is ascertaining whether students have learned the material we want them to learn. So, while *we* know the answer to, "What major factors did the court use in allocating punitive damages?" we are really asking students to tell us whether they identified those factors. We could help students engage in the dialogue by naming what we want them to learn, such as by asking, "The court used several factors in rejecting the claim for punitive damages. I'm wondering if you identified the same factors or interpreted this opinion differently. Marcel, please start us off by identifying one of the factors the court seems to have used." If you don't wish to call on a particular student, you could invite any student to respond, "Could someone start...?"

Ask one question at a time

Discipline yourself to stay with one question at a time. While repeating a long or complex question is helpful, adding more questions compounds student confusion. Writing the questions in advance helps avoid such problems.

Ask a range of questions

Open-ended questions are more likely to generate discussion than yes/no questions. Vary the kinds of questions and the time it takes students to respond. Some questions are effectively posed in a quick and ongoing repartee—think of a lively dinner table conversation—rather than a long question followed by a longer answer.

Elicit different levels of thinking

Ask students questions along the range of thinking hierarchy. (See Illustrations 3-2 and 3-3.) Depending on where you are in the learning unit (see Chapter 2) and the context of the class, develop questions from lower and higher levels of thinking. As you progress through the course, ask students questions at increasingly more complex levels. Embed material about a concept studied earlier in a question as you ask about the current class topic, for example: "Let's review the tests administrative agencies use to … [name tests briefly]. Let's apply those factors to …"

Allow sufficient wait-time (at least three to five seconds) after you ask a question

Most of us struggle with silence in the classroom. We ask a question and quickly call on the usual students who raise their hands. Alternatively, we may call on students, expecting immediate responses. We usually wait only a second or two before we fill the silence by commenting or rephrasing the question. One second is insufficient time for most students to generate a meaningful response. Giving students time to process your question usually results in more students participating. To address the awkwardness of silence, explain this process to students, "I am going to wait for five seconds to give you time to think," or, "I see that Ee Ming and Rafael both have answers to this question. How about some others? I'll wait."

Another way to provide students with time to process the question is to ask them to write a response for 30 seconds or to engage in a think-write-pair-share exercise as described above. These exercises give students time to reflect and work through their responses.

Encourage and promote effective responses

Actively listen to students' responses. Smiling, nodding, being quiet, and making eye contact encourage students to elaborate. Leaning forward, writing students' responses on the board, and inviting others to help their classmates can also help build student confidence and sense of belonging. Acknowledge students' effective responses, both when they respond and later, e.g. "Mason made an excellent point. Remember how they said...." Encourage and coach students to develop their responses. "Great start! Now can you help me out by explaining how you got there?" Show delight when your students develop particularly insightful points and acknowledge insights new to you; your students will remember those moments, both as a sign of your respect for them and as a reflection of your own self-confidence in your expertise. Conversely, when students respond and we look elsewhere, lean away from them, fiddle, or interrupt, we're suggesting their responses aren't worth our attention.

Respond appropriately to ineffective answers

If possible, when students give a "wrong" answer, guide them to a better one. Focus on the answer, not the student, and acknowledge any positive aspect of the response. A gentle sense of humor can help diffuse a potentially uncomfortable moment for the student, "Oh, that answer is so-o-o close! But I wonder if it could use something more. Take a look further down the page where it says ..." Try hints, such as, "Why do you think the court mentioned _____ fact?" "Is there anything in the federal rules you might use to support your argument?" You can also invite the student to call on "co-counsel" to help, and then return to the student to end the discussion with a positive contribution. (For more suggestions on giving corrective feedback, see Chapter 10.)

Use discovery sequence instruction

To implement discovery sequence instruction, give students a series of examples and non-examples of a concept. Label each as either an example or non-example and ask the students to infer the principle or principles that reconcile the examples and non-examples. For example, give students a set of contracts, some of which are governed by Article II of the UCC and some of which are not. Tell the students which are which and ask students to infer the principles that govern when Article II applies. You could give students a set of effective and ineffective responses to a hypothetical or draft contract terms and ask the students to explain the principles that distinguish the effective responses. You can combine this technique with a think-write-pair-share exercise or small group learning activity. Because the students acquire deep learning when they figure things out for themselves, such experiences capture students' attention and produce strong and lasting memories.

Visuals

Here we address some essentials about visuals in the classroom, including PowerPoint and clothing.

PowerPoint and other visuals

Visuals can be highly effective, disastrous, or somewhere in between. There is a wealth of information about how to effectively use visual media, including PowerPoint. Any of these tools can work well; the key is using these tools intentionally and thoughtfully. Review your class learning objectives. Consider how visuals may help students meet those learning objectives. Then learn about and practice using the technique and reflect on how well visual and other media worked in class. Some terrific classes include lots of visuals and other media; some excellent classes use very little media. You can spend hours developing beautiful, media-rich classes, but if using media means you're the one doing all the lawyering in the class, it is likely not the most effective use of your time.

For all images, whether a computer projection, movie clip, or board, it's important all students can "read" the visual. Check the sight lines from everywhere in the room. Must students crane their necks to see the screen? Does a whiteboard's glare hide content? Can students decipher your handwriting? Is a screen large enough for students to accurately read and interpret the content? These considerations relate to a frequent principle in this book: Less is more. Use bigger letters, numbers, and images. Have fewer of them.

When projecting text, use principles for effective graphics:

- As suggested in Chapter 3, projecting words using text boxes, bullets, white space, numbered lists, and color helps students get the most from the visual.
- Use a font without feet like Arial or Helvetica. While fonts with feet (like the one on this page) are easier to read in a document, fonts without feet are easier to read when enlarged. (You'll notice that most road signs use fonts without feet.)
- Limit yourself to six lines of type or less. Six lines is not much text, but this limit increases the likelihood your students can read the slide. Limit your text to the important points. You can amplify verbally, let students fill in gaps, or add essential points on another slide.
- In class, unless you have a good reason for doing so, avoid looking at the projected text and reading it. Students can do that. Instead, face the students, use the text as a focal point, and engage students in discussion. Pause to let them read the projected words.

If you are using any kind of media during class, practice first and be prepared to have an alternate strategy if your plan fails. No one enjoys watching someone fidget with problematic technology.

Similarly, when using images, be intentional about what you use and what messages they send. As with projecting relatively few words, a few clear images are better than a mob of confusing ones.

A final thought about using PowerPoint or other presentation software : you may be tempted to use slides to transmit information—e.g., a statute's wording, an excerpt from an opinion, or three points you want to make in a lecture. If you only transmit knowledge using PowerPoint, however, your students may conclude your course is mostly or exclusively about acquiring knowledge. Just as writing on a board sends a message about what you think is important, the content of your slides can influence your students' perception of your course. By including slides with questions, problems, visual metaphors, or a checklist addressing distinct analytical steps, you show students that answering questions, applying skills, and solving problems are important in your course.

Dress

How we dress is an issue for all teachers and is especially important for teachers who are women, of color, nonbinary, relatively young, inexperienced, or otherwise do not conform to some students' preconceptions about law professors.

Some colleagues won't teach without wearing a suit. Others teach comfortably in jeans and a casual shirt. Some insist on wearing different clothes to each class. What you choose to wear depends on your personality and comfort level, your school's culture, where you are in the semester, and what is going on with your students. No matter what, be yourself; there's no one right way to dress for the law school classroom. If you tend to be casual, however, don't suddenly start wearing conventional and formal dark suits. On the other hand, at least for the beginning of the course, you may want to lean towards the more formal side of your personality. Likewise, if you tend to be more formal and conventional, stick with who you are. Your school may have a dress culture; consider how others dress and, if you have questions, talk to your colleagues about these unspoken norms. If you want ideas about how your students might perceive teachers your age, you can find helpful images on the internet. How do politicians dress? Actors playing lawyers? Other people in public positions of authority to whom your students respond positively?

The best clothes to wear are those which are comfortable and make you feel confident. For some of us, putting on the suit contributes to our self-confidence: "Even if I am scared out of my wits, I'll at least look like a law professor." Some women feel most confident wearing pants; others feel they project a desired image of professionalism with skirts. A friend of ours, a young woman new to teaching, felt she needed to look as much like a 50-year-old as possible. Her approach was to wear the power suit, heavy jewelry, and silk scarves associated with top women business executives. Similarly, some people feel better wearing a jacket; others feel confident wearing high heels. Whatever you wear, try it out first. (That nice jacket may make it hard to write high up on the board or will become beastly hot with all your gestures.)

Most of us dress more formally at the beginning of the semester. The first class is like a professional job interview: What will make the best first impression on the students? As the semester continues, and students start to show signs of stress, we may shed the formal attire and adopt more casual and comfortable clothing. One teacher deliberately puts on his cardigan sweaters for the days when his students are most stressed out. You may also want to choose more formal clothing when teaching a large class and be more casual when holding office hours or teaching an upper-division seminar.

Timing

When teaching a live class, track chunks of time along with your learning objectives. For example, you might divide a 50-minute class into three sections of 13 minutes each, leaving 10 minutes for the opening and closing of the class session. Rather than setting the exact timing for each instructional activity (hard to do unless you have experienced the instructional activity several times), we suggest you consider what you want students to be doing and learning for each 13-minute chunk. Remember to engage students in active learning activities for the most important learning objectives.

Because some of us worry whether we'll have enough material to "fill the time," the authors plan more instructional activities than the class time allows. If you are focusing on what the students are doing and how they are learning the material, you will be less concerned about having enough material. Instead, you will wonder how you can possibly help students learn sophisticated skills within the time available. We suggest you prioritize and schedule the timing along with your learning objectives.

For example, assume you have 40 minutes for the body of class and plan the following instructional activities:

- Small group discussion: 7 minutes
- Whole class discussion: 6 minutes
- Mini-lecture summarizing and clarifying: 10 minutes
- Think-Write-Pair-Share: 3 minutes
- Whole class discussion: 5 minutes
- Point/counterpoint: 9 minutes

In class, however, you realize students need more time for their small group discussions. Because students seem engaged and on task, you decide to extend the time to ten minutes. The whole class discussion similarly reveals several questions and misunderstandings. You let that continue for 15 minutes. It's now 25 minutes into the class and you are more than 10 minutes behind your plan. What do you do?

Return to your learning objectives. What do you want students to learn by the end of this class? Of the instructional activities you have planned, which one is most likely to help students achieve those learning objectives in the remaining 15 minutes? Rather than cramming the planned instructional activities into the time remaining, omit one or more of those activities and focus on the one you think will be most effective. If you plan for this in advance, you can determine which instructional activities are most important, which ones would be helpful, and which ones are less important, but would be great if time allows.

Use time effectively for most of your students. Often teachers don't limit discussion or questions because they fear that doing so is disrespectful to the student asking questions. However, you disrespect the entire class if the discussion meanders off on tangents unrelated to your learning objectives. Several techniques help keep students on task and allow you to limit discussion. One is saying something like, "Last comment goes to Lavanya," even when three other people have their hands up. Another is stating, "Let's hear two more contributions. I'd like to hear from students who have not yet contributed to the class discussion." If you decide not to call on students who volunteer most often, talk to them outside of class, letting them know you appreciate their eagerness and enthusiasm but may not always call on them because you want a variety of students to be heard in class.

Occasionally, you may have extra time in class. To your surprise, students complete their learning activities faster than you planned. Now what? Again, return to your learning objectives. What will help students understand the material at a deep level? One suggestion is asking students to prepare answers in writing. Students often believe they have finished a group assignment once they've discussed it with their peers. However, because articulating ideas *in writing* is such an important lawyering skill, asking students to write a summary of the group's key points is valuable skills practice. When they move from talking to organized, analytical legal writing, students frequently identify gaps in their analysis you can clarify. Another solution to having extra time in class is preparing a supplemental instructional activity to reinforce key learning objectives.

A final word about timing. Some teachers find it helpful to practice their class sessions. They rehearse, refine their class plan, and adjust their planned timing for each part of the class. No matter what else you do, end the class on time. Leave five minutes at the end of class to summarize and provide closure.

Closings: the last five minutes of class

Some of us find it easy to skip this step. The students are fully engaged in the instructional activities described above. We look at the time and see we have three minutes left. We rush through a few final points as students start noisily packing up.

Instead, as suggested in Chapter 3, use the last five minutes of class to consolidate students' learning. In many ways, closings mirror the openings. We tell them what they have been working on and what they have shown us about their learning. We can summarize important points, preview how this class will fit with the next, or provide them with feedback. Alternatively, we can ask students to complete a minute paper about the most important point they learned (see Chapter 10), invite them to summarize material individually or in small groups, or spend a few minutes writing notes to themselves about what they learned.

As with any part of teaching the class, variety is helpful. We recommend developing several approaches to closing class and offer three examples.

Summarize key points

In the last few minutes of class, summarize the class's key learning points. You might use a skeletal outline on the board or a slide and verbally add to it. (This could be the same outline or slide you used at the start of class.)

> *Today you focused on the skill of identifying ambiguity in contracts. You noticed ambiguities in the words used, such as "damage to property or physical injury." The phrase was ambiguous because "damage" alone included physical and economic damage.*
>
> *You also noticed ambiguity created by grammatical use . . .*
>
> *You noticed the problem with spatial terms, such as "within 25 miles" which could mean a traveling distance or a physical radius.*

You noticed ambiguities other students and I hadn't seen.

You've analyzed obvious and sophisticated ambiguities. While excavating ambiguities may seem overelaborate, you learned ambiguities can cost a party millions of dollars.

You've worked through all but the final problem, which is the most complex. Please review that problem for our next class; we'll start with it....

Summarizing may take less than five minutes. The worst that can happen is you allow five minutes for closing and let students leave a minute or two early. Alternatively, you could invite anyone to ask a final question.

Give students time to consolidate their learning

Instead of summarizing, ask the students to reflect and consolidate the class objectives.

Today you had a chance to evaluate different proposed temporary restraining orders. In groups, you examined five different examples of temporary restraining orders, and evaluated each version's advantages and disadvantages.

Please take a minute to write a few notes to yourself. If in practice or on an exam you needed to draft a proposed temporary restraining order, what important things would you want to remind yourself to do?

Give students a few minutes to write. You could then ask students to compare their notes with someone outside their small group or invite the class as a whole to contribute a few important points.

Allow students to reflect on their learning

This technique allows students to practice the skills they need to become self-regulated learners.

Today, you were assigned to play the roles of constituents seeking to resolve a toxic landfill problem. Some of you represented the landowner, others the neighbors, the city, legislators, the company that produced the toxins, and consumers who would benefit from the toxins. Take a minute to think about what you learned from this exercise. Then, write down one thing you learned.

As with the previous suggestion, you could then invite students to compare their notes with each other, share with the whole class, or thank the students for participating and let them leave when they have finished writing.

Closing modification: the very last class

The last class of the semester, like the first class, is special. For some students, this class may be the last time they are in one of your classes. The end of the last class is your chance to leave a final impression. Consider leaving ten to fifteen minutes for the very last closing.

Some teachers like to give words of advice to students, telling them to remember why they are in law school and what their dreams are once they are in practice. Many teachers like to summarize the course, talking about what the students have learned, thanking students for their efforts, and revealing what the teacher most appreciated about teaching these students. One of our colleagues uses the last class to provide a "best of" review, where she describes some highlights of the course, and then invites students to name the one most striking thing that happened to them all semester (inside or outside of class).

Other teachers use the last class as a chance to build students' confidence. They may tell students about the mistakes they've made and suggest how to navigate the stress of final exams. They may tell stories about practice and life. They may offer their assistance and support for future years. They may ask a final question. One of our colleagues stands at the door and shakes the hand of each exiting student. Like any other aspect of teaching, be authentic. Do something you enjoy doing. Try different approaches to ending the course. Reflect and learn from the experience.

Final notes on teaching the class

All teachers have good days and bad days. Avoid seeking perfection, and instead try to gradually increase the value you add to the limited time you have being physically present with your students. You are the single most expensive, most adaptive, and most empathic educational resource available to them. Consider ways to engage students as lawyers in the classroom. Find something to celebrate in every class. Immerse yourself in the ongoing process of developing as a teacher.

Checklist for teaching the class

Illustration 5-3 is a checklist for teaching the class.

Illustration 5-3: Teaching the Class Checklist

Teaching the class: Who in the room is acting like a lawyer? Who is doing most of the talking in the class?

- ❑ **Create a positive learning environment**
  - ❑ Know and use students' names
  - ❑ Be conscious of the messages you send
  - ❑ Be enthusiastic
  - ❑ Model taking risks and acknowledging weaknesses
  - ❑ Envision yourself as a "guide on the side"
  - ❑ Be transparent
  - ❑ Be authentic
- ❑ **Openings—the first five minutes**
  - ❑ Arrive early
  - ❑ Consider the opening message you send
  - ❑ Modify for first and other special days
- ❑ **Body—the heart of the class session**
  - ❑ Use a variety of instructional activities
  - ❑ Use activities that engage the students
  - ❑ Surround mini-lectures with other activities
  - ❑ Use effective questioning techniques
  - ❑ Use visuals students can "read"
  - ❑ Prioritize your timing according to learning objectives
- ❑ **Closings—the last five minutes**
  - ❑ Summarize and consolidate students' learning
  - ❑ Modify for the last class
- ❑ **Engage in ongoing practice, reflection, and evaluation**

Teaching the Class Resources

These three books provide excellent summaries of the research on teaching and learning in higher education and detailed guidance for engaging students in a wide variety of learning exercises. While focused on college teaching, the exercises are easily adapted to law teaching. The first book addresses everything from promoting equity and inclusion and universal design to using visuals effectively and font size and type for slides.

- Elizabeth F. Barkley & Claire Howell Major, Engaged Teaching: A Handbook for College Faculty (SocialGood 2022)
- Elizabeth F. Barkley & Claire Howell Major, Student Engagement Techniques: A Handbook for College Faculty (Jossey-Bass 2d, 2020)

- Claire Howell Major, Michael S. Harris & Todd D. Zakrajsek, Teaching for Learning: 101 Intentionally Designed Educational Activities to Put Students on the Path to Success (Routledge 2d. ed. 2021).

These two books are from the legal education literature on teaching and learning.

- Michael Hunter Schwartz, Gerald F. Hess & Sophie M. Sparrow, What the Best law Teachers Do (Harvard University Press 2013).
- Gerald F. Hess, Steven Friedland, Michael Hunter Schwartz, and Sophie Sparrow, Techniques for Teaching Law 2 (Carolina Academic Press 2011).

Chapter 6

Online Asynchronous Course Design and Delivery

Teachers who are effective in the face-to-face environment can be effective as online teachers, but it is not automatic, and it does not happen overnight.

—Judith V. Boettcher and Rita-Marie Conrad,
The Online Teaching Survival Guide

Introduction

Most law professors have some online component to their courses, and most law students expect and have experience with courses' online features. Using our institution's online Learning Management System (LMS) or another platform, we post course materials such as the course syllabus and list of assignments, handouts, course supplements, and links to other relevant media such as videos and podcasts. We may also use the course LMS to quiz students, capture students' assignments, post grades, moderate discussions, and post announcements. With traditional face-to-face or "onsite" courses, we and the students consider the online part of the course as background—the main event is the face-to-face classroom experience.

During the worst of the COVID pandemic, online teaching became the main event; most of us were suddenly trying to learn how to effectively harness technology to teach from a distance. In many cases, we transferred our face-to-face classes to synchronous Zoom sessions, learning how to share documents, put students in breakout rooms for collaborative exercises, incorporate polling, use chat, and hold online office hours. Post-COVID, the ABA loosened restrictions on distance learning, currently allowing law schools to grant "up to 50 percent of the credit hours required for the J.D. degree" for online courses (ABA Standard 306). Due to the combination of the ABA's looser standard and many law teachers' online teaching experience during the pandemic, more law schools currently offer online or blended hybrid classes, a trend likely to continue. In addition, many law professors have and will continue to add online-line components to their onsite courses. In this chapter we're not talking about COVID-era "emergency" online teaching; instead, this chapter addresses how to intentionally design and teach a completely or almost completely remote course.

In particular, this chapter focuses on designing and teaching asynchronous online law courses because teaching those courses requires the biggest change in our perspective on teaching, and because such courses require significantly more organization and attention than most hybrid courses. One chapter limits how much we can include on this topic; certain areas, such as privacy and copyright issues, as well as artificial intelligence and other emerging technologies, are beyond its scope. Fortunately, a wealth of resources provide detailed guidance about teaching online asynchronously, and more are published every day.

Many of this book's other chapters apply to teaching online asynchronous courses and before designing or teaching an online course, we urge you to first read Chapters 1, 2, 4, and 10. Reading these chapters will give you foundational information about how students learn (Chapter 1), designing a course effectively (Chapter 2), inclusive teaching (Chapter 4), and assessing students' learning (Chapter 10). Here we first identify the advantages of teaching online asynchronous courses and the major differences between teaching online and teaching onsite. We then address how to get started, how to design an online asynchronous course and its separate components, and important points about how to teach the course once it is under way. As repeated throughout this book, our main goal is to help our students learn. While this chapter focuses on online asynchronous courses, you can incorporate many of the concepts in this chapter into a blended or hybrid course, where some of the course is fully asynchronous online, some may be synchronous online, and some is conducted face-to-face.

Before delving into specific suggestions about how to effectively teach online asynchronous courses, keep the following points in mind:

1. teaching an online course is and should be a very different experience than teaching onsite;
2. motivated students can learn as effectively—and possibly even better—from a well-designed and executed asynchronous online course as from an onsite course;
3. designing ways to provide online students with a comparable learning experience requires you to invest significant time and work before the course starts;
4. "being present" and creating a sense of community online is vital to students' learning;
5. during the course, most of your "teaching time" consists of giving students feedback on their regular online submissions;
6. student engagement can occur in a variety of ways; and
7. starting small, capturing what works, and making small improvements each semester can enable you to become effective in helping students learn from an asynchronous online course.

Advantages of online asynchronous and hybrid courses

Online asynchronous and hybrid law courses have multiple advantages. They allow students to learn, study, and submit work remotely; collaborate on projects; and earn JD credits at more of their own pace. Students who otherwise would be unable to attend law school because of distance, jobs, or caregiving responsibilities, can participate in remote online learning. Asynchronous courses provide students with great flexibility, allowing them to pursue a legal education if in-person alternatives are unfeasible. Many online students have long wanted to earn a JD, but their circumstances and the demands on their time have made pursuing that dream impossible. Depending on a law school's programs, students may now earn a JD without having to move or quit their jobs. Offering online courses and programs increases the diversity of our student body and the legal profession.

More introverted students and those who learn by carefully processing information before speaking can also benefit from an online teaching environment. Many of those students are challenged by onsite courses where they are expected to respond quickly and accurately to their teachers' cold calls, think on their feet, and speak articulately about complex material in front of 50 or so classmates. These students benefit from having the time to think about and process questions before committing to an answer.

Law schools and faculty also benefit from online asynchronous and hybrid courses. Gone is the tyranny of course schedules or locating appropriate classroom space. In addition, law teachers can directly and frequently experience what their students are learning. In most online courses, students must regularly submit concrete learning artifacts, producing tangible evidence of what they are learning. Students benefit from seeing their classmates' different perspectives on problems and their different approaches and skills in analyzing them. Law teachers arguably can better ascertain where students need further guidance, clarify misunderstandings, and capture students' progress. As a practical matter, teachers who cannot be present due to other obligations, physical limitations, attending conferences, or weather can still connect and help their students learn.

Above all, teaching online can make most of us better teachers. Teaching effectively online requires us to be much more intentional and explicit about what we want students to learn and why we use our chosen materials and techniques. Because we capture tangible evidence of students' learning, we can also change our course design and engagement methods to enhance student learning. The experience can be terrifying, exciting, and intellectually engaging.

Major differences in teaching asynchronously online and teaching onsite

For most of us, the major differences between teaching onsite and teaching online are the loss of the in-person, in-class shared experience, and the way we spend our time during the course.

Loss of the in-class experience

Many of us greatly enjoy teaching students in person. Onsite, we are present in one space with our students at regularly scheduled times and spaces. We interact with them directly and they do with each other as we teach given courses. While we are inexpert at deciphering students' reactions in person, we can identify some behaviors suggesting we modify, speed up, or repeat our teaching and learning strategies. We can modify our classes in real-time, weaving in current news events or recent court, agency and legislative actions. We can respond to difficult events in students' lives and other demands on their time, such as midterms, job searches, or due dates for writing projects. Onsite, we can build a positive learning community through our voices, using students' names, showing empathy, moving around the classroom, engaging students in small groups, and using a wide range of emotive, expressive, and interpersonal skills. For many of us, teaching onsite is an exciting, stimulating, and inspiring environment. We talk to our students and they to each other before and after class. We can respond to students' questions as they arise and redirect them when they go astray. Together we share a rhythm and structure to the days and weeks—we will all be in Room 204 from 11–12:15 on Tuesdays and Fridays for the entire semester. Onsite we have immediate communication of information and ideas and feedback. Needless to say, teaching is different in an online asynchronous course.

When we teach asynchronously, we lose that collective in-person energy and excitement. If we schedule regular online synchronous office hours, we can interact online in real-time with some of our students, such as holding office hours on Zoom every Thursday from 8:00–9:00 p.m. Eastern Time. Other than office hours, unless our courses also require attending onsite classes for a few days a semester, we miss out on that in-person connection with our students. Many of them are also far removed from each other. Most of us miss the energy of simultaneously engaging with other humans in exploring course material.

In preparing to teach an onsite course, many of us think a lot about what will go on in the classroom. What questions will we ask? How do we predict students will respond? How will we engage students at increasingly complex tasks over the semester? How will we interact with them? How will we spend our limited time together? Are we funny, irreverent, conversational, formal? What will the students call us and how will we address them? What will we wear?

When we prepare to teach an online asynchronous course, we must plan how to mediate our teaching and students' learning through technology. Rather than responding to most students' inputs in real-time, we hear or see their work after they have completed it—on a screen. Unable to pivot during class to ask questions we hadn't thought of, we have to script almost everything in advance. Instead of planning the minutes in a classroom, we design learning exercises for students to complete individually or with others.

Using "teaching time" differently

Teaching an online asynchronous course, we interact with students through technology. Instead of being in class for 90 minutes twice a week, we review and respond to work they have completed hours and days before. During the semester, we spend a lot of time working at a computer observing and giving students' feedback on their weekly submissions.

Teaching onsite, we can add quizzes, assignments, formative assessments, revise slides, adjust reading assignments and modify other aspects of the syllabus and course design as the course proceeds. Teaching online asynchronously, we can modify our courses, but it is considerably more difficult as we need to have planned the whole course in advance. Before the course starts, we also need to spend time making short teaching videos, designing student engagement exercises, and planning ways to give our students feedback on those exercises. As one expert educator stated, teaching online is not like putting food in a slow-cooker and leaving it until the food is done; teachers must be present and actively engaged in an online course at least several times a week.

Learning how to teach an online asynchronous course

Because we have been onsite students for around two or more decades, starting in preschool, we've observed and been immersed in onsite teaching and many of its forms. We have teaching models we can refer to, often fashioning our onsite teaching on what worked well for us when we were students, or what our favorite teachers did. If we have experience teaching in other domains, educated ourselves about the science of teaching and learning, or attended conferences or teaching seminars, we may develop ways of teaching law students that look nothing like the law school courses we attended. While not recommended, based on our experience of being onsite learners, some of us walk into our first onsite law school course without any training in teaching and learning.

Conversely, relatively few of us have experience being immersed in online asynchronous learning. We likely haven't watched movies or shows about asynchronous online teaching, and, while we may have learned how to unclog a pipe from watching YouTube videos, few of us can jump into teaching an online asynchronous online law school course without a lot of preparation and guidance. While online asynchronous courses first became available about forty years ago, in the early 1980s, very few of us know what being an online student feels like. We rarely "have a good, practical sense of the look, pacing, and feel of online courses."

You may have taught online before and need little training. You also may be fortunate to teach at an institution with abundant resources, including excellent instructional designers, videographers, and graphic artists who will help you create professional materials. If not, depending on your fluency with designing asynchronous courses and using different teaching and learning technology, you may need specific training. Teaching asynchronously requires us to develop and use different skills—we need to facilitate student learning without the interpersonal direct contemporaneous experience. We must be more intentional and work harder to communicate with students. Unlike teaching onsite, students are less in a relationship with us and more in a relationship with the course itself.

One of the best ways to learn about online teaching is being a student in an online asynchronous course. As a student, you develop some sense of what online teaching is about, and what works, at least for you. Your institution may offer a course or learning modules for teaching online; spending time immersed in such a course is enormously helpful. Another way to develop skills teaching online is to incorporate more online learning within a traditional onsite course. That approach allows you to gradually design learning modules and materials, gather data about student learning, and continue to develop and build new modules. Regardless of the way you gain a deeper understanding of this relatively new teaching medium, plan on investing considerable time in the process, making mistakes, and learning from them.

Designing an online asynchronous course

Some teachers approach teaching an online asynchronous course as "doing what they've always done, just online." In fact, designing an online asynchronous course requires a different approach. This section addresses the main components of online course design. While all types of courses can be taught online, including skill development courses, simulations, seminars, clinics, or externships, our focus here is on teaching doctrinal courses, whether first year, required or elective. An excellent resource for teaching a variety of courses is Tessa Dysart and Tracy Norton's compilation, LAW TEACHING STRATEGIES FOR A NEW ERA: BEYOND THE PHYSICAL CLASSROOM. Directed primarily towards general higher education audiences, many other resources have extensive suggestions and materials for teaching online. Some of them are listed at the end of this chapter.

Follow general course design principles

As noted above, to design asynchronous online courses effectively, having foundational knowledge about student learning (Chapter 1), effective course design (Chapter 2), incorporating issues relating to racism and diversity (Chapter 4), and assessing students' learning (Chapter 10) better enables you to design an effective online course. As with any course design, creating an online asynchronous course is an iterative process, requiring us, and our students, to be flexible and adapt as we go. We are all learning how to become better at teaching and learning from a distance of time and space.

Assuming you are designing a new course rather than teaching one designed by someone else, before you start, find out how much autonomy you have. Depending on your institution, you may have complete control over how you design all aspects of your course. Alternatively, your institution may require certain course components, such as using a specific LMS, making videos for each unit or module of instruction, requiring online synchronous "office hours," or demanding a certain number of student assessments. Other programs may have even more highly structured conditions for online courses, such as required technologies, time limits within which to respond to students' questions, specific methods of feedback, established rubrics, and set course grade weights. Regardless of how much autonomy you have over designing a course, you or others at your institution will need to ensure the course complies with ABA Standard 310 regarding calculating credit hours.

As explained in Chapter 2 on effective course design, whether you are creating an online, hybrid, synchronous, or asynchronous course, it is essential you identify what you want students to learn and how they will show it. Break the course into units—or modules, as most online educators call them—sequence learning modules in ways that work for you and your students, select relevant course materials for students to learn from, and plan formative and summative assessments. If your law school offers the same course online and onsite, the online course should be substantially equivalent to the onsite course in terms of learning goals, topics, and number of credits.

Choose your Learning Management System

More than likely your law school has adopted a specific Learning Management System (LMS). These online learning platforms, such as Canvas, D2L Brightspace, TWEN, or Blackboard, include a variety of features, such as course navigation systems, learning modules, online quizzes, group discussion platforms, wiki pages, online links, places for announcements, depositories for student assignments, grade calculators, rubrics, class emails, instant messaging, video recording and editing, and synchronous video conferences.

Even if your institution's chosen LMS has limitations, using it can be very helpful. First, you have access to resources within your school to support the LMS, such as educational technology experts. Second, you can learn from and troubleshoot problems with colleagues who use the same LMS. Third, students will have access to instructional support for the LMS when they experience problems. Especially when new to teaching online asynchronous teaching, many of us would rather outsource technology and LMS troubleshooting to those who have greater expertise and focus our energies on student engagement. Fourth, it may be easier for your students if their other teachers use the same LMS. Having all their courses on the same LMS makes it easier for students to navigate the LMS and easily locate relevant assignments, links, and materials. Law school is challenging enough on its own for most students; for online students, adding more technological challenges adds to their cognitive load, reducing the time and energy they have to focus on successfully learning your course goals. To ease online students' cognitive load, don't require them to learn about a new system's navigation, collaboration, and other communication and media tools.

Conversely, if you are an early adopter of new technology who needs no support to use an LMS, and your institution places no restrictions on technology, there is no reason you can't design the LMS of your dreams. You may decide to create virtual worlds, interactive games, and any number of elaborate structures that will fully engage students who love and may prefer interactions mediated by technology. Those of us who are less tech-savvy, however, benefit enormously from others helping make our course websites more effective and bailing us out when we mess up.

Your LMS may have many functions you have previously not explored. Don't feel you need to use them all and never adopt a new technology tool unless it helps students learn. Use technology because it will help students master your course learning goals, not because of its dazzling features. You don't need to adopt a cool new technology just because a colleague uses it. We are fortunate today to have access to an extraordinary array of new technologies, but given the speed with which new technologies arrive, it's impossible to keep up with all technological developments. And bear in mind that not all students are equally adept at using technology. We recommend starting with a basic set of tools well supported by your institution. In THE ONLINE TEACHING SURVIVAL GUIDE, authors and educators with decades of online teaching experience, Judith Boettcher and Rita-Marie Conrad, recommend starting with three or four tools, becoming proficient with them, and then gradually adding to them as you continue to teach online.

As you continue to develop proficiency with online teaching tools, invite students to share their learning experiences with online tools, some of which they may have used in previous educational settings. As with many other aspects of teaching, asking for student input and listening to their feedback and insights can serve you well. Whichever tools you use, review them every two-to-three years to see if they continue to help students learn. As Professors Boettcher and Conrad state, technology "tools are similar to pets, plants, and cars. They require investments of money and training, and regularly updating them in sync with the world around us."

Online asynchronous course components

Some of the components of an online asynchronous course will be the same as an onsite course; the focus here is on three main components which are more prominent or new to this environment. Once you have identified your LMS or "course container," include the same kinds of materials and information as you would in your onsite course's LMS, such as the course syllabus; a list of assignments and due dates; supplemental course materials; links to relevant podcasts, blogs, videos, and articles; and a gradebook. Then add the major course components for an online asynchronous course such as mini lecture videos, frequent student exercises and assessments, and course communication tools.

Create video mini lectures

Make video mini lectures about course content to convey the kind of information you would share with students in an onsite course. As with an onsite mini lecture, for each course module, point out important takeaways, synthesize authorities, and clarify common areas of misunderstanding. Above all, keep your videos short—ideally five-to-seven minutes. Based on her review of multiple research studies, in Small Teaching Online, educator Flower Darby recommends videos be no longer than six minutes. While videos take time to make initially, you can reuse your videos the next time you teach online or make them available as supplements to your onsite students. The advantage for students is they can pause, rewind and review video mini lectures at their own pace and on their own schedule.

Limiting videos to about six minutes is effective for multiple reasons. (1) Students have increasingly short attention spans for any kind of lecture, and paying attention to a video is harder than paying attention to a human in the same room. (2) If you need to revise or update your course, you can edit and replace short video clips much more easily than editing a longer video and splicing in new content. (3) Short videos, appropriately labeled, also allow students to find and review those specific video segments addressing topics with which they struggle. (4) Short videos can be followed by low-stakes short formative assessments designed to assess whether the student grasped the video's foundational learning points. If the student cannot accurately answer a five-question multiple-choice quiz on the reading and accompanying video, the student can quickly rewind and review the video, rather than having to search through a lengthy video to find the relevant topic.

Some advocates of online asynchronous education argue all videos should be made only by professional videographers and editors. Because students are accustomed to seeing slick videos on social media, they argue that showing them anything less than professional quality videos will cause students to disengage, become frustrated, or lose respect for the teacher and course. Certainly, professionally-made videos will probably have higher quality sound and images, but not all of us have access to those kinds of resources. Instead, we take the time to create the most professional videos we can. It is not easy to create such videos. Because our words are captured on a screen, may be viewed by a much larger audience, and may need to be usable for several years, we need to be much more precise and concise than we would be when speaking to students in a classroom. Some professors, including experienced online educators, report that it takes them about an hour to make two-to-three minutes of effective video. Each six-minute video could take up to three hours to make, and that estimate excludes the work done in preparing notes, scripts, and images before shooting video. We recommend starting with a limited number of mini lecture videos addressing the most important course material and adding videos as you continue to develop your course.

Other educators encourage us to create more informal videos, arguing that having a stray hair or verbal stumble helps students experience us as more accessible and human. Informal mini lecture videos show more about who we are. You may choose to have a mixture of formal and informal videos, depending on your teaching approach, location of the video within the course (beginning, middle, or end), or topic. Regardless, follow the principles of Universal Design for Learning (UDL) "a framework to improve and optimize teaching and learning for all people based on scientific insights into how humans learn" (https://www.cast.org/impact/universal-design-for-learning-udl). For the visually impaired and those who prefer to process new material visually, include closed captioning or a script and tag all images with descriptions.

Making the videos is challenging for many of us. When giving a mini lecture during an onsite course, you and your students are all participating in the moment. You are speaking directly to other humans in the room. You may move around the room, insert students' names, illustrate your points through gestures and props, modulate your voice, make eye contact with different students, and repeat or skip parts of your mini lecture depending on your perception of students' attention. In contrast, most video lectures involve us looking into a camera lens and speaking into a void. This takes some getting used to, especially if you are trying to look at the camera while also checking your notes, using slides, showing images, etc. Practicing helps. Even when we do have professionals helping us, recording us as we read from a teleprompter, we may struggle to look and sound anything other than stiff and awkward.

If your preferred mini lectures consist of narrating over slides, include minimal text on each slide and pause to allow students time to read the slides. Afterward, speak conversationally about the slides' content, amplifying points, giving examples, and exploring nuances about the topic. Above all, avoid reading the slides. When we see written material on a screen, our brains automatically seek to read and understand it. Trying to comprehend the written onscreen text while listening to someone speaking is distracting and reduces our ability to understand either the text or the spoken word.

As you teach the course, if new laws or court decisions impact course content, add a mini-lecture video with those updates. Similarly, if students routinely struggle with a subject, such as conflicts in legal ethics courses, make an additional mini-lecture video. For sustainability, avoid referencing specific page numbers from texts, current dates, or including other references that require you to redo videos each time you change any part of the course. The casebook you use may come out with a new edition, changing its content and pagination, or someone else may teach the online course you developed. We suggest you keep each video independent of the other mini-lecture videos, making each be more like short stories than book chapters; when possible, avoid referring to one video when making another.

Most LMSs allow us to upload videos for student access. If doing so on your LMS creates a storage problem, you can upload your videos to a private YouTube channel. Alternatively, consider making audio files available for mini lectures, which consume less bandwidth and may work better for students accessing courses on their phones. While some of us have excellent internet access and bandwidth almost all the time, students who are on military assignments, live in rural areas, or live off the grid may have limitations. To combat this, most institutions offering online courses have specific hard and software requirements for all students. Even with those requirements, however, we have had students struggle to post course assignments from their phones while sitting in the car at their child's soccer game or be kicked off a site during a thunderstorm.

Watching your own videos can be brutal. Many of us don't love how we look in photographs, let alone how we look and sound on video. You may be inclined to spend hours trying to improve your videos, but your efforts may yield minimal gains. It's hard to see ourselves the way our students will; be kind to yourself and don't expect perfection. If possible, invite a friend to review one of your videos and give you candid feedback about one or two things you could change to make the viewing experience better. Learn from the experience. A student who viewed one of the first mini lecture videos one of us made later took another of our online courses after we had much more experience making videos. He voiced his surprise, commenting, "You're so much more relaxed and animated on these videos!"

Design student engagement exercises

When we teach onsite, we want all students in the classroom to be actively engaged, participating in the kinds of higher-level thinking that leads to long-term, deep understanding. In doctrinally focused courses, most of us use class discussions, whole class or small group, to enable students practice applying, evaluating, and synthesizing legal rules and theories. While we hope all students are paying attention and learning from us and their classmates, the reality is some or even many of them can hide in the back of the room or behind their laptops.

In an online asynchronous course, we don't have the luxury of that kind of interaction. Instead, we need to design other ways to engage students in their learning. These exercises usually consist of student experiences that engage them in practicing the skills on their own time and then learning from our feedback. When considering the kind and content of exercises you assign to students, review your course goals and what you want students to learn. In essence, part of designing an online asynchronous course is creating weekly or bi-weekly assessments of student learning. Instead of verbally answering questions in class, students repeatedly engage in the course through learning artifacts such as individual or collaborative writing assignments, graphic representations, or audio or visual presentations. Just as we don't have the luxury of leading in person discussions, students in online classes don't have the luxury of opting not to participate. In online asynchronous courses, students can't hide because they have to regularly read, write, edit, critique, question, peer review, and collaborate.

One often-used model for engaging online asynchronous students is requiring them to submit responses to a teacher-designed discussion prompt once a week, followed by responding to two or more students' submissions a few days later. These discussion submissions can work well, depending on how you write the discussion prompt, the prompt's connection to course content, and the specific directions students need to follow to earn credit for their response. Often, however, when the prompt is less well drafted, lacks a meaningful connection to the course topics, and can be responded to with little effort or new learning on students' part, it can be perceived as busywork. As one of our online asynchronous students told us, a straight-A, highly motivated student with a PhD, "Every Thursday night we have to post something and then respond to two classmates' by Sunday night. But they're really easy to do and don't take much time." The student's perception was that she and her classmates were required to post something to show they were engaged in the course, but they learned little from the process. Some online students appreciate why we require these discussion posts and take them seriously, but based on our experiences teaching online, many don't.

As with any kind of formative assessment or student learning exercise, when designing effective discussion prompts, consider what you want students to do to produce their learning artifacts. For example, in a criminal law course, ask students to read statutes and articles about mandatory prosecution in domestic violence cases. Citing to those authorities, ask students to advocate for or against mandatory prosecution. The goal is not just for the students to argue one side or the other but to engage in the process of closely reading primary and secondary authorities; analyzing data about domestic violence crimes; organizing arguments based on facts, law, and policy; and finally writing well-reasoned persuasive arguments using correct writing mechanics. Alternatively, you could design an exercise as an opportunity for engagement but not completion, allowing students to submit a response with bullet points, short phrases, or rambling sentences.

Some exercises might be directly connected to the practice of law, such as writing some of the documents below, or you can ask broader questions like the one above on mandatory prosecution for domestic violence crimes. During an online Remedies course, for example, asking a discussion question like, "How much weight should public interest considerations carry in determining whether injunctive relief is appropriate?" may engage students in deeper thinking about the underlying goals and theories of remedies and equitable relief. A related discussion question students answer the following week could ask them to research and synthesize three court opinions where judges relied on public interest considerations in granting or denying equitable relief.

When designing most of your discussion prompts or student exercises, align them with your course's most heavily weighted summative assessments, such as final exams. In an online Constitutional Law course, for example, if the final exam asks students to analyze a constitutional law issue using two different justices' philosophies, design discussions that give students practice in identifying how justices apply different constitutional law philosophies to different contexts. Likewise, an online Property course that bases a large portion of a student's final grade on future interests could include multiple discussion questions comparing the merits and limitations of different kinds of instruments creating those interests.

However, if students are primarily assessed on identifying relevant facts from a variety of documents and then applying majority and minority rules to those facts, students would be better advantaged by having assignments related to writing similar analysis. For example, during a module on permanent injunctive relief, students could be asked to submit responses to problems asking them to identify the relative hardships and burdens on the parties if equitable relief is granted. Or in a preliminary injunction module, identify the arguments and address the counter arguments for why a client is likely to succeed on the merits.

Similarly, instead of posing less engaging discussion prompts, we can use a variety of instruments that will help students build the kinds of skills and knowledge they need to succeed in the course and in law practice. Regardless of the exercises you assign, make them relate to your course learning goals, have real-world relevance, and require students to use skills and knowledge to complete them effectively. Ideally start with simpler assignments early in the course and develop complexity over time, interleaving topics to help students apply big course concepts and individual rules.

With all exercises, follow the principles about designing effective assessments and consider the different kinds of assessment in Chapter 10. Identify what you want students to do, tell students why you want them to do it, and give clear directions. If students earn credit or grades for an assignment, provide them with explicit criteria in advance. Tell students the estimated amount of time you expect them to spend on the exercise. If you require citations and certain formats, explain what they are and why you are requiring them. Depending on your class size and the number and frequency of assigned exercises, consider imposing a word limit and explicitly articulating your rationale for it. After one of us required students to submit weekly written responses to multiple problems from our coursebook and then received an excellent but 27-page response, we decided to limit the number of problems and words. Some students complained they couldn't do justice to the questions within the 300-word limit. Others appreciated that future employers might only want as much text as would fit on a phone screen and valued having the opportunity to practice writing concisely and making intelligent judgments about what to exclude.

Along with giving very clear directions, we recommend giving all students the same deadline. One course we taught required students to submit assignments by 11:59 p.m. in their time zone. Submitting assignments on time was one of the three requirements for students to earn credit for their work, the other two being following all directions and showing a good faith effort. Given our LMS and that students were located all over the US and abroad, it took hours to determine whether a student submitted their work on time. The next time we set all deadlines for 11:59 Pacific Time.

In addition to the assessments described in Chapter 10, below are a few concrete suggestions about ways to actively engage students with course material without having those assignments turn into busywork.

Written responses to hypotheticals

Teaching onsite, many of us pose hypothetical scenarios to students. We typically ask students to respond verbally to those scenarios, comparing the new facts to the authorities assigned for class, identifying underlying policies for certain rules and outcomes, or synthesizing a line of cases, among other tasks. While leading the discussion of a hypothetical, we can start with less challenging questions and follow up with harder questions or new facts. On the spot, we can tweak the questions based on students' responses, correct misunderstandings, direct students to read material more closely, find and cite to authority for their propositions, or call on a friend to help answer the question.

To simulate this kind of engagement in an online asynchronous course we can post the written hypothetical to the class, asking them to post written responses to specific questions by a certain deadline. Set the LMS so that students can't see their classmates' submissions until they have independently completed and posted their own work. Use one discussion forum for the whole class, or create multiple discussion fora, assigning different groups of students to each discussion forum. When the assignment deadline has passed make some or all responses available to all students so they can learn from each other and build upon their ideas.

After students post their responses to the initial question, we can add facts to the hypothetical and ask students to respond three or four days later to explain whether those new facts change their analyses and why. Alternatively, if a hypothetical problem has multiple correct answers, once students have posted their responses, we can ask them to evaluate the merits of different answers. If you use a coursebook that has problems, you can assign those problems for students to answer in their written discussion posts. Because students will be answering the problems in writing, and because it will help students focus on the relevant task, you may want to add more information about the facts, questions to be addressed, issues to avoid, and other material that will yield better learning. Depending on your course learning goals and the size of the class, you could ask students to complete module exercises individually, in pairs, or small groups. For suggestions about forming and structuring small group exercises, see Chapter 3 on designing individual class sessions. Students could individually draft and post their answers by a certain date, then collaboratively compile a response representing their best ideas. On a job, in other educational settings, and through other organizational activities, many students already have experience collaborating using cloud-based word processing applications such as Google Docs or Teams. We've often found that at least one student in a small group knows how to use these tools and is more than happy to teach their classmates how to use them effectively.

There are many advantages to having students submit written responses to hypotheticals or complete any kind of law-related writing assignment. First, having to put their thinking in writing helps students deepen their analysis. Second, it gives students more practice writing about legal topics, from which almost all of them can benefit. Third, you can more easily evaluate what students understand by seeing their thinking made visible in writing. And fourth, with their permission, you can use students' work as templates, models, or future sample answers.

Portions of or complete legal documents

In addition to showing their engagement and understanding through written responses to hypotheticals, students can apply their learning to drafting a client letter or email, a provision of a contract, part of a complaint, a set of jury instructions, etc.

If you expect answers in a specific format, consider providing students with a template they can download and use. For example, in a Remedies course, students could be assigned to draft a proposed temporary restraining order. In a Torts course, students could draft a demand letter to an insurance company explaining their client's injuries and how they arrived at their estimated damages. To build complexity and scaffold students' learning, students could be asked to draft one part of a document the first week, revise the first part and add another part over the second and third weeks, and so forth.

Outlines, charts, matrices, and concept maps

While some students think linearly and find lists and outlines most helpful to develop deep understanding, others benefit from organizing and representing different concepts and their relationships using other formats, such as charts, graphs, matrices, and concept maps. You could require students to use a particular format, such as a concept map, or allow students to demonstrate the connections among and between concepts using their choice of graphic. Students could complete these in discrete parts, starting with one or two simple concepts, and then adding complexity over days or weeks. For example, in an online Torts course, after working through negligence modules about ways a plaintiff can prove a defendant breached their duty of care, students could show the difference between proving breach through a defendant's violating a relevant statute and acting unlike an ordinary reasonable person under the same or similar circumstances. Having to represent concepts visually helps some students learn more deeply. Seeing how others graphically represent concepts and relationships enables other students to gain perspectives they otherwise would miss. And you benefit from seeing novel and creative ways in which students make connections.

Multimedia exercises and assessments

Depending on your course goals, you may also ask students to upload videos or audio files showing students engaged in various simulations. In Property, students could make an audio file of them using plain language to explain adverse possession to a client or upload a photo of an easement. In Civil Procedure, students could make videos of their arguments in support of a motion to dismiss. The possibilities are endless.

Other forms of assessments

In addition to generating learning artifacts students can show their engagement and learning through online multiple-choice and short answer quizzes. Having one or more short—five to ten—question quizzes per module requires students to assess their learning and us to gain data about areas where they struggle. Some of us use quizzes as part of a conditional release technique (also called adaptive release). With this approach students have restricted access to online course components until they successfully complete an online quiz. Some of us allow multiple attempts until students answer all questions correctly; others require a certain percentage of correct answers, and others just require completion. Students can't access another module or course component or see examples of their classmates' work until they complete the assigned tasks.

You can also engage students more informally with course material, such as assigning all students to summarize the previous module's main takeaways in a maximum of 250 words, describing what they already know about a new module, posting descriptions of effective study techniques to a discussion forum, uploading a recent news story related to a course module, sharing articles or other resources that extend students' knowledge, and identifying resources other students may find helpful. As noted earlier, design exercises that you believe will help students learn, and be transparent about what you are asking students to do and why.

When designing exercises, bear in mind that you will need to respond in some fashion to every course assignment (see more below on giving feedback in Teaching the Course). As one student told us, "If I know you are going to read what I submit, I put more effort into it." While designing student exercises, also design and prepare ways to provide feedback, such as writing sample answers, preparing rubrics, and drafting detailed scoring sheets. These too take considerable amounts of time. Take notes so you can learn what's effective the next time you teach the same or another course.

Design effective course communication tools

As teaching expert Claire Howell Major expresses in TEACHING ONLINE: A GUIDE TO THEORY, RESEARCH, AND PRACTICE, "Communication is what makes or breaks an online course.... Making sure that communication actually happens requires careful planning and structuring, as well as maintaining a high level of effort throughout the course." Teaching onsite, we can communicate directly and simultaneously with our students every class, usually once or twice a week. Among things we communicate, we can preview the next class's material, pose questions for students to consider as they prepare for the next module, modify course assignments, respond to students' questions, or identify the potential topics on a final exam. In online asynchronous courses we have to work harder to communicate the same information. Without the benefit of a back-and-forth exchange or conveying messages through our voices and body language, we must be more intentional and precise about how we communicate. It's hard to convey an authentic welcoming smile in writing. Subtleties are lost, and sarcasm falls flat.

We can, however, use a variety of communication channels to regularly and repeatedly connect with our students. Through our LMS, we can send individual and whole class emails; post short written, video or audio announcements; have a general discussion forum for FAQs and student questions; provide feedback and words of encouragement; identify common mistakes and misperceptions; make video clips giving overviews of new modules, explaining the purpose of an assignment and how it relates to our course learning goals; and use all of these to reinforce core objectives repeatedly throughout the course.

In SMALL TEACHING ONLINE, educator Flower Darby explains how she communicates with students about upcoming assignments. By posting a short video with the following components, she ensures more students will complete the right assignment, deliver higher quality work, and reduce her need to explain further. In her pre-assignment informal videos she says,

> **"Here's what I want you to do,"** and describes the assignment. In a law school course, this could be stating something along the lines of, *"I want you to write the opening paragraphs of a cease and desist letter."*
>
> **"Here's why I want you to do it,"** and explains why the assignment will help students learn. *"Writing the opening paragraphs of a cease-and-desist letter will help you briefly summarize your client's problem and legal demand."*
>
> **"Here's how to do it,"** and provides detailed instructions about what she wants to see in students' work. *"Follow the criteria in the posted rubric, cite relevant portions of the Trademark Statute, use the attached letter template, and write in plain language. Use a maximum of 300 words to identify your client's right to their trademark, how the recipient infringed on your client's mark, what you want the recipient to do, when you want it completed, and what will happen if the recipient doesn't comply within the deadline.*

You could put all that information in writing, but because students are already required to read significant amounts of complex material, watching and listening to your directions may be a much-welcomed change. As described below about teaching the course, plan to use a variety of communication methods regularly and often.

As you become comfortable teaching online asynchronous courses, consider engaging your students in creating effective communication tools. More comfortable using Teams than accessing an online course's LMS and its less intuitive layout, one semester a student voluntarily posted all course announcements, updates, samples, feedback and other material generated during the semester to Teams. He said it helped him track assignments and due dates and manage his time effectively; other students stated it helped them do the same.

Teaching the course once it is under way

Every source we consulted about online asynchronous teaching emphasized the importance of having a teacher presence in the course and creating and maintaining a positive learning community while the course is in session. Based on our own and others' experience, another key component of teaching online asynchronously is managing your time so you can effectively respond to and provide feedback on students' learning. These are discussed below.

The importance of teacher presence

Even more than in an onsite course, the teacher in an online course is more of a "guide on the side," serving as a coach, guide and mentor. But students need to know their guide is paying attention and cares about them. According to online teaching leaders Professors Boettcher and Concord, "Regular, thoughtful, daily presence plays a significant role in learner satisfaction with learning experiences." Due to the disconnected, and, to many of us, strange and unnatural nature of online asynchronous courses, creating and maintaining a presence in these courses is essential.

Some expert teachers recommend being present in the course every day by commenting on student work, sharing ideas, or referencing relevant current events. They recommend preparing communications in advance and setting scheduled release times during the course. Alternatively, you could log into your course for a few minutes every day to communicate with your students. These regular communications don't have to be long, complex or significant. They can be as simple as offering words of support, providing study tips, directing students to a resource, or reminding students of due dates. At the very least, plan to show your presence in the course at least twice a week.

At the beginning of a course, introduce yourself to your students through a short informal video or slideshow. Share your philosophy about online asynchronous teaching. If you are comfortable talking with students about your families, pets, and interests outside of law school, do so. Tell them about your background before becoming a law teacher, your teaching journey, and why you enjoy teaching them. Tell them how they can succeed in your course and what you expect of them. Be authentic. Most students enjoy learning about who you are as a person.

During the course, show your presence by responding to students' emails, usually within 24 hours during business days. Post a summary of the highlights of a learning module, discuss students' submissions, or post an audio recording that previews the following module. Check in on students who fall behind or show they are struggling. Hold online synchronous chat or video office hours where students can ask questions. Encourage students to ask questions and nudge you if they haven't had a response within a certain number of hours or days. Consider meeting individual students through a ten-minute videoconference or phone call. Your presence shows students you care about them and their learning.

In the same vein, if you will be less available due to spending time attending a conference, or going to a friend's wedding, give students advance notice. Explain to students you're not abandoning them, just going offline for a few days, and give them a date when you'll be back and present in the course.

The first few times one of us taught an online asynchronous class, we scheduled 15–20-minute individual videoconference meetings with all 37 students. Students signed up through the appointments feature of the course LMS, and all were asked to complete their meetings within the first three weeks of the course. These individual meetings took considerable amounts of time but were well worth the investment.

Before each meeting, these students, whose average age was 38 and many of whom had other graduate degrees, were asked to upload their resume, CV, or description of their backgrounds to a dropbox only visible to us, not their classmates. We looked at students' backgrounds before our individual meetings, and asked our online students about why they wanted to earn a JD and what other demands they had on their time. Their answers were fascinating, and allowed us to make a personal connection, even if brief, with each one of them. Many commented how much they appreciate speaking to their teacher alone.

When the class size increased to over 70 students a few years later, we stopped holding individual meetings due to the amount of time they took. However, the next time we taught the course, we reinstated these meetings, limiting them to 10 minutes, and spacing them over a longer period of time. While it takes considerable time to speak individually with each student, making even a brief connection with our students increases our ability to work with them, especially when they get behind or struggle to learn course material.

Creating and maintaining a positive learning community

Closely connected to having a presence in the class is creating positive and safe learning communities where students can try new things and make mistakes. As explained in Chapter 5, Teaching the Class, creating positive learning communities significantly helps students learn. As humans, we are wired to make connections to other humans, and our interactions with others help us see different perspectives and test out ideas. Our brains are social, and we need to interact with other humans to deepen our learning. Students need to interact with us and their classmates to help them learn; looking online at course materials, videos, and texts is rarely sufficient.

Without the benefit of us casually interacting with students, and students interacting with each other in an onsite course, it's especially important to be intentional about creating ways to build community in an online asynchronous course. and support interpersonal relationships between you and the students, your students and you, and the students with each other. Learning is a social enterprise.

There are multiple ways to build and maintain community. At the beginning of the course, ask students to make two-minute videos introducing themselves to their classmates. Because some students may already know each other, some of us ask all students to share one piece of information about themselves that others don't know, and that they are willing to disclose. You could also ask students to post an audio file explaining the meaning and origins of their names, talking about their favorite interests, or what they hope to learn in the course. Some of us like to ask students to tell us and their classmates about their favorite foods and how they procure them. Unlike sports, hobbies, and close family members, everyone must eat to survive, and students' food stories are refreshingly vivid and mouthwatering.

Nontraditional students, first generation students, and students who come from less well-represented groups may especially feel like they don't belong. They may well doubt they truly belong in law school. When they interact with other students, however, they often realize their confusion is shared and their ideas are valued. To help students connect to each other, you could assign pairs or small groups of students to ask each other a question about how they plan to succeed in the course, what they know about the course topic, or what they are curious about. Facilitating students' connection to each other reduces attrition and feelings of isolation or not belonging.

Another way to facilitate community and students' interaction is to set up a "student café" or "lounge" discussion board where students can pose and answer their classmates' questions. Sometimes students will develop their own independent communication channels, closed to anyone outside the class, where they can share complaints, ideas, and advice. The advantage to having a course-related student café discussion forum is that you can monitor it for culturally sensitive language and offensive comments. If invited, you can also weigh in on students' comments and questions.

Not all approaches will work for all students. Try different ones and learn from your efforts.

Managing your time during the course and responding to students' work

One of the most common questions teachers ask about online asynchronous teaching is whether teaching online takes more or less time than teaching onsite. The answer is "maybe." As with preparing any new course, designing the course and its components, monitoring discussions, communicating with students multiple times a week, and giving feedback on student work will take the most time the first time you teach it. During the course, the size of the class, nature of students' assignments, quality and quantity of feedback you provide, and your familiarity with teaching online will shape the amount of time you spend. According to some experts in online teaching, with a significant initial investment in designing the course, you can continue to tweak and update your course and give students feedback in about the same amount of time it takes to teach onsite.

One of the challenges to accurately assessing how much time it takes to teach an online course is our changed perception of time. We have to work harder to communicate. Gone are uninterrupted chunks of time when we are present in class, focused solely on teaching and learning. Instead, we sit at a computer, getting interrupted by emails, news alerts, and other distractions. Because it takes more time to complete a task when we divert our attention elsewhere and then return to the task, we also may be working inefficiently. We lack the rhythm and structure of teaching onsite and can easily focus on tasks other than helping our invisible and distant students learn.

To teach effectively online it helps to create set routines for engaging with the course and providing students with feedback. Just because our course runs 24/7 doesn't mean we should or can be present in it every waking hour. After completing one semester of online asynchronous teaching, one of our colleagues realized the only way she could ensure she could provide students with timely feedback was to devote one day a week to teaching her online asynchronous course. The bulk of her students' assignments were due by 11:59 p.m. Sunday. Not being a night owl and raising two young children, responding late at night was not an option. On Mondays and Thursdays she commuted over an hour each way to teach onsite. She carved out almost all of Tuesday to provide students with feedback, held online office hours Tuesday nights, and checked her online course LMS and emails briefly during the other days. She usually collected two or three days of students' questions at a time and posted those questions and her responses to her LMS twice a week.

Whatever your approach, we strongly recommend you don't get behind. Students often have work due every week. That requires us to respond by commenting on individual students' submissions, releasing a sample answer and explanation, using a rubric to assess students' work, or providing whole class feedback. If we don't respond, students assume we haven't read their work or care about their efforts. Our lack of reliable feedback and engagement will likely make them frustrated and less engaged in their learning. In addition, unless you have support staff doing it for you, you need to track students' progress through the course. Looking at students' data on your LMS, you can see how many times students have logged into the course, where they have spent time, and how close they are to completing a course module. We recommend you keep track of how you spend your time teaching an online course. Yes, this itself takes more time, but a log can help you see where you are spending your time and how you might structure your time more efficiently the next time.

In terms of providing students with feedback on their student engagement exercises, follow the suggestions from Chapter 10, Assessing Students. That chapter contains a wide variety of ways to provide students with feedback on their learning. Most of those forms of feedback refer to written material; we encourage you to vary your feedback using audio and video recordings as well.

As you develop your skills teaching online asynchronously, be patient and kind to yourself. Learning to teach online is challenging and you will get better over time. Keep it simple at the beginning so you can become comfortable and more adept as you go.

Checklist for online asynchronous course design and delivery

Illustration 6-1 is a checklist for online asynchronous course design and delivery.

Illustration 6-1: Online asynchronous course design and delivery

- ❑ **Familiarize yourself with asynchronous online learning**
    - ❑ Recognize teaching online is different from teaching onsite
    - ❑ Enroll in an online asynchronous course
    - ❑ Learn about teaching asynchronously online
- ❑ **Follow general course design principles**
- ❑ **Choose your Learning Management System**
- ❑ **Design the online course**
- ❑ **Create short videos on discrete topics**
- ❑ **Design student engagement exercises**
    - ❑ Written responses to problems and hypotheticals
    - ❑ Portions or complete legal documents
    - ❑ Outlines, charts, matrices, and concept maps
    - ❑ Multimedia exercises and assessments
    - ❑ Other forms of assessments
- ❑ **Design effective course communication tools**
- ❑ **Teaching the online asynchronous course**
    - ❑ Be present in the course
    - ❑ Create and maintain a positive learning community
    - ❑ Manage your time and regularly respond to students' work
- ❑ **Engage in ongoing practice, reflection, and evaluation**

Teaching Online—Resources

Designed for higher education in general, the five books below provide excellent and detailed guidance about teaching online.

- Elizabeth F. Barkley & Claire Howell Major, Engaged Teaching: A Handbook for College Faculty (SocialGood 2022)
- Judith V. Boettcher & Rita-Marie Conrad, The Online Teaching Survival Guide: Simple and Practical Pedagogical Tips (Jossey-Bass 3d. ed. 2021)
- Flower Darby, Small Teaching Online: Applying Learning Science in Online Classes (Jossey-Bass 2019)
- Claire Howell Major, Teaching Online: A Guide to Theory, Research, and Practice (Johns Hopkins University Press 2015)
- Linda B. Nilson & Ludwika A. Goodson, Online Teaching at Its Best: Merging Instructional Design with Teaching and Learning Research (Jossey-Bass 2d. ed. 2021)

The text below includes excellent suggestions and nuts and bolts ideas about teaching online to law students, including teaching first year courses, legal research skills courses, upper-level courses, seminars, simulation courses, clinical supervision, externships, and bar preparation programs.

- Tessa L. Dysart & Tracy L. M. Norton, Eds., Law Teaching Strategies for a New Era: Beyond the Physical Classroom (Carolina Academic Press 2021)

Chapter 7

Student Motivation, Attitudes, and Self-Regulation

Introduction

> "It's easy to teach 1Ls. But how do you motivate burnt-out 3Ls?"
>
> "One day in class, I called on three students, and none of them were prepared. I just wanted to walk right back out of the room! What else could I do?"
>
> "I want my students to develop a sense of professionalism and a commitment to the lawyer's responsibility to serve the community. But how do you teach values?"
>
> "My students just want to be spoon-fed. They don't want to do any of the work for themselves. How do I get my students to take control over their own learning?"

Whenever we do faculty workshops on teaching—for our colleagues, at other law schools, at conferences—someone invariably asks us these kinds of questions. In our experience, it is not at all unusual for smart, dedicated, passionate law teachers to express concerns about motivating their students, about changing or developing student attitudes and values, and about training law students to be self-motivated, reflective, lifelong learners. This chapter is our effort to address those concerns.

We have chosen to join these topics in a single chapter because each addresses a different facet of what law teachers perceive to be some of the emotional issues in the law school learning process. Motivating students, influencing them to change or adopt new attitudes, and inspiring professional growth all focus on the students as people and our role in the students' personal development. In many ways, this work has become even more urgent as we adjust to students who spent much of their undergraduate learning in online, isolated environments in recent years.

This chapter begins with the research on motivating students. We introduce the research on intrinsic vs. extrinsic motivation and suggest the gold standard for motivation, known as "flow," to which law professors can aspire. We then suggest some concrete things law professors can do to motivate their students and to facilitate flow.

We then turn to a discussion of the research on attitude change, discussing the spectrum of possible attitude changes, the facets of attitude change, and the techniques law professors can use to facilitate attitude change.

Finally, based on the motivation and attitude change materials, we suggest concrete ways law professors can motivate students to re-think what they know about being learners and to choose to become self-actualized, reflective, lifelong learners.

Motivating students

Introduction

On the one hand, motivating students arguably is not its own, separate subject but, instead, is a natural outgrowth of adopting the good teaching principles we describe in this book. As you read this discussion of motivation, you will hear echoes of other ideas explored throughout this book. On the other hand, motivation is a specialized field in educational psychology. Educational researchers have conducted hundreds of focused studies in an effort to tease out the triggers of student motivation. Some basic principles have emerged.

Educational experts describe the goal of motivation instruction as increasing the likelihood that students achieve the state known as "flow." In the academic context, flow refers to a mental and emotional state in which the student experiences a task as exciting and challenging yet attainable. The student feels confident yet pressed to grow, engaged yet not over-stimulated. Students who feel a sense of flow immerse themselves in the learning process. They feel less inhibited than normal and also feel in control. Even though the work may be challenging, they experience the work as effortless. In many instances, a student who experiences flow is so engaged in the learning process the student loses track of time. Most of us have had at least a few class sessions in which both we and our students have lost ourselves in the thrill of learning.

> **Thinking exercise:** When have you experienced flow? For example, you may have felt a sense of flow when you were immersed in preparing for class and figured out how to fully engage your students or while writing a law review article regarding a subject about which you are passionate.

One important distinction experts draw is between students' extrinsic vs. intrinsic motivation. Extrinsic motivation emphasizes things teachers do to reward student engagement and to impose natural consequences for student disengagement. In our experience, law professors interested in fostering student motivation tend to use *only* extrinsic motivational tools, such as emphasizing grades, administering pop quizzes, considering class participation in assessing students' grades, or rewarding (with a small grade boost) those students whose class participation throughout the semester was extraordinary. Some teachers go one step further, privately thanking, right after each class session, those students who unmistakably engaged themselves in the class discussion.

While extrinsic motivation tactics can make a difference, they seldom produce the sustained engagement possible when students operate from intrinsic motivation. In educational settings, intrinsic motivation refers to qualities and circumstances within the student or the learning activity that stimulate engagement. When our students seem to enjoy learning for its own sake or because they are interested in the subject, they have found intrinsic motivation.

Unfortunately, many students often do not fall in either the enjoy-learning-for-its-own-sake category or the particular-interest-in-the-subject category. Recent studies have focused on techniques teachers can use to stimulate the development of intrinsic interest by these other students. These studies, taken together, prescribe a wide variety of choices for inspiring and motivating students; below, we describe the techniques best supported by this research. As you study these principles, you will encounter many of the ideas addressed elsewhere in this book. Many of the techniques that produce better learning also motivate students. Because the discussion below is about motivation, we focus on the motivational implications of the principles we have introduced elsewhere.

Specific techniques

Teacher attitudes that motivate students. Teacher passion and confidence significantly influence student motivation. As we explain in Chapters 1 and 5, students frequently describe their most inspiring teachers as passionate about their subjects and student learning and as confident in themselves and in their students' ability to learn. These attitudes help students discover the excitement that led their professors to become lawyers and law teachers in the first place and to feel confident in their ability to learn. Inspiring teachers make it seem as if their courses are an adventure in which everyone, including the teacher, will learn exciting new things.

Teacher passion for a subject can inspire students to be watchful for the transformative ideas, issues, problems, and solutions that have excited their teacher. Students take cues on such matters from how we present them. Students are more likely to be excited if the law teacher sounds excited and explains why. The optimal moment for communicating this passion is during course transitions—when a course or a new topic starts; at this moment, the students are still deciding what they think about the subject.

Teachers can show passion for student learning by expressing excitement about students' insights, by making themselves available to students, by actively and explicitly looking for new ways to help students learn, and by treating student learning as the principal goal in their classes. If a student suggests a new insight or a new way of understanding a concept or explains a difficult concept well, expressing delight in this success and acknowledging the student's influence on our thinking can motivate not only that one student but others as well. The students are then more likely to be motivated to engage in the kinds of behaviors likely to produce such a reaction from their teacher.

Law teachers can show their confidence (or a lack thereof) in themselves and their students by what they choose to teach, by the particular teaching methods they adopt, by the language they use as they teach, and by how they otherwise interact with their students. For example, the choice to teach difficult materials and to ask students to solve challenging problems manifests confidence in both the teacher and the students. The students get the idea that the teacher believes the students can learn hard things.

Likewise, when teachers create learning activities in which students develop their own insights and must manifest their developing expertise, such as cooperative learning exercises, peer feedback experiences, and peer-to-peer teaching, the teachers convey their belief that the students are capable. Well-designed cooperative learning experiences show faith in students because they allow students to negotiate meaning among themselves—the students construct ideas rather than passively receiving them. When a teacher organizes a learning experience that places students in the role of teachers, the students infer that the teacher respects their abilities.

Very simple things, such as our body language in class, how we react to questions in class (as challenges or as learning opportunities), how we deal with student frustration (with encouragement, not disdain), and our comfort in demonstrating our expertise while acknowledging our errors also express our confidence or lack thereof. Respectfully listening, finding and reinforcing the insights embedded in students' comments, and engaging students' questions all concretely manifest a belief in our students' capabilities and insight.

These confidence-boosting techniques are crucial because so many students experience law school as overwhelming and become disheartened. By adopting these techniques, teachers can help students develop (or regain) what educational psychologists refer to as their "internal locus of control" with respect to their learning. If the student credits or blames factors outside his control, such as peers, teachers, and other conditions, the student has an external locus of control. If the student recognizes that successes (and failures) are products of persistence, effort and strategy choice, i.e., factors the student can control, the student has an internal locus of control. Having an internal locus of control means the student is a confident learner; as a result, the student is more likely to be motivated by the process of learning as an end in itself.

Authentic experiences, variety, and active learning. As detailed throughout this text, students learn more and learn it better when they engage in a variety of authentic lawyering experiences that involve active learning.

By situating students in their new roles as lawyers, authentic experiences explicitly connect students' new learning with their career aspirations. The concreteness of this link attracts students' interest. Students develop the motivation to learn because the connection between what they are learning and what they want to be doing is direct and the consequences of not learning seem more significant. This strategy is particularly effective with law students and other graduate students because their employers, clients, and peers will expect them to use what they have learned.

Variety and active learning experiences can be motivating because they capture students' attention and minimize distraction. Variety in teaching methods serves to recapture students' attention and motivate students to continue trying to learn, especially if the overall cycle of teaching methods includes techniques preferred by the students. Active learning motivates students because it prevents them from mentally withdrawing. Instructional designers argue that an unappealing instructional experience is ineffective; students who must constantly sift through passive, single-method teaching are less likely to find the subject engaging and therefore less likely to permanently integrate what they are learning with who they are.

Structuring student autonomy. Student autonomy is highly correlated with student satisfaction and therefore motivation. Giving students power to make choices about how the class will be taught and what they will learn is particularly effective for motivating students. Having chosen for themselves what will be happening in the class and what they will be learning, the students willingly engage themselves. They also feel better about themselves because their professor has shown respect for their autonomy and competence, and the experience gives them more energy to invest in the learning process. Giving students choice also increases the likelihood that they will perceive that they are learning things that are relevant to their experiences and goals.

Disclosing learning goals, providing students with mechanisms to self-evaluate their progress, and explicitly explaining the criteria by which students will be evaluated (i.e., creating rubrics) also foster student autonomy. This information empowers students to control their own learning process. Students may also interpret these disclosures as evidence of your confidence that the class will be successful and the students will learn.

Goal-setting. Student goal-setting has been a subject of frequent study. Students who set mastery learning goals not only get higher grades than students who set grade goals or who do not set goals at all, but also enjoy the learning process more; accordingly, they are more engaged. Mastery goals motivate students to persist until they learn well and, in fact, probably because they have chosen to persist, the students attach greater value to what they are learning. Consequently, you can motivate students by convincing them to set mastery goals, to monitor the attainment of those goals throughout the semester, and to evaluate their success.

Participation (role-playing). Engaging students in role-plays can be particularly effective for motivating students. Asking students to assume their future lawyer role helps students identify the importance of what they are learning. But role-playing also can be useful for motivating students in other ways. Asking students to take the various roles involved in a transaction or dispute can motivate them to master difficult concepts by providing context with which they may not be familiar. This technique is especially effective if the students bring strong but incorrect preconceptions to the area of law. For example, many students assume that the proper measure of damages in a breach of contract case is the non-breaching party's out-of-pocket expenses; many do not even consider the benefit of the bargain as a possible measure. By engaging in a role-play as buyers and sellers, students not only internalize the benefit of the bargain idea but also gain more robust insights into its limitations. Perhaps most importantly, role-playing can help students understand the perspective of clients, outsiders, judges, opposing lawyers, and others with whom the student will need to effectively interact.

Challenge, incongruity, and conflict. Of all the techniques educators suggest as tools to motivate students to learn, the challenge, incongruity, and conflict technique is the one law professors most commonly use. The law school Socratic method focuses heavily on introducing students to considerations and ideas that either actually contradict their viewpoints or seem to do so. This technique effectively stimulates student interest because challenge is one of the two key components in producing flow. However, students cannot develop flow if they perceive success as unattainable. One problem with the law school Socratic method is that, in some classrooms, the law teacher fails to ensure that the students also enjoy success in addressing the incongruity and resolving (or at least understanding) the conflict. Just as challenge is motivating, unending failure is de-motivating. In fact, the research strongly suggests that law students suffer real losses in their sense of autonomy and competence as a result of the law school Socratic approach.

Challenge works best as a motivational tool when the challenge is *both* reasonable and continuous. By sequencing course materials and learning activities so that the students' learning tasks are increasingly difficult, law teachers can make sure students get both the benefits of being challenged while also being reinforced for their persistence.

In addition, incongruity and conflict are not the only ways to challenge law students. Authentic lawyering experiences in which students must translate doctrinal concepts into work products lawyers regularly create (such as contracts, wills, pleadings, arguments, letters, etc.) often are more challenging than merely understanding the doctrine.

Most law teachers have taught classes in which some students could more rapidly master many of the concepts and skills than their peers. In fact, each of us have had classes (such as remedies) in which some topics come easily to some students (e.g., the calculation of damages) while other topics seem to be easier for different students (such as weighing the factors involved in determining the appropriate scope and content of an injunction). If your students are mastering the various skills and subjects in your course at widely varying paces, maintaining the optimal balance of challenge and success can be difficult.

The literature suggests a few possibilities for addressing this problem. Many law teachers do not realize that, under the stress of law school, praise and attention can keep students quite motivated. Students who are enjoying substantial success feel rewarded, and students who are struggling view such praise as confirmation that they are enjoying at least some success. Finding ways to reward success that seem to naturally flow from the students' success benefits their learning; arranging natural consequences intrinsic to success in learning the material is even likely to be more effective. One possibility is allowing students who demonstrate mastery to move on in a way that doesn't leave the other students feeling even further behind. Consider creating challenging and realistic problems specific to each subject area so that students can learn at their own pace. Another possibility is to ask the speedier students to mentor the students who have not yet finished. This near-peer mentoring approach benefits both groups of students.

> **Thinking exercise:** What can you do to maintain challenge for your students who have learned a topic quickly while not overwhelming your students who need additional time to master that particular concept?

Reinforcement. Reinforcement also can be effective in motivating students. In general, however, reinforcement tends to focus students on extrinsic rather than intrinsic goals and therefore is less likely to persist as a motivator. Effective reinforcement includes praise, public recognition, and unexpected prizes. Reinforcement also can take the form of eliminating an obstacle or hurdle that is unattractive to your students, such as allowing students to pass their way out of having to complete an exercise. In contrast, threats, surveillance practices, and punishments are less effective in stimulating motivation. These techniques tend to produce student anger, negativity and, in some instances, rebellion.

Two other principles of effective reinforcement are worth noting. First, intermittent reinforcement, in which the grant of a reward is uncertain and therefore a surprise, is the most powerful form of reinforcement. If you have gambled money or played golf, you probably already understand intermittent reinforcement; golfers and gamblers' occasional success is exciting especially because they have no idea when they will again enjoy success. Thus, rather than always reinforcing student success or effort, consider doing so randomly. Second, students need the most reinforcement when they are first learning a new skill. This early reinforcement encourages them to persist when they encounter difficulty.

Illustration 7-1 summarizes the choices available and our sense of the considerations that can guide your strategy planning.

Illustration 7-1: Techniques for Motivating Law Students

Technique	Keys to Using Technique Effectively	Significant Caveats (if any) in Using Technique
Teacher passion and confidence	• Display passion for subject and for student learning • Relay confidence in teacher and in students • Foster internal locus of control over learning	• Must be expressed authentically
Authentic experiences, variety and active learning	• See Chapters 1, 3, 4, 5, 6, 7, and 8	No significant caveats
Fostering student autonomy	• Give students choice of coverage and methods • Disclose objectives and rubrics	No significant caveats
Goal-setting	• Encourage mastery learning goals	No significant caveats
Participation (role-playing)	• Use law practice experiences • Use strategies to overcome erroneous student misconceptions • Make an effort to expand student perspectives	No significant caveats
Challenge	• Consider a pointed use of Socratic-style questioning • Expand to law practice challenges • Create challenge for students who learn quickly by creating additional exercises or structuring mentoring relationships	• Balance challenge and success
Reinforcement	• Use praise, public recognition, unexpected prizes • Reinforce regularly at outset; intermittently thereafter • Avoid punishment	• Be mindful of the risk of emphasizing extrinsic rather than intrinsic goals

Teaching for attitude or value change or development

Law schools and teachers commonly assert that they want their students to develop the attitudes and values of professionalism, commitment to public service, sensitivity to diversity, respect for the rule of law, and belief in the value of reflection and lifelong learning. Other law teachers, however, believe that values cannot be taught or assessed. The research suggests students can be taught values. As you might expect, however, simply telling students to have a value is seldom effective. In fact, even if students agree a particular value is worthy of adoption, they may not adopt it.

General principles of attitude learning

Determining whether attitude-focused instruction has changed students' minds is difficult. It is impossible to determine in a direct way whether students' attitudes have changed. While a survey would capture some sense of students' opinions, there is reason to doubt attitude survey results. Students who have received instruction directed at attitude change, especially the very smart students who attend law school, are likely to know how their law schools would like them to respond to such survey questions. Consequently, experts in attitude instruction focus on *evidence* of attitude change. Students have acquired a desired attitude if they consistently choose to engage in behaviors that express the desired attitude. For example, if the goal is to convince students to be self-regulated learners, students who, without being asked to do so, set mastery goals, reflect on their learning process, seek opportunities for practice and feedback, and adapt their learning approaches based on the task, the time available, and their past results, have acquired the desired attitude.

More specifically, attitude experts conceptualize changes in student attitudes along a wide spectrum as depicted in Illustration 7-2. At one end of the spectrum, the student merely engages in behavior that evidences the attitude. In the context of self-regulated learning, the student follows the teacher's directions to engage in self-regulating activities. At the opposite end of the spectrum (a result seldom seen in attitude instruction), the student has become so committed to the attitude that the student has become a role model or advocate for the behavior. A law teacher who teaches self-regulated

Illustration 7-2: Spectrum of Behavior Evidencing Attitude Change

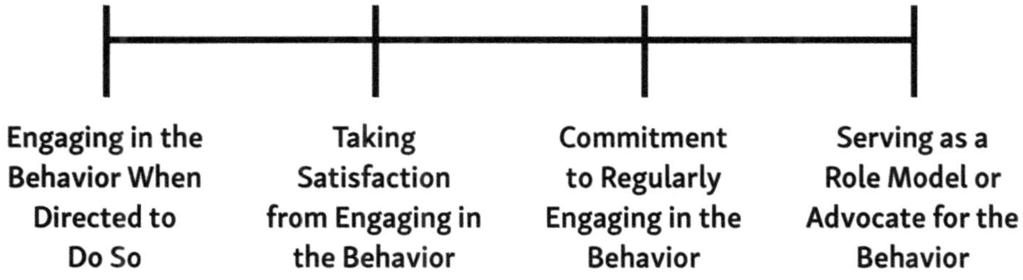

learning would fall into this category. In the middle of this spectrum are lesser degrees of dedication to the value, such as taking satisfaction when engaging in the behavior or committing to the behavior (choosing to engage in the behavior when no one else is watching).

Teachers sometimes feel frustrated when they believe their students lack motivation. Motivation is affected by underlying attitudes. For example, a hopeful attitude has been shown to predict academic performance of law students beyond previous academic achievement. A hopeful attitude means that not only do students see the clear path of steps needed for mastery, but they also believe they personally will experience success if they follow the steps (self-efficacy). This attitude can be distinguished from mere optimism, in which a student believes the learning steps can help random students succeed, but does not believe the same is true for himself. When students feel hopeless, they may struggle to maintain motivation. They think: Why bother to spend the time if I will fail anyway?

Techniques for producing attitude change

Three common techniques have been shown to influence attitudes: persuasion (trying to convince students to change by arguments and other messages), role modeling (using others to demonstrate the efficacy of adopting the attitude), and experience (creating an occurrence that juxtaposes the benefits of the desired attitude with students' existing attitudes). The discussion below considers each of these possibilities in the order of least to most effective. Persuasion is the least effective technique and, in fact, can be ineffective if the students are highly committed to their existing views. Experience is the most effective technique, especially if the experience positively juxtaposes the desired attitude against the students' previously held attitudes. Role modeling is somewhere in the middle.

Persuasion. Persuasion has two facets: the characteristics of the arguments and the source of the arguments. Effective arguments for change must be easy to understand, well-structured, and convincing, but the key to success is whether the arguments address a need or problem the students regard as personally significant. Because the students often do not perceive a need or problem, it is helpful to think of persuasion as needing to address two issues: (1) the existence of a need or problem, and (2) the advocated behavior that addresses the need or solves the problem. Finally, research suggests that persuasion is most effective if the persuader explicitly articulates the attitude change for which they are arguing.

The source refers to the person who is making the argument. A source is most effective when it has one or both of two characteristics: credibility (expertise or education) and attractiveness (similarity to students or fame). The research suggests that teachers can establish the persuader's credibility. Accordingly, if you use a guest practitioner as a persuader, for example, make sure you tell the students about the speaker's expertise.

Upper division students are commonly used for persuasion because of their similarity to the students. How many times have you had students adopt even wild suggestions from an upper-division student who claims to know a secret for doing well in your class?

If you choose to use attractive persuaders, select a diverse group of persuaders and encourage them to open up with the students. A major factor in attractiveness is whether the students perceive that the persuader shares their attitudes with respect to issues other than those about which the persuader is speaking. By selecting a diverse group of persuaders and encouraging the persuaders to be open about themselves, their career goals, and their values, you increase the number of students who are likely to be influenced.

While persuasion can be effective and probably is the most commonly-used attitude-change technique, it typically only addresses the emotional elements of attitude change. Persuaders only address why an attitude change is a good idea. Modeling adds in the cognitive element.

Modeling. Modeling, in the context of law school learning, refers to having a former student or a practitioner demonstrating and being rewarded for engaging in the target behavior. Credibility is as important for modeling as it is for persuasion. High credibility role models, people the students regard as worthy of imitation, are particularly effective as role models. Note that the above description of role modeling emphasizes the importance of students not only observing the role model engaging in the behavior but also observing the role model being reinforced for doing so. The combination of demonstration and observed reinforcement emphasizes the relationship between the two. For example, if students see a successful upper-division student engaging in self-regulation and witness the student being rewarded by good grades or exciting career opportunities, they are more likely to adopt the desired behavior. In this way, modeling addresses both the cognitive and the emotional elements of attitude change.

Law professors have three potential sources of role models. First, it is important to recognize that you function as a role model. You represent the profession to your students (especially for first-year students). For example, the way you go about fulfilling your teaching role, in terms of your professionalism and commitment, is an opportunity to communicate your values. Students quickly decide for themselves whether you are engaged, prepared, and committed. In addition, students notice whether you practice what you preach in terms of service to our communities, institutions, peers, and them.

Second, as explained above in connection with the discussion of persuasion, more advanced students can be effective role models. Having such students report their adoption of the attitude and rewards that followed can convince some students to change.

Third, practitioners can make excellent role models. In particular, we suggest using former students who have become successful practitioners. For example, having alumni reflect on something they did in practice (take a deposition, argue a motion, try a case) and brainstorm how they will change his approach the next time they need to perform the task again would be an effective way to model the value of reflection. Similarly, having practitioners discuss their pro bono work can be effective. In this way, practitioners help students transfer the adoption of the value in law school to the form the value takes in law practice.

Experience. Experience refers to students actually trying out the desired behavior and experiencing its benefits for themselves. Experiences are most effective if the conflict between the students' existing values and the desired value is readily identifiable and the students receive or discover the benefits (rewards) from engaging in the alternative behavior. Because such experiences expose a discrepancy between the students' existing values and the desired value, many educational researchers use the term "dissonance" to refer to this strategy.

The keys and the challenges are to design experiences that are authentic, give students as much autonomy in the process as possible, and allow students to experience the benefits of adopting the desired value. An experience is authentic if the students are engaging in the behavior in a way that is similar to what they might choose to do in the future. For example, using actual course feedback (e.g., a grade on a paper, comments on a practice exam) as a springboard for getting students to engage in self-regulation increases the likelihood students will make the connection between the self-regulation activity and their other efforts at learning. An experience gives students autonomy if the students have some choice in the process. For example, asking students to engage in public service but to choose for themselves the particular form of public service in which they will engage gives students the autonomy that increases the likelihood they will adopt the value. If the students do not experience any reward from adopting the behavior, experience is unlikely to change their attitudes. Natural rewards, rewards inherent in adopting the desired attitude, as you might expect from reading the above discussion on motivation, are more effective than grade or other extrinsic rewards because the natural rewards develop student's intrinsic interest in adopting the behavior.

Experience can address all three elements of behavioral change. Most obviously, experience addresses the behavioral element of attitude change because the students are actually implementing the desired behavior. Experience also addresses the cognitive element because the students are trying out the techniques for themselves and can receive coaching in their efforts in implementation. Experience most effectively addresses the emotional element because, rather than being told about the benefits or seeing someone else get the benefits from implementing the desired behavior, the students actually experience the benefits for themselves.

Conclusion regarding motivational teaching strategies and attitude learning

Taken together, the recommendations explored above suggest a complex set of practices. The discussion below, describing what law professors can do to engage students to become self-regulated learners, reflects an implementation of many of the ideas explored above, both with respect to motivation and with respect to attitude change. Thus, it not only stands alone as an implementation of a commonly-stated law teacher goal but also serves as an example of how the preceding ideas can be implemented.

Engaging students to become expert self-regulated learners

This discussion offers some very specific recommendations of things law professors can do to help their students engage themselves in self-regulating their learning and, eventually, choose to be self-regulated learners. Of all the discussions in this book, this section is the only one to focus on a specific learning goal, getting students to adopt the attitudes, habits, and activities of self-regulated learners. Accordingly, the discussion is very concrete. Because it is relatively easy to teach students the skills involved in self-regulated learning and quite challenging to convince students that self-regulated learning is worth their time and effort, this discussion is organized according to the three techniques for producing attitudinal learning: persuasion, role modeling, and experience.

Persuasion

Practitioners who work in the field and are respected by the students can serve as credible persuaders and therefore be a useful part of a campaign to convince students to engage in self-regulation. In particular, practitioners can make the link between self-regulation in the context of law school and self-regulation in the context of law practice. Excellent practitioners continuously reflect on their learning and lawyering efforts, treating each one as an opportunity to improve. Practitioners also engage in reflection while they are practicing. For example, it is common for trial lawyers to take notes both on what witnesses say and on the lawyers' reflections about the witness' demeanor and opportunities for cross-examination. This approach increases the likelihood students get the idea that self-regulation is a core skill for lawyers.

Upper-division students who have done well in law school can serve as attractive persuaders. They can be particularly useful for convincing students that self-regulation, when used properly, doesn't mean students must work harder; self-regulated learners just work smarter. They can identify the ways in which self-regulation actually has improved the effectiveness *and* the efficiency of their study efforts. It is particularly important, in this context, that the upper-division students you choose are similar to your students so they are more likely to develop hope that the same outcomes could occur for themselves. Consider racial, gender, sexual-orientation, gender identity, age, and disability diversity in choosing students, and also try to choose at least one student with family obligations, one with work obligations, one who is first gen, and one who used to be cynical about self-regulated learning. Convincing upper-division students to share is easier than you might imagine. The students feel flattered to be asked.

Role modeling

While it is possible to structure learning activities in which a practitioner demonstrates a self-regulation skill, most teachers rely on upper-division students and themselves as role models. Upper-division students can be effective role models because they have developed the desired skills in the same context in which the students need to develop the skills. Exercises in which the upper-division students demonstrate how they continue to self-regulate their learning in their current courses and then supervise the students in using the skills are particularly effective. This approach addresses all three facets of attitude change.

Most consistently, we strive to be reflective law teachers. We regularly seek information about student learning through quizzes, classroom assessment techniques, student advisory groups, in-class multiple-choice questions, and other mechanisms, and we reflect (explicitly and out loud) on the implications of these data for our efforts to be effective in our teaching role. We teach using graphic organizers and outlines and reflect aloud on their role in our own legal learning (e.g., "I never fully grasped this case until I created this chart" or "I created this flowchart so I could think through all the ways this issue might arise").

The most effective tool for getting students to become self-regulated learners is having them try the techniques and experience how those techniques improve their learning process.

Experiencing: getting students to take their "metacognitive pulse"

The remainder of this chapter consists of a series of exercises designed to be self-regulated learning "experiences" as we used that term in the above discussion of attitudinal learning. In each exercise, the goal is to engage students in reflective, self-regulated learning in the context of one of their regular courses. We also assume that the exercises would be directed and supervised by one of the students' regular law teachers. These two principles are particularly important. Studies consistently have found that the best way to get students to make such practices a permanent part of their learning process is to have the students adopt the practices in the context of one of the students' regular courses in a session taught by one of their regular teachers. Stand-alone courses and orientation experiences may be effective in getting a few students to change. For the most part, however, because the students do not see learning experiences in stand-alone courses and orientations as a part of their formal education, the students are likely to adopt the recommended practices only for the course or orientation or, at best, only for one semester.

In fact, students are most likely to permanently adopt such practices if they have experiences in several of their classes. This approach ensures that students do not perceive the experiences (and the suggested activities and attitudes) as idiosyncratic to one teacher. If all or most of the students' law teachers teach the students to engage in self-regulated learning, the students will perceive that this skill set is at the core of what they should be learning.

We refer to these exercises as getting students to take their "metacognitive pulse" because the exercises are intended to function in ways that are similar to checking your heart-rate while exercising; the students engage in a self-regulation skill and quickly reflect on the implications for their learning (i.e., they engage in metacognition). In general, these exercises have two key components: (1) guided practice, and (2) reflection on results.

One last point about progression is worth considering. As we explained in Chapters 2 and 3, instruction should be sequenced from easy to hard so that students receive reinforcement and experience success as they progress towards mastery. In the context of building students' self-regulated learning skills, this progression is slightly modified: students should progress towards independence as they build their reflection skills. Thus, students should be directed to adopt particular strategies early in their process and, later, encouraged to select and implement their own choices of strategies.

Guided journaling. The simplest way to get students to engage in reflection is to ask them to keep a journal about their learning process. Make sure you give them specific writing prompts rather than just telling students to write in their journal or just engage in reflection. Novice self-regulated learners need more guidance, and the research suggests that students often perceive unguided journaling as mere busy work. Generally, for each entry, encourage students to write about three topics: (1) description of the practice—what students did; (2) reflection on the experience—the effectiveness of the strategy, how the strategy compares to other, alternative strategies; and (3) future planning—how the students' results and reflections will affect future efforts to accomplish the same general task. It is also useful to get students to write about and assess their progress towards achieving their development of self-regulation skills.

Another crucial condition for productive student journaling is that the students' reflection process must be spread out over time. Sometimes, when busy students are assigned to keep a journal, they procrastinate and complete the entire assignment just before it is due. This approach greatly decreases the chance that students will learn from the experience and increases the likelihood the students will see the experience as busy work. Consequently, it is better to prompt students to engage in the reflection in a way that reminds them to journal on no less than a weekly basis and encourage them to establish a routine for their journaling.

Moreover, the most significant benefits occur when students look back over past journal entries and draw larger conclusions about their learning processes, strengths, weaknesses, and areas for improvement. Students are unlikely to engage in this behavior absent prompting. Consequently, we encourage you to direct your students to review a series of past journal entries and identify larger themes in their learning processes.

Students also are more likely to value the experience if they know how the journal will be used: Will it count towards their grade? Will the entries be shared with the rest of the class? Will anyone respond to their entries? Who? In particular, feedback on entries is considered a crucial prerequisite to making the experience valuable for students. Finally, it is worthwhile for you to be explicit about how the journaling will benefit them.

Attention-focusing exercise. This exercise is a quick and simple way to help your students see the value of self-monitoring for attention. This exercise focuses on the students' role in retaining focused attention. The exercise is most effective at a time when you have been covering some very dry material by lecture or by traditional law school Socratic-style interactions. In the middle of the discussion or lecture, ask the students to write down what they were thinking about in the immediately preceding moment. Encourage them to be honest and communicate that you are assuming some of them weren't focusing on the discussion. Solicit a few examples and then ask the students to write down what the exercise teaches them about self-monitoring for attention.

Reflective reading exercise. A series of five studies on law student reading have found that successful law students read court opinions differently than their less successful peers and much more like successful practitioners and judges. Two key reading characteristics of the successful students are: (1) they are more likely to argue with the author of the opinion while reading the opinion, and (2) they are more likely to vigilantly monitor their comprehension, by brainstorming examples of the principles discussed in the cases. Consequently, a nice variation on case briefing expectations would be to ask students to come to class with three points made by the courts with which they disagree and two real-world examples of each of the legal concepts discussed by the courts. You may also want to ask students to develop two non-examples (see Chapter 2 for an explanation of the term "non-examples"). In class, rather than doing a typical facts-issue-holding discussion, engage students in comparing, with each other, their critiques, examples, and non-examples. Conclude by having the students compare how well they understood the cases for which they have done traditional case briefs and the cases they read for this exercise. These reflections will guide students in making good choices in reading future cases. Even those students who feel they learned better by briefing will benefit; their sense of the value of briefing (to them) will be enhanced. You can provide students additional data by having them take short, three-five question multiple choice tests on both sets of cases.

Note-taking reflections exercise. This exercise addresses two learning process issues. First, a significant number of students treat note-taking as a dictation exercise; they try to write down every word rather than trying to understand and thoughtfully and reflectively thinking about what they should write down. Second, students also learn more in class when they engage more deeply with the discussion. Consequently, starting a class by asking students to divide their handwritten notes or laptop page so they have space for notes and space for reflections and prompting them to use the reflections space to note when they are confused or cannot generate an example of the concept they are learning. Ask students, at the end of class, to review their reflections and comment on whether taking notes in this way helped with their learning process. As an alternative, you simply can ask students to look over their notes at the end of class and identify any gaps in their understanding. It's particularly helpful if you also ask students to decide for themselves how they will remediate any confusion (e.g., review a hornbook).

Organizational strategies exercise and debriefing. A particularly effective exercise for teaching students the value of imposing structure on their learning and for taking time to process the course material is to have 25 or 30 students each name one concept the class has studied and, as they do so, write the name of the concept on the board (in random order). Then, cover up the list and give the students two minutes to see how many of the items they can recall from memory. After the students correct their answers, conduct a class discussion in which you and the class create a mind map or hierarchy chart to structure the same concepts into categories, sub-categories, and sub-sub-categories. After you have done so, cover up the list and the mind map and give the students another two minutes to see how many of the concepts they can recall. Most students will do better the second time (although you often will have one or two outliers who do worse or do the same). Conclude the exercise by having students explain why most students did better the second time—(1) because they have imposed structure and (2) because they have mentally processed the materials.

Time management/self-monitoring logs. In a frequently-replicated set of studies, professors have asked students only to add one additional practice to their study practices, keeping a time management self-monitoring log such as the log reproduced below. The key components are: getting students to focus on mastery goals, on consciously deciding how they will study, and on evaluating their learning as it is ongoing. Other possible topics on which students can reflect include: where and with whom they will study, the presence or absence of distractors, when they will take breaks, and how they will remediate any confusion.

Concept and Mastery Learning Goal	Study Strategy(ies)	Planned Time and Place for Study	Actual Study Time and Place	Ability to Focus	Results of Study Efforts

Comparison of strategies exercise. To become expert self-regulated learners, students need to become experts in knowing which strategies work best for them. This goal requires students to try to compare their results in using the wide variety of strategies available to them. Thus, if you have students outline one week and do hierarchy charts three weeks later, having each student compare and share how well each strategy worked for that student will reveal to the students not only their individual preferences but also the variety among their peers.

Exam or paper results exercise. Returning an exam or paper presents a particularly apt moment to engage students as self-regulated learners. At this moment, students are most interested in continuing those things that worked for them on the exam or paper and changing those things that did not work. Unfortunately, getting students to self-assess their work isn't easy. You may even need to establish some sort of a reward system: for example, you can ask students to complete a reflection exercise and promise those who do so access to a model answer to the exam or you can provide the model answer to facilitate student self-assessment and offer an additional practice and feedback opportunity to students who engage in appropriate reflection.

There are several keys to maximizing student learning in this context. First, a crucial skill of productive learners is their ability to self-assess their learning; expert learners know when they don't know. Consequently, before the exam, ask the students to predict their results and, afterwards, ask them to compare their results with their predictions and grapple with the inconsistency (if any). Second, expert self-regulated learners attribute learning successes to effort and persistence and struggles to insufficient persistence or strategy choice errors. Accordingly, provide students with a list of possible causes of their failures to learn—all of the items should be related either to persistence or to strategy choice. Third, based on their results and their assessment of the causes of those results, students need to plan how they will improve their studying efforts in the future. For most students, it is also useful to ask them to remediate any confusion, i.e., correct any errors in their original paper or essay.

Free-writing on lessons learned. This lesson focuses on helping students self-assess what they have learned in a class session as they are finishing the session. Ask students an open-ended prompt, e.g., write about class today or, somewhat more narrowly, write about what you learned in class. Give the students a few minutes and encourage them not to edit or otherwise limit themselves. The idea is to do a true free-write in the hope that their concerns and ideas about the class session will come to the forefront of their minds.

Conclusion regarding self-regulated learning exercises. You can ask students to engage in any self-regulated learning experience. For example, you can ask students to set and reflect on their attainment of mastery learning goals. You can ask students to invoke self-efficacy by recalling a challenging learning task and why they succeeded in learning. Or you can ask students to complete online or pen-and-paper assessments of their learning style preferences or personality types and reflect on the implications of what they have learned for law school. The key conditions to developing students' self-regulation skills are integrating these exercises into students' regular coursework, providing them with the opportunity to reflect, and giving the students feedback.

Checklists

Illustration 7-3 includes three checklists you can use to implement the ideas in this chapter: a motivation checklist, a teaching values checklist, and a teaching self-regulated learning checklist.

Illustration 7-3: Motivation, Attitudes, and Self-Regulation Checklists

Teaching for Motivation Checklist

This checklist summarizes things law professors can do to better motivate students.

- ❑ **Adopt attitudinal strategies**
  - ❑ Project passion and enthusiasm
  - ❑ Display and boost confidence
- ❑ **Create authentic lawyering experiences**
- ❑ **Use a variety of teaching techniques**
- ❑ **Structure opportunities for student autonomy**
- ❑ **Encourage student goal-setting**
- ❑ **Create non-threatening challenge, incongruity, and conflict to spark interest**
- ❑ **Provide reinforcement**

Teaching Values Checklist

This checklist lists the three techniques law professors can use to facilitate student attitudinal change.

- ❑ **Persuasion**
- ❑ **Role Modeling**
- ❑ **Experience**

Teaching for Self-Regulation Checklist

This checklist summarizes the things law professors can emphasize to build students' self-regulated learning skills.

- ❑ **Persuasion**
- ❑ **Role modeling**
- ❑ **Experiences**
  - ❑ Guided journaling
  - ❑ Free writing
  - ❑ Attention-focusing exercises
  - ❑ Reflective reading exercises
  - ❑ Reflective note-taking exercises
  - ❑ Organizational strategies reflection exercises
  - ❑ Time management/self-monitoring logs
  - ❑ Comparison of strategies exercises
  - ❑ Exam or paper results exercises

Teaching for Motivation, Attitudes, and Self-Regulation—Resources

These two books contain extensive treatments of instructional design principles applied to motivating students, teaching them to be self-regulated learners, and teaching for attitude change.

- Patricia L. Smith & Tillman J. Ragan, Instructional Design (3d. ed. 2005).
- Walter Dick, Lou Carey, James O. Carey, The Systematic Design of Instruction (6th ed. 2005).

These three articles address motivating students.

- Michael Hunter Schwartz, *Teaching Law by Design: How Learning Theory and Instructional Design Can Inform and Reform Legal Education*, 38 San Diego L. Rev. 347 (2001)
- Gerald F. Hess. *Value of Variety: An Organizing Principle to Enhance Teaching and Learning*, 3 Elon L. Rev 65 (2011).
- Gerald F. Hess, *Heads and Hearts: The Teaching and Learning Environment in Law School*, 52 J. LEGAL EDUC. 75 (2002).

This book focuses on teaching students to be self-regulated learners.

- Dale H. Schunk and Barry J. Zimmerman, Self-Regulated Learning: From Teaching to Self-Reflective Practice (1998).

This article addresses teaching law students to be self-regulated learners.

- Michael Hunter Schwartz, *Teaching Law Students to be Self-Regulated Learners*, 2003 Mich. St. D.C.L. L. Rev. 447 (2003).

Chapter 8

Experiential Teaching and Learning

Introduction

Experiential education integrates theory and practice, combining academic inquiry with real-life or simulation experiences. Experiential education opportunities permeate legal education; experiential education courses include clinical courses, externship programs, pro bono and other service experiences, simulation courses such as client interviewing and counselling, negotiation, legal writing, pretrial, trial, and appellate practice courses. In addition, doctrinal-focused courses can include experiential exercises, materials, and methods, including legal documents, videos, pictures, field trips, interviews, role-playing, and student presentations and performances.

Experiential education helps students engage in the complexity of practice, gain a deeper understanding of the context of a legal problem, practice a variety of skills and values, develop practical wisdom and judgment, recognize areas of confusion, and become actively involved in their learning. Experiential exercises are particularly effective for some students; students who struggle with learning through verbal discussion and reading and writing often excel when they are placed in the role of an attorney. Experiential exercises can also help students gain the kind of authentic confidence that comes from competence. And because real-life problems and illustrations often put students in the role of practicing attorneys, real-life exercises are frequently highly engaging and motivating.

Consider the contrast between a course without and with an experiential component. A student in a family law course can master the doctrine and theory of shared custody and apply them to a hypothetical set of facts by writing a memo or essay. However, a student in the role of an attorney negotiating a shared custody arrangement for a disappointed and angry client must use doctrine and theory as well as a host of other skills. To participate effectively in a shared custody situation, the student must listen and show respect for the client, communicate in terms the client can understand, respond appropriately to the client's strong emotions, honor the client's goals as much as possible, absorb and respond to new information, navigate the myriad of questions surrounding shared custody arrangements, negotiate with opposing counsel, and be patient with a time-consuming process, in addition to many other skills and values. These kinds of experiences help students bridge the gap between law school and practice.

Students gain important skills, knowledge, attitudes, and self-awareness from law schools' in-house clinics, externship programs, and pro bono and other service experiences where students work with real clients under the supervision of practicing lawyers. In addition, simulation courses such as legal writing, client interviewing and counseling, pretrial and appellate advocacy, judicial opinion writing, patent practice, and negotiation offer students opportunities to practice knowledge, skills and values under more controlled settings.

Recognizing the importance of experiential education, the American Bar Association currently requires all law students to earn a minimum of six credits of experiential learning through clinics, externships, or simulation courses. The ABA sets out common characteristics that must be part of every clinical, externship, or simulation course: the courses must be primarily experiential in nature; integrate doctrine, theory, skills, and legal ethics; engage students in the performance of professional skills; develop the concepts underlying the skills; give students multiple opportunities to perform; provide opportunities for ongoing student self-evaluation and reflection; and provide supervision and feedback from a faculty member or supervisor. The list of resources at the end of this chapter includes books that offer extensive ideas to make clinical, externship, and simulation courses effective.

Because we believe it is important to incorporate experiential learning throughout the curriculum, this chapter focuses on concrete ways to bring real-life and simulation experiences into doctrinal courses. We recognize that reading statutes and cases are real-life experiences; in this chapter, we focus on additional exercises to provide depth and breadth to students' learning. This chapter first identifies a number of experiential methods and illustrates them with specific examples from doctrinal courses. It then follows with suggestions about experiential design choices and process. The list of resources at the end of this chapter includes books that provide many specific ideas for including engaging experiential exercises in a large range of law school courses.

Experiential exercises and methods

We have used and observed colleagues using a wide variety of experiential exercises lasting as short as a few minutes or as long as an entire semester. As with other ideas in this book, we recommend that you be intentional about incorporating experiential exercises in class, start slow and small, reflect upon the experience, and adjust over time to improve students' learning. Illustration 8-1 identifies a variety of experiential or real-life methods to use in a doctrinal course, and suggests how students might engage with those methods. Note that many of the experiential methods and exercises below overlap, and that this list is not exhaustive. In general, more complex experiential exercises will involve multiple methods and engage students in a wider range of skills and values. More details about each of these methods and examples of how they can be used in doctrinal courses follows Illustration 8-1.

Thinking exercise: Consider a doctrinal course you teach. Identify two kinds of experiential methods that might be appropriate for your students.

Specific examples of experiential exercises

The same experiential method or experience can be used for multiple purposes in multiple ways. For example, students could read an actual contract as an example of what one might look like, revise and edit the contract to improve it, draft an additional provision, role-play different sides in negotiating the contract and its enforcement provisions, or draft a client letter about the contract's validity and purpose.

1. Current events and real-life stories

Having students or teachers bring in current events helps students connect more abstract doctrine to real-life events and shows students how the doctrinal topic is relevant. Reading or listening to the news, creating media alerts for new developments in particular topics, and asking colleagues and practitioners about current events can be a quick, easy, and low-cost way to incorporate real life into your course. You can also add a tab on your online learning platform to post real-life cases that students share. That bank of links can be used to start class or as discussion prompts to boost class engagement.

Examples of current events and real-life stories

- In a professional responsibility course, the teacher reads the names of the attorneys disciplined by the state bar for violating the principles the class is studying that day.
- Students each research and briefly present a photograph, video, news story, or case decided within the past five years that addresses portions of a criminal law, administrative law, tax, or other course.
- A teacher calls the attorneys on the major cases assigned and tells the students about the attorneys' perspectives on the litigation.
- Once each week, a teacher devotes the first five minutes of class to student comments and questions about current events related to the course.
- A teacher relates course material to what the teacher, a colleague, or a former student actually did in practice.
- Students research facts about safety warnings for a new toy or device such as a hover board.

Illustration 8-1: Some Experiential Methods Appropriate for Doctrinal Courses

Experiential Methods		
Experiential methods		Possibilities for student engagement
1.	**Current events and real-life stories**—news stories, examples from practice, videos, photos	Research, read and view, report to class, connect to doctrine
2.	**Documents**—claims, contracts or contract clauses, forms, letters, pleadings, trusts, etc.	Read, review, analyze, comment upon, apply to rules
3.	**Drafting documents** or parts of documents—public comments, code proposals, letters, opinion pieces, emails, questions, etc.	Outline, draft, revise, self- and peer-critique
4.	**Field trips**—agency hearings, legislative sessions, courts, medical examiner, construction sites, neighborhoods, prisons, hospitals, etc.	Develop questions, attend, observe, ask questions, photograph, videotape, summarize and share information
5.	**Guest speakers**—potential clients, experts, lawyers, adjudicators	Develop questions, attend, ask questions, summarize and share information
6.	**Interviews**—potential clients, lawyers, legal constituents, legislators, regulators, judges, engineers, social workers, etc.	Research, develop questions, conduct interview, summarize and share information learned
7.	**Problem-solving**—current or realistic problems facing lawyers and clients	Research, develop questions, collaborate with practitioners; prepare, generate and present alternative solutions
8.	**Short role plays**—advocating, negotiating, interviewing, counseling, etc.	Practice being attorneys or clients in short problems
9.	**Simulations**—more complex role plays	Prepare and explain material to clients and constituents, advise supervisors, negotiate agreements, gather and respond to new information, practice research and writing under time constraints
10.	**Student presentations**—informing, explaining, advocating, demonstrating lawyering skills in front of others	Prepare, practice and engage in giving presentation with audience; provide feedback to peers; role-play decision-makers and other constituents

- As part of course preparation, students learn about the lives of the litigants in major cases, such as Helen Palsgraf.
- Students discuss how doctrine will affect current issues such as voting rights or transgender access to single-sex schools and public bathrooms.

As this list reflects, real life examples can be brought to the class by the professor or the students, and can serve as examples of concepts, provide new insights about the concepts, or stimulate a discussion. These techniques can also be combined with other experiential learning techniques as exemplified below.

2. Documents—reading and reviewing

Students are often fascinated to see real-life documents related to course material. Real-life documents provide a context and experience different from reading about a document in a case. Even when students have been exposed to legal documents in their lives, such as with credit card agreements, making the connection between those documents and their contracts or consumer protection law course material helps them see their own documents and the course material in a new light.

Examples of using real-life documents

- Torts students analyze and critique releases signed by members at a local fitness center. (This exercise is also an example of a current event, and could include a field trip.)
- In civil procedure, a teacher brings in a real-life complaint and asks students to identify the federal rules associated with different paragraphs.
- A contracts teacher shows the rock group Van Halen's "no m&m" contract with concert venues; another teacher shows the Harry Potter book contracts.
- Students bring in their credit card agreements, automobile insurance policies, and apartment leases, applying relevant doctrine to analyze the provisions.
- A land use teacher brings in recent zoning board decisions and maps about variances permitted in the neighborhood near the law school.
- Students read actual deeds, wills, trusts, security agreements, environmental impact statements, and other documents frequently prepared and analyzed by lawyers.

3. Documents—drafting

Students can read course materials, view documents, and masterfully identify substantive and procedural legal knowledge, but they learn the same material in a different way when they have to draft a document or portion of a document themselves. It's one thing for students to apply and analyze a hypothetical about an international trademark license; drafting an international trademark license requires different and higher level skills such as evaluating and creating.

Examples of document drafting exercises

- Students make written public comments on a proposed current federal environmental regulation. (For details about this exercise, see Chapter 9.)
- Students propose written changes to state model probate rules.
- Students draft affidavits in support of a child relocation motion.
- In groups, students prepare a short email to a public employer about discrimination based on race and gender.
- Students draft civil litigation documents such as complaints, answers, motions, interrogatories, requests for documents, etc.
- Students draft a cease and desist letter or a potential trademark client.
- Students representing a lender with a mental disability prepare mediation summaries for a dispute about an automobile loan.
- Students write and submit opinion pieces about local tribes' access to health care.
- Students draft basic estate documents, including advance directives, for each other.

4. Field trips

Students often report that field trips stand out as some of the most memorable learning moments in a course. Field trips break up the standard pattern of the regular classroom experience. In addition to having the field experience connect real-life to doctrine, students have a much richer sense of how legal problems arise in context. Field trips can engage a range of senses and embed a relevant experience in multiple neural pathways and thereby assist with long-term retention. Students are exposed to things such as the setting of a business, the smell of a police station, the slow pace of board hearings, and the wide variety of judging and lawyering styles on display in courts. Field trips can also show students clients' settings and environments.

Field trip examples

- A teacher takes students to the morgue, where they observe an autopsy of a crime victim.
- Students attend meetings of the international trade law section of the state bar association.
- An administrative law judge conducts hearings at the law school; disability law and administrative law students are required to attend.
- Health law students visit the local hospital's emergency room on a weekend evening.
- First-year students are required to spend two hours observing and commenting upon a local trial court's hearings.

- Food law students visit two dairies, one organic, one not.
- Poverty law students visit and volunteer at a local food bank.
- Education law students attend a school board meeting.

One of the best ways to make sure students engage deeply in field trip experiences is to require students to write reflective essays detailing their observations, the legal implications of those observations, any ethical or other issues, and their evaluation of any lawyering performances.

5. Guest speakers

As with field trips, students value learning exercises that add variety to the classroom dynamic. They appreciate hearing from speakers who have relevant experience in the field and can relate course principles to law practice. Sometimes, the same message given by a teacher resonates significantly more with students when delivered by a guest speaker. The expanded use of Zoom offers additional opportunities to virtually "host" guest speakers from all over the country.

Examples of using guest speakers

- A prosecutor, defense attorney and probation officer discuss common challenges and joys of working in the criminal justice system.
- A civil legal aid attorney speaks to remedies students about representing very low income disabled clients in a health care class action.
- In intellectual property, an economist talks to students about valuing clients' intellectual property portfolios.
- A teacher's friend comes to class to talk about her medical malpractice claim against her dental surgeon for removing the wrong tooth.
- An architect speaks to a construction law class about how the Americans with Disabilities Act affects building design.
- A state supreme court justice speaks to first-year students about the role of professionalism and civility in law practice.
- A city attorney talks to a First Amendment class about reasonable time, place and manner restrictions.
- Plaintiffs' and defense attorneys talk to a civil rights course about excessive force claims against police officers.
- A panel of lawyers speaks to a professionalism course about networking.
- A panel of clients speaks to a client counseling and interviewing class to provide the clients' perspective on attorney-client communications.

6. *Interviews*

Interviews provide students with opportunities to focus research on a topic or person, prepare thoughtful questions, uncover material not included in course materials, and practice summarizing information gained from conversations. Moreover, interviews give students the opportunity to practice interviewing and relational skills, forge relationships, make professional connections, and develop confidence.

Interview examples

- Students are assigned to interview an attorney in the attorney's office about the attorney's career path, challenges, and successes.
- A mock client (an actor, student, colleague) comes to a required first-year class and is interviewed by students who have prepared questions in advance.
- Staff attorneys for the state legislative office, insurance department, or other agency are interviewed by groups of administrative law students.
- In class, employment law students interview in-house counsel about Family Medical Leave Act policies.
- Students interview a child psychiatrist about a child's learning disabilities in preparing for a simulated school individual education program team meeting.
- A social worker is interviewed by students about the advantages and disadvantages of people with disabilities living in group homes or receiving services while living independently, and the major mistakes lawyers make when representing people with disabilities.
- In an admiralty law class, students interview officials from the Harbor Department to learn about the Harbor's major legal problems with container ships.

7. *Problem-solving*

Students are usually motivated to learn when they are asked to consider complex scenarios and shape a variety of solutions based on real-life challenges lawyers face. Students also tend to remember and internalize important knowledge when they have to apply strategies to solve real-life problems. In addition, asking students to solve problems in groups promotes collaboration, teamwork, diversity, and respect.

Examples of student problem-solving

- Working in groups, students research and prepare a one-page email about the carbon monoxide dangers of a specific waterski boat model, and advise a mock supervisor whether they have sufficient information to bring a products liability defective warning claim against the manufacturer. Students also conduct factual research about the dangers of the boat design and the properties of carbon monoxide poisoning.

- Given facts about a private nuisance affecting a residential homeowner and given a mock client's goals, remedies students make brief presentations to classmates and the teacher about the various possible remedies.
- Students in business organizations interview a mock client, then research and prepare memos to a mock supervisor about the main issues facing a business entity. Embedded in the problem are multiple issues, legal issues from other doctrines, and red herring issues. Students have to evaluate which issues are the most significant and write about how they can be resolved.
- Given a mock client's wishes about distributing her assets upon death, trusts and estate students compare the advantages and disadvantages of using a trust or will. Students also advise the client about the consequences of failing to create any trust or will documents.
- Representing different parties to a dispute about personal jurisdiction, civil procedure students identify what additional facts they need to obtain, how those facts would affect jurisdictional analysis, and how authorities read for class support or conflict with their analysis.

8. Short role plays

In playing a role, students tend to become more involved in an exercise. They can practice a wide variety of skills, focus on particular skills in isolation, make mistakes in a safer environment than in the workplace, and develop a great appreciation for different points of view, particularly if they role-play a position with which they would otherwise disagree.

Short role play examples

- Taking turns playing the role of attorney and client, pairs of students spend ten minutes conducting initial interviews of an employer and employee client engaged in a labor dispute.
- Pairs of criminal law students act as prosecutors and defense attorneys in negotiating a plea agreement.
- Two students advise a third student about an entertainment law dispute.
- In the role of agency officials, sports law students explain decisions and reasoning about a doping complaint filed against an athlete.
- Evidence students argue motions advocating for and against suppressing medical records.
- Sexual discrimination students put themselves in the role of managers teaching employees about sexual harassment.
- Students in election law represent different constituents in a redistricting hearing.

9. Simulations

More complex than simple role-plays, simulations typically engage students in a variety of other experiential methods, such as reading and drafting documents, conducting interviews, role-playing, problem-solving, and presenting information. Simulations range from the comprehensive and complex to more discreet applications. Some teachers engage students in semester-long simulations during which students experience a wide range of challenges lawyers encounter in practice. Other teachers have students engage in shorter simulations, such as drafting and negotiating a contract, making oral arguments, making a presentation for a simulated client, or conducting a mock client interview.

Example of simulation with multiple steps

- Students are provided with a few basic facts about a mock military client facing a court-martial for sexual harassment.
- Before interviewing the client, a librarian gives a short in-class presentation about practice-based resources related to military justice. For homework, students conduct outside research and prepare interview questions.
- In class, small groups of students compare their research findings and brainstorm the most important questions to ask the client.
- Students next take turns interviewing the client in class to learn more about the client's circumstances and goals.
- Reconvening in small groups, students compare and analyze the client's facts and goals, and prepare to advise the client.
- Following a class in which a few students take turns advising the client, all students are put in the role of the military prosecutor and assigned to prepare arguments against the client.
- In the final simulation of the experiential module, students play the roles of the client, client advocate, witnesses, military prosecutor, and administrative discharge board officials.
- At the end of the simulation, students write reflective papers responding to specific prompts about their experience in the different roles.

10. Student presentations

When students have to make presentations in front of the whole or part of a class, they often perform at a higher level than when asked to present to the teacher alone. Moreover, the choice to trust students as "teachers" communicates a high level of confidence in students' abilities.

Examples of student presentations

- Students prepare concept maps about significant art law topics, show images to class, explain, and respond to questions.
- Students debate whether parties should be allowed to use their peremptory challenges to potential jurors for any reason or should be prohibited from striking potential jurors on the basis of race or gender.
- Choosing individual privacy law topics, students research and prepare short lectures to class.
- Groups of students engage their classmates in an interactive ten-minute lesson about current events tied to the day's reading assignments.
- Students demonstrate reasonable and unreasonable stop-and-frisks and engage classmates in identifying distinctions.
- In class, an individual student presents a real and fictional current event on climate change, challenging the class to identify which is which.
- Small groups of students design hypotheticals about which they ask their classmates and then analyze for the class.

Thinking exercise: What experiential methods have you encountered as a learner? Which ones most helped your learning? Why?

Designing experiential exercises and methods

As with many aspects of teaching and learning, there is no one right way to design and conduct experiential exercises. While we recommend that you consider the design considerations below, we encourage you to use your own approach in developing exercises and using experiential methods. Bear in mind that the way you expect an exercise to work may be very different from what actually happens for students.

Considerations for designing experiential exercises

1. Learning goal/s and objective/s
2. Experiential method/s
3. Overall structure
4. Relevant and significant material
5. Clear goals, directions, and expectations
6. Teacher preparation
7. Student preparation

8. Feedback
9. Reflection for students
10. Reflection for teachers

1. Focus on learning goals and objectives

As with other aspects of course and class design (see Chapters 2 and 3), connect experiential exercises and methods with your course learning goals. Be clear in your own mind what specific course goals the exercise addresses. Likewise, be clear with students about the goals of the exercise. For example, goals of a complaint drafting exercise may be for students to (1) apply their knowledge of federal rules in a realistic setting, (2) draft a clear, concise legal document, and (3) comply with the ethical standards that govern civil litigation.

In general, the more time the experiential exercise takes, the closer it should relate to important learning goals. For example, different students could spend several minutes presenting a current event related to administrative law at the beginning of each class. Because of the variety and brevity of the presentations, many of them may relate to less significant course learning goals. By engaging in this assignment, though, each student will have the opportunity to practice connecting administrative law to real-life examples and presenting that information in an organized coherent way to the teacher and classmates, skills that may be important course goals. Conversely, if deep understanding of *quasi in rem* jurisdiction is not an important learning objective in civil procedure, it would likely be less effective for students to spend a whole class on a *quasi in rem* jurisdiction simulation. But if the law, policy, skill and ethics of engaging in discovery in civil litigation are important course goals, then having students participate in a simulation may not only be motivating and engaging for its own sake, but is likely to produce significant learning.

2. Choose the experiential method/s

Illustration 8-1 and the more detailed descriptions in the first part of this chapter provide ideas about ways to infuse real-life experiences in a doctrinal course. If you are new to incorporating experiential methods, start by using one that seems most compatible with your teaching approach. Because experiential exercises may invite new teaching challenges and surprises, we recommend you begin with a method that feels comfortable. As is true of other active learning exercises (see Chapter 5), experiential learning exercises require the teacher to relinquish some control over the class, and it is challenging to predict how long an effective exercise should last.

It may be easier to envision an experiential exercise when you understand one a colleague has already designed. Tweaking those exercises and making them fit your course goals and students may be more efficient than designing one completely on your own.

3. Design the overall structure

Once you have identified why you want students to have a real-life exercise and what method(s) you want to use, consider specifically what you want students to do and when. To understand easements, property students could take a photo of an easement after they have learned about them and post it to a course website. Or they could research a city's housing and zoning laws and canvas a neighborhood to determine how certain property laws appear to affect its composition mid-semester. Several weeks into a patent law course, students could attempt to draft claims for a new pizza box design. At the beginning of the term, immigration law students could complete a citizenship test, later draft immigration forms, and toward the end of the semester take a field trip to observe an immigration detention facility. Scheduled throughout the term, criminal law students could accompany police officers on their beats. Constitutional law students could listen to Supreme Court oral arguments and read parties' and amicus briefs on topics related to those they are currently learning about. Tax students could be asked to summarize a current tax problem related to the material they are studying in the course and orally present it and answer questions about it from a simulated client or supervising attorney.

4. Find relevant and significant material

Students are more likely to be engaged in experiential exercises if they seem important and relevant to the topic. For example, because most negligence cases are settled before trial, it may be more effective to have torts students prepare a demand letter or settlement proposal to a defendant's insurance company rather than prepare closing arguments for a trial.

Practicing attorneys, former students, colleagues, recent cases, continuing legal education materials, bar journal articles, and scholarly articles can be useful sources for real-life exercises. Letting students know that the role-play you assigned was based on an actual matter helps the students put themselves in the role of lawyers and connect course knowledge, skills, and values to the problems.

5. Provide clear goals, directions, and expectations

Be clear about what you expect students to do and what the results of the real-world exercise should look like. It's much more effective to direct students to "spend an hour researching facts related to the design defects of a John Deere Model 800J lawn tractor" than it is to ask them to "research relevant facts related to the problem." Explain what the result of students' work should be, such as "by the end of class, each group must post a one-page document listing the two most significant remedies available for the breach of the building sale contract and the main reasons why those remedies are most important."

Upper-level courses, in which students can be expected to have greater knowledge and skills and are closer to practicing law, might call for less explicit instructions. In those circumstances, you may want to create more complex problems, what learning experts call "ill-structured problems." Students not only must produce a work product but also must determine what facts they need and how they will get or develop the facts, and they must identify and assess the options available to them for addressing the client's needs. Such problems provide a more realistic experience. For example, an insurance law teacher might assign students to write a client advice letter about the various insurance options available to the client. The teacher's instructions could be that the students need to find and evaluate the options, explain what the client needs to have explained, and write a letter "long enough to appropriately convey the important information using words the client can understand." For such assignments, it helps to provide directions and guidance consistent with what students might experience in a summer internship or initial job as an attorney.

To write clear directions, work backwards from what you want students to accomplish. Break down the different steps so that students can be successful. For example, if you want students to all spend about 15 minutes engaged in a paired role-play where one student attorney advises another student playing the role of a bankrupt and suicidal client, you should provide students in the different roles with different directions, specify how the students are to behave, and explain what they are to accomplish by the end of the role-play. In designing an experiential exercise that lasts more than a few minutes, it helps to put the goals, directions and performance expectations in writing and have someone else—assistant, teaching fellow, colleague, or friend—read the material and see if that person understands what you have written and knows what he or she would need to do.

6. Identify what you have to do to adequately prepare for the exercise

Are there special materials needed? Do you need to find a different classroom with flexible seating? Do you need to recruit speakers, attorneys, judges, clients, witnesses, etc.? How much research should you do? How will you connect this exercise to the course material and goals? Depending on the complexity of the exercise and other teaching methods used in the course, consider what additional preparation you will need to do and how much time you should allocate for it.

7. Identify what students have to do to adequately prepare for the exercise

If the experiential exercise you choose requires you to bring in current events related to your course every day, students may have no additional preparation. If, however, you want students to actively engage in the exercise, having them prepare for the exercise leads to higher engagement. For example, your expectation could be that throughout the course, each student brings in two current events related to the course. Or, rather than have students sit through a hospital risk management attorney's guest lecture about health law, have students research the attorney and bring questions to class to ask. Prepared students bring more depth and sophistication to real-life experiences so consider what will best help students be effective. Consider too what will happen if students do not prepare adequately.

8. Determine what feedback students will receive

Students' performance in an experiential exercise might be graded as a separate assignment, considered as part of a class participation grade, required as part of the course, or completely ungraded. You may decide to provide individual comments, rubrics, group or whole-class feedback, or none. For more ideas about giving feedback, see Chapter 10.

9. Determine how students will reflect upon the exercise

One of the hallmarks of effective experiential learning is that students reflect upon their experiences and learn from them. Being self-aware and thoughtful about what they have experienced leads to greater learning gains. For longer and more involved experiential exercises, we recommend that you ask students to reflect upon their experience and how they might apply what they have learned to future practice. As is true of all reflection exercises, a more specific prompt (e.g., What did you observe the lawyer do that surprised you? How will this experience influence you in the future?) is more effective than a directive to "reflect on your experience."

10. Reflect and self-assess the experience

Just as students learn from reflecting about their experiences, we recommend that you consider and write down the features of the experiential exercise that worked well, the parts that went poorly, and where you might make changes in the future. For more on using reflection and teaching journals to improve your teaching and student learning, see Chapter 13.

Thinking exercise: Consider students' performance on recent final exams and a course overall. What important knowledge, skills and values are not as strong as you hoped? How might you include experiential exercises to enhance future students' performance?

Illustration 8-2: Experiential Teaching and Learning Checklist

Experiential Teaching and Learning

- ❑ **Foundational considerations**
  - ❑ Understand the value of experiential exercises to promote deep learning of concepts, theory, skills, and values
- ❑ **Consider the variety of experiential methods**
  - ❑ Current events and real-life stories
  - ❑ Documents
  - ❑ Drafting documents
  - ❑ Field trips
  - ❑ Guest speakers
  - ❑ Interviews
  - ❑ Problem solving
  - ❑ Small role-plays
  - ❑ Simulations
  - ❑ Student presentations
- ❑ **Design the experiential exercise**
  - ❑ Connect to learning objectives
  - ❑ Choose appropriate methods
  - ❑ Design overall structure
  - ❑ Select relevant and significant material
  - ❑ Describe clear goals, directions, and expectations
  - ❑ Identify teacher preparation
  - ❑ Identify student preparation
  - ❑ Determine feedback methods
  - ❑ Determine student reflection
  - ❑ Reflect and self-assess

Experiential Teaching and Learning—Resources

This chapter is informed largely by these seven resources. The following four books focus on clinical, externship, and simulation courses.

- Carwina Weng, Danielle R. Cover, Margaret E. Rueter, Chris Roberts, Learning Law Through Experience & Through Design (Carolina Academic Press 2019).
- Leah Wortham, Alexander Scherr, Nancy Maurer & Susan Brooks, Learning from Practice: A Text for Experiential Legal Education (3d ed. West 2016).

- Deborah Maranville, Lisa Radtke Bliss, Carolyn Wilkes Kaas & Antoinette Sedillo López, Building on Best Practices: Transforming Legal Education in a Changing World (LexisNexis 2015).
- Roy Stuckey and Others, Best Practices for Legal Education (Clinical Legal Education Association 2007).

The following three books contain many ideas for incorporating experiential exercises in a wide range of courses.

- Emily Grant, Sandra Simpson & Kelly Terry, Experiential Education in the Law School Curriculum (Carolina Academic Press, 2017).
- Gerald F. Hess, Stephen L. Friedland, Sophie M. Sparrow & Michael Hunter Schwartz, Techniques for Teaching Law 2 (Carolina Academic Press 2011).
- Gerald F. Hess & Steve Friedland, Techniques for Teaching Law (Carolina Academic Press 1999).

Chapter 9

Deep, Lasting Learning

What constitutes exceptional, significant learning? How can we foster deep, lasting learning for our students? These are important questions for us as teachers. We all struggle to develop courses and classes that produce profound, persistent learning. Recent scholarship in legal education and higher education addresses these issues.

What is exceptional, significant, lasting learning?

Scholars in adult and college education have begun to define deep levels of learning. In *Creating Significant Learning Experiences*, L. Dee Fink posits that a key to improving higher education is for teachers to thoughtfully design courses so students have significant learning experiences. Significant learning has two characteristics. First, courses should cause significant change in students which persists after the course is over and students have graduated. Second, what students learn must have value in their lives. Value in this context might take the form of enhancing students' personal lives (such as developing a thoughtful philosophy of life), enabling students to contribute to the community (whether local, national, or global), or preparing students for work (developing professional knowledge, skills, and attitudes).

In *Understanding and Promoting Transformative Learning*, Patricia Cranton defines transformative learning in the context of adult education. "Transformative learning is ... a process by which previously uncritically assimilated assumptions, beliefs, values, and perspectives are questioned and thereby become more open, permeable, and better justified." (*Understanding and Promoting Transformative Learning*, page 2.)

In *How Learning Works*, the authors define mastery as the attainment of a high degree of competence in a particular area. To achieve mastery, students "need to develop a set of key component skills, practice them to the point where they can be combined fluently and used with a fair degree of automaticity, and know when and where to apply them appropriately." (*How Learning Works*, page 95.)

In What the Best College Teachers Do, Ken Bain conceived of exceptional learning as a combination of intellectual and personal development. Intellectual development includes "understanding a sizable body of material, learning how to learn (to expand understanding), to reason from evidence, to employ various abstract concepts, to engage in conversations about that thinking (including the capacity to write about it), to ask sophisticated questions, and the habits of mind to employ all those abilities." Personal development includes "understanding one's self (one's history, emotions, dispositions, abilities, insights, limitations, prejudices, assumptions, and even senses) and what it means to be human; the development of a sense of responsibility to one's self and others (including moral development); the capacity to exercise compassion; and the ability to understand and use one's emotions." (*What the Best College Teachers Do*, pages 189–190.)

Exceptional learning in legal education

In the first phase of our research for WHAT THE BEST LAW TEACHERS DO by Michael Schwartz, Gerald Hess, and Sophie Sparrow, we solicited nominations of law teachers who produced exceptional learning in their students. The nomination form included a working definition of exceptional learning in law school, modeled on Bain's definition. We invited the nominators to articulate their definitions of exceptional learning. More than 150 teachers, students, and deans responded to our invitation.

> **Thinking and writing exercise:** How do you define exceptional learning in the context of law school? Articulate your vision of exceptional learning in a paragraph.

Many of the nominators gave thoughtful examples and explanations of exceptional intellectual and personal development in law school. Intellectual development begins with a deep, nuanced understanding of core legal concepts and skills. Core concepts include analytical frameworks, underlying theories, and ambiguities in areas of substantive and procedural law. Core skills include legal analysis, legal research, drafting, fact investigation, advocacy, counseling, negotiation, and the development of professional judgment. Successful learners can critically analyze problems, synthesize ideas from different areas of law, and view legal challenges through various perspectives. Ultimately, exceptional intellectual development prepares students to apply concepts and skills in law practice and life after graduation.

Personal development begins with students' self-awareness of their strengths, weaknesses, cognition, assumptions, biases, and emotions. Exceptional personal development can be transformative, building students' confidence, allowing students to achieve personal and professional goals beyond what they thought was possible. Exceptional personal development inspires students to become lifelong learners. Finally, exceptional personal development includes students' acquisition of the core values of the profession and the development of a professional identity based on those values.

Lasting learning in legal education

As part of our data gathering for *What the Best Law Teachers Do*, we interviewed dozens of current and former students of the twenty-six law teachers we studied. We asked those students and alumni to identify lasting learning (if any) that they gained from those teachers. The lessons that stuck with them included subject matter, skills, and values.

> **Thinking exercise:** Think back to your own experiences as a law student. Identify several "lasting lessons" that you took from your legal education.

Some students and alumni identified subject matter that stuck with them. However, they did not focus on discrete rules of law (the elements of battery, hearsay exceptions, the *Erie* doctrine). Rather, their lasting learning included the idea that legal rules are indeterminate and constantly changing. They learned frameworks for analysis to address future problems in an area of law. Their teachers inspired these students to pursue careers in particular fields of law, including election law, immigration law, and civil rights. One of Professor Heather Gerken's students put it this way:

> *Learning from her and working with her had, and continues to have, a profound impact on my life. Substantively, I learned the entire field of election law from Heather—a field in which I now practice, thanks in large part to Heather. She introduced me to an area of the law that I found absolutely fascinating.... Beyond the substance and doctrine of the class, however, what has stuck with me was Heather's love of the field of election law. She was genuinely excited to discuss the cases and issues and made it all seem like so much fun.* (*What the Best Law Teachers Do*, pages 292–293.)

For many students and alumni, the focus of their lasting learning was skills. Students learned transferable analytical skills including close reading of cases and statutes, attention to detail, problem solving, and nuanced analysis of court opinions and statutes. Many alumni noted drafting, writing, and advocacy skills that they learned in law school and employ in law practice. One alum summarized the effect Professor Hiroshi Motomura had on the student's practice.

> *I learned how to use scholarship to the advantage of my clients, how to introduce the ideas into writing on behalf of clients, how to analyze the law with a fresh approach and to put it into a context that helped the Immigration Judges make the decision that helped my clients. I think I was able to do quite a bit of good work, especially for asylum seekers, who almost literally faced the death penalty if they lost their immigration cases. I don't think there is any way I could have done this without what I learned from Hiroshi Motomura. His work has saved lives.* (*What the Best Law Teachers Do*, pages 297–298.)

The most common types of lasting learning, by far, concerned personal development, values, and professionalism. Take-away lessons for students and alumni included:

- developing a strong work ethic;
- striving for excellence;
- bringing passion to their work;
- maintaining a balance between confidence and humility;
- treating clients with compassion and humanity;
- recognizing the significant impacts of the law on client's lives;
- being respectful in every interaction with clients, lawyers, judges, staff, witnesses, and everyone else in the profession;
- making conscious choices about their professional identities;
- living healthy, balanced lives;
- exemplifying integrity and responsibility; and
- embracing an ethic of service and a quest for justice.

One of Professor Patti Alleva's students articulated the following lasting lesson.

> *[A]s long as you're doing your best, and zealously advocating for your client, and you're doing everything you possibly can to put your best foot forward and give them a fighting chance. That's what it all comes down to. You're not always going to be, you know, victorious, but you're going to give it your best. And that's what she's taught me from the word go. I think that makes everybody who has interaction with Professor Alleva, not only a better law student or better future lawyer, but a better person in general, 'cause it affects your everyday life.* (*What the Best Law Teachers Do,* page 304.)

> **Thinking exercise:** What "lasting lessons" do you think students took from the last couple courses you taught?

How can teachers foster deep, lasting learning for students?

The higher education and legal education literature provide guidance for teachers to design courses to foster deep, lasting learning for students. Four design principles run through that literature:

1. Choose learning objectives that address significant, lasting learning;
2. Create a challenging, supportive, collaborative teaching and learning environment;

3. Engage students in rich, textured learning activities; and
4. Incorporate frequent formative feedback.

Choose learning objectives that address significant, lasting learning

Identifying learning objectives that address significant, lasting learning is the first step for teachers to design courses to foster deep learning for students. We cannot overemphasize the importance of this step.

Our conscious decision to choose specific, deep learning objectives for a course has several implications. First, as we discussed in chapters 2 and 3, the first step in intentional course and class design is to identify learning objectives. Lasting learning should be built into courses and class sessions from the beginning of the design process. Second, most teachers feel pressure to cover large volumes of content in their courses. We believe that foundational content should be included in learning objectives for many courses. But core content objectives should not be the *only* learning objectives. Instead, courses should also include lasting learning objectives beyond foundational knowledge. Third, we should be thoughtful and selective when choosing lasting learning objectives for our courses. Although there is no "correct" number of lasting learning objectives for a course, we believe that at least three such objectives are appropriate for most courses.

An example of the importance of choosing lasting learning objectives for our courses is illustrated by an experience two of us had in designing a required curriculum for a new law school. For each required course, the faculty identified foundational concepts and skills that the course would address. For example, Commercial Law was to include core principles of law (such as creating a security interest and priority among secured creditors) and the skills of statutory analysis and document drafting. In addition, based on surveys of lawyers and judges, the faculty identified a list of professional values important to success in the practice of law (honesty, reliability, diligence, tolerance, quest for justice, etc.). As a final step in the curriculum design process, each faculty member who taught required courses selected two or three of the professional values from the list and committed to incorporating them in their courses. The simple act of selecting professional values for our courses created an incentive for us to give those learning goals equal priority with other course objectives. As we taught our courses, we continued to search for methods to address professional values in meaningful ways. (See Chapter 11 for a description of emphasizing values through daily reminders.)

The particular deep learning goals appropriate for a course depend on many variables, including the nature of the course, the students, and the teacher. The following questions address some of the relevant considerations.

- Is the course required? Recommended? Elective?
- Is it a survey course (Evidence)? A specialty course (Transactional Drafting)?

- Are there prerequisites for the course?
- Has the faculty allocated specific learning objectives to the course?
- Is the subject tested on most bar exams?
- Where are the students in their legal education? First-semester, first-year? Second-semester, third-year?
- What background, experience, or prior learning do students bring to the course?
- What types of jobs do most students secure after graduation?
- In what areas does the teacher have the most expertise? Least expertise?
- What concepts, theories, skills, values is the teacher particularly passionate about?

After considering the nature of the course, students, and teacher, think expansively about appropriate lasting learning goals for your courses.

- In your wildest dreams, what learning would students take away from your course?
- What learning do you hope persists after students graduate?
- What learning would most help students in their professional lives? In their personal lives?

Many of the twenty-six teachers we studied in *What the Best Law Teachers Do* articulated lasting learning goals for their students. Some of those goals focused on legal doctrine. For example, Professor Julie Nice seeks to have her students achieve mastery of one aspect of Constitutional Law and to view mastery as a transferable skill.

> *I want [students] to have a good overview of Constitutional Law then some really good deep knowledge of how to zoom in and really master one of the doctrines in Constitutional Law and that's a transferable skill.... I say to them, "You all know how much depth went into the commerce clause and equal protection and so you learn two of the templates for structure and individual rights. And now those are the templates you'll use if you need to practice something we did not spend much time on...." What I'm trying to get them to see is if they were the master of a subject matter that they practice in they would want to have that kind of command.* (*What the Best Law Teachers Do*, pages 288–289.)

Professor Roberto Corrada wants students to see that to be effective lawyers, they need to not only consume legal doctrine, but to discover and develop the law as well.

> *What happens when a law student becomes an attorney with little ability to gather knowledge (and indeed, a strong preference for knowledge gathered by others—in a nutshell or hornbook) and no idea that he or she might be able to change and effect law (as producers of knowledge themselves) for the betterment of their immediate client and society itself?* (*What the Best Law Teachers Do*, pages 289–290.)

Others aimed to develop enduring analytical and advocacy skills in their students. Professor Ingrid Hillinger focuses on enduring statutory analysis and transactional skills.

> *I tell them on the first day in Article 9 [that] by the end of this course whether you've seen a provision or not, you're going to know how to deal with statutory language. You're going to know where to go in the code and what to do there.... You're going to have a system and a sense of other laws that sort of impact the system and you're going to have a sense of what a transactional attorney does, which is risk identification and how you minimize or try to circumvent risk.* (*What the Best Law Teachers Do*, page 291.)

Professor Cary Bricker aims to develop transferable oral and written advocacy skills.

> *I want them to come away with a sense of... knowing they can communicate in any form. We teach it in particularly a litigation setting, but I want a student to graduate and go to a school board and be the person who stands up and makes a coherent, persuasive presentation. I want them to be an associate in a law firm, who's going to ... take this big collection of facts, and isolate legal issues, and come up with legal memoranda that really work, that are persuasive.* (*What the Best Law Teachers Do*, pages 290–291.)

Many of the teachers we studied focused on professionalism and values. For example, Professor Beth Enos set out these objectives for her students:

> *I want them to be lawyers (and people) with integrity and compassion. I want them to understand that the parties in cases are real people, and that the choices that the lawyers and judges make have real consequences. I want them to be humbled and sobered by the responsibility they have not only to their clients but to the profession and to the wider community.* (*What the Best Law Teachers Do*, page 300.)

Several teachers, including Professor Paula Lustbader, sought to empower students.

> *My job is to empower them to make the difference they came here to make. I want them to question the status quo. I think most of my students come in doing that and I want to keep them doing that. And to question what's right and what's just. And who's not being heard, who's being silenced.... I want them to find their right work and have fulfilling, satisfying lives.... I want them to believe in their passions. I want them to believe in each other.... I want them to believe that they can be the change agents and transformative.* (*What the Best Law Teachers Do*, page 301.)

There are hundreds, perhaps thousands, of lasting learning objectives appropriate for law school courses. Law is an enormous, complex field. And the practice of law is a challenging, sophisticated profession. When making choices about significant, deep learning objectives for a particular course, it may help to categorize those objectives into (1) knowledge and analytical skills, (2) practice and relational skills, (3) professionalism, values, and identity.

Illustration 9-1: Lasting Learning Objectives

Categories and Subcategories	Sample Learning Objectives
Knowledge and Analytical Skills Analytical frameworks Underlying policies Theoretical approaches Perspectives on law Legal analysis Legal argument Case analysis Statutory analysis Constitutional interpretation Critical thinking Creative thinking Problem solving Close reading Attention to detail	Students will be able to: • Develop an analytical framework for an area of law relevant to a client's problem • Use underlying policies and theory to support arguments on behalf of a client • Generate multiple reasonable approaches to help achieve a client's goals
Practice and Relational Skills Legal research Written communication Oral communication Listening Legal drafting Fact investigation Interviewing & Questioning Negotiating Counselling Trial advocacy Practical judgment Organizing & managing projects Strategic planning Leadership Teamwork Cultural humility	Students will be able to: • Efficiently find applicable cases, statutes, and regulations relevant to a client's problem • Employ applicable negotiation styles and strategies to resolve a dispute • Build cross-cultural skills by practicing habits of cross-cultural lawyering
Professionalism, Values, and Identity Honesty & integrity Self-motivation & diligence Reliability & responsibility Seeking fairness & justice Passion & respect Balance & stress-management Self-confidence & humility Empathy & tolerance Commitment to *pro bono* & social justice Self-reflection	Students will: • Always show respect for clients, lawyers, judges, staff, witnesses, etc. • Engage in self-reflection to continuously improve as professionals • Incorporate *pro bono* as a significant aspect of their professional lives

For each of the three categories, Illustration 9-1 lists many subcategories and several examples of lasting learning objectives. Dozens of subcategories of learning objectives can be found in Chapter 2 of *Best Practices for Legal Education: A Vision and a Roadmap* and Chapter 6 of *Building on Best Practices: Transforming Legal Education in a Changing World.*

Thinking and writing exercise: For a course that you will teach, articulate a set of deep, lasting learning objectives.

- Begin by considering the nature of the course, the experience of your students, and your own passion and expertise.
- Think expansively. In your wildest dreams, what learning would stick with students in their personal or professional lives?
- Identify at least one lasting learning objective in each of the three categories (1) knowledge and analytical skills, (2) practical and relational skills, and (3) professionalism, values, and identity.

Create a challenging, supportive, collaborative teaching and learning environment

Students' motivation directly affects the depth and persistence of their learning. Student motivation tends to be highest in a teaching and learning environment that is challenging, supportive, and collaborative.

A challenging learning environment begins with clear expectations that students will achieve deep, lasting learning goals. A student of Professor Julie Nice explains the motivational effects of these expectations.

> *One thing that I really appreciate is that at the beginning of class, the beginning of the semester, she tells you what she expects from you. She has, I think, really high expectations of us. And she says this is what you're going to get out of my class.... And you should be able to analyze critically by the end of the class these specific situations, specific scenarios. And that just gets you excited as a student, excited that this is what you're going to be learning and it makes you actually help her reach her goal and in turn you become a better student."* (*What the Best Law Teachers Do*, pages 127–128.)

A teacher's high expectations can have dramatic effects on students' preparation and performance. High expectations are essential to an effective teaching and learning environment. But high expectations alone are not enough. Students will be more motivated to excel when they perceive that the teacher's expectations for lasting learning are both high and achievable. In other words, student motivation increases when they believe that what they are learning is meaningful, that their teachers expect a lot from them, and that they can succeed if they work hard.

It is important for teachers to communicate high expectations for every student in the course along with the belief that every student can succeed. These uniform expectations and confidence that each student can achieve great things can be powerful motivators for students. Students of Professor Cary Bricker explain:

> *[S]he expects a lot from each and every student.... I think anyone that has had Trial Ad, or Advanced Trial Ad, or Defender's Clinic with her will tell you that in mock situations with her she expects a lot and she's tough on you but she's tough on you because it makes you learn more.... Everyone walks out of her class feeling like, "Wow. That was amazing. I feel like I've grown a lot."* (*What the Best Law Teachers Do*, pages 131–132.)

Students respond to teachers who model high expectations. Teachers who demonstrate high expectations for their own performance inspire students to achieve important lasting learning goals. Students of Professor Patti Alleva and Professor Rory Bahadur describe the link between teachers' modeling high expectations and student motivation.

> *[S]he set an example of utter exactness, forcing me to strive continually for greater alacrity of thought and clarity of expression. And also she was always engaged, excited, ready, and willing to help. She served sort of as an ideal upon which one could attempt to model oneself, an archetype. And she makes you want to be a better lawyer, and you want to learn, not just to learn but to please her, to become a better advocate for your future clients by learning the intricacies of the law.* (*What the Best Law Teachers Do*, pages 140–141.)

> *[W]hen you see the amount of time and effort you have to appreciate and respect him.... It wasn't that I was scared of him, that's not why I prepared. I prepared every day because I respect him as a person and ... you can just tell how bad he wants you to get it.... Because he is just so into it and I haven't found or studied from another teacher that's like that and no other teacher has ever been able to make me want to learn as much as he has.* (*What the Best Law Teachers Do*, pages 140–141.)

Most students excel in teaching and learning environments that are not only challenging but supportive as well. A fundamental characteristic of a supportive environment is mutual respect between students and teachers. Professor Julie Nice beautifully articulates the power of mutual respect.

> *Mutual respect is where it begins and ends. I treat my students with an incredible amount of respect. I tell them in each class, "I believe you're here because you actually want to be here in law school and in this course and that you want to develop your knowledge and skills and you want to expand your own repertoire. I believe you are really bright and interesting people. And I am going to treat you with that kind of respect and I know you'll treat one another with that kind of*

respect...." I think it's our job to set the tone of mutual respect. I think it's really important to their motivation, sense of encouragement when they feel seen as human beings.... It's like watering the flower. They respond so powerfully to those little drops of water. (*What the Best Law Teachers Do*, page 81.)

Students describe teachers' attitudes that lead to a supportive teaching and learning environment, including respect for students, caring deeply about student learning, concern for students' well-being in and out of the classroom, and confidence in every student's promise and potential.

Using a variety of verbal formulations, students describe teachers who manage to create an environment that is both challenging and supportive. (*What the Best Law Teachers Do*, pages 126–127.)

- *She is remarkably good at keeping balance—really tough but she is empathetic. Love and challenge.* Student of Professor Tina Stark.
- *[H]e challenges you but at the same time cares about you.* Student of Professor Steve Friedland.
- *[T]here's that high expectation of professionalism but it's coupled with a recognition of the emotional needs that students have.* Student of Professor Nancy Levit.
- *She ... really cares about her students. The class requires a lot of preparation, and she has very high expectations, but it is definitely worth it to put in the work.* Student of Professor Heather Gerken.
- *He does a wonderful job of challenging us and respecting us.* Student of Professor Andy Leipold.

Thinking exercise: What actions, big and small, can you take to establish and maintain a challenging and supportive teaching and learning environment in your courses?

"Collaborative" is a third attribute of a teaching and learning environment that fosters deep, lasting learning. Most of the outstanding law teachers we studied view their relationship with students as collaborative rather than hierarchical. They see their students as colleagues and peers. They treat students as adults and professionals. Their students notice and appreciate this collaborative environment.

- *[H]e treats people like you're an attorney already, and you're a young professional.* Student of Professor Steven Homer.
- *[S]he feels like a peer. She doesn't feel like someone who's standing in front of me preaching to me, and her attitude is more of let's work together to arrive at the best solution for you.* Student of Professor Cary Bricker.

- *Professor Bahadur treated me like an adult.... He told us that "you guys are going to be attorneys; we'll be colleagues."* Student of Professor Rory Bahadur.
- *[She] treats students like junior colleagues... like they are part of the firm she is in.* Student of Professor Tina Stark.
- *[H]e honestly, genuinely treats you like a peer.* Student of Professor Hiroshi Motomura.
- *It was from day one, we were colleagues and we were going to do this together.* Student of Professor Andy Taslitz. (*What the Best Law Teachers Do*, page 105–106.)

One way that we can create a collaborative teaching and learning environment is to involve our students in course design decisions. As discussed in Chapter 2, course design involves choices about objectives, materials, assignments, teaching and learning activities, roles and responsibilities of teachers and students, and an assessment scheme. Typically, teachers make all of the design decisions. However, teachers can involve students in some or all of those decisions.

The benefits of teacher/student collaboration in course design is supported by the literature on learner-centered teaching, transformative learning, and empirical research on motivation and performance. By sharing power and responsibility with students in the course design process, teachers communicate their respect for students and convey their confidence in them. Involving students in designing their education can increase students' intrinsic motivation and positive attitudes toward the course, the teacher, and law school. Ultimately, student engagement in course design can enhance the classroom environment and student performance.

The teacher's level of comfort with the notion of sharing design responsibilities with students will vary from person to person. Further, students' ability and willingness to participate meaningfully in design decisions changes during law school as students become more self-directed in their learning. Most first-semester, first-year law students expect their teachers to make all of the course design decisions. As students progress through their legal education, their interest in and ability to participate in course design decisions grows.

Teachers and students who are ready to engage in collaborative course design can do so in a variety of ways, from small to large. For example, students can participate in identifying relevant material for the course—articles, websites, and videos. We can build student choice into assignments—students can select their topics for writing assignments and presentations. Students' options in assignments can allow them to build upon their strengths and interests.

We can provide students with a draft syllabus and ask students to weigh in on all or some of these questions:

1. What are your goals for the course?
2. What roles and responsibilities do students have to achieve the goals of the course?

3. What roles and responsibilities does the teacher have to achieve the goals of this course?
4. What teaching and learning activities should we use in the course?
5. What evaluation methods should be used to assess student performance?

> **Thinking exercise:** Do you currently involve students in course design decisions? Are you comfortable doing so in the future? If not, why? If so, in what aspects of course design are you willing to collaborate with students?

Engage students in rich, textured learning activities

Students are more likely to achieve significant, lasting learning if they engage in learning activities that are rich and textured. We begin by defining the concepts of "rich" and "textured" learning activities, recognizing that these concepts overlap and interact with one another. Then we present several extended examples of assignments designed to produce lasting learning.

Illustration 9-2: Rich Learning Activities

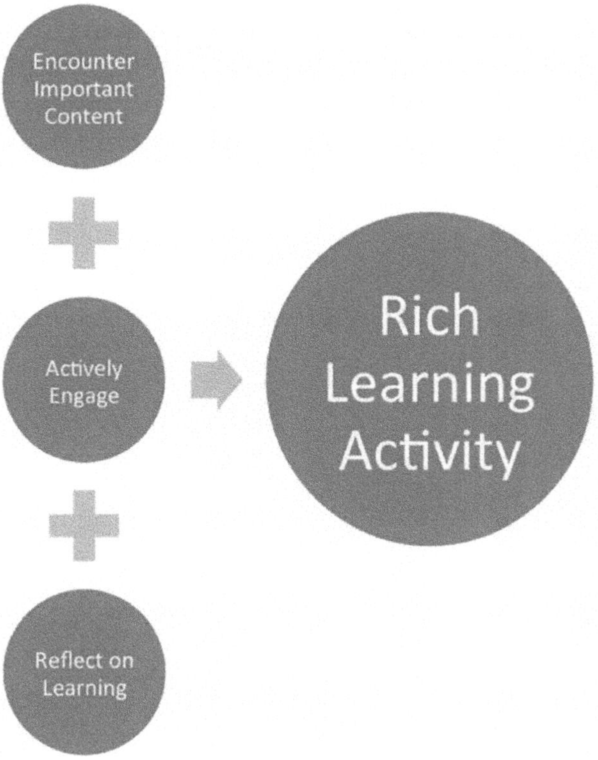

Our conception of rich learning activities, which we adapt from L. Dee Fink, has three phases: (1) students encounter important content; (2) students actively engage with the content; and (3) students reflect on their learning. Each of these phases could take place outside of class, in an on-line class, or in a face-to-face class.

In Phase 1, students encounter important content, which could include ideas, principles, policies, theories, perspectives, values, strategies, etc. In this context, content could address learning objectives related to knowledge, skills, or values. Students can encounter content in many different ways. Students could read cases, statutes, articles, or stories. Students could view videos, pictures, diagrams, or demonstrations. Students could listen to lectures, presentations, or podcasts.

In Phase 2, students work with the content by engaging in active learning activities. Students ask and respond to questions, produce outlines and diagrams, participate in discussions and debates, analyze hypotheticals and problems, make arguments orally and in writing, draft transactional and litigation documents, conduct fact investigations and discovery, interview and counsel simulated or real clients. These examples just scratch the surface of potential active learning methods. Other examples appear throughout the book. Students can engage in active learning individually, in small groups, or in a large group.

In Phase 3, students reflect on their learning. Reflection solidifies learning for students. For example, students can complete a "minute paper" at the end of a class session in which they articulate a key lesson from the class—"Explain the policies that underlie attorney-client privilege." (See the discussion of minute papers in Chapter 10.) Reflection can help students identify strengths and weaknesses in their performance, after a midterm exam, a draft of a paper, or a witness interview. And reflection can help students think through how to improve their understanding and performance in the future. (See Chapter 7 for many examples of reflection activities, including reflective writing.)

Illustration 9-3: Textured Learning Activities

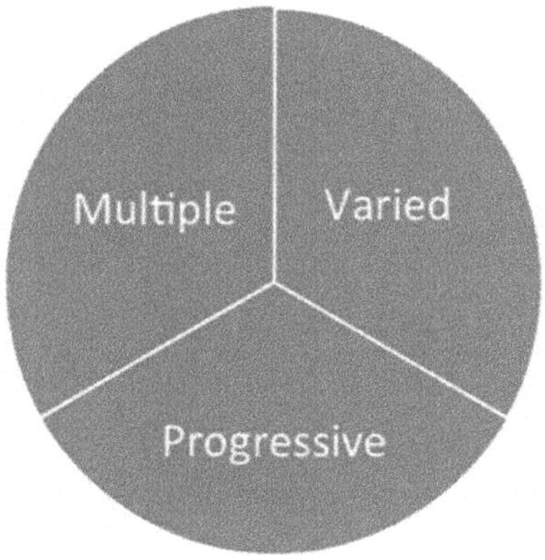

Our conception of textured learning activities has three components: multiple, varied, and progressive.

In the context of textured learning activities, multiple means that students will encounter and work with the relevant concept or skill or value more than once in the course. The more important the learning objective, the more learning experiences directed at the objective the students should have throughout the course. Varied means that the students will employ more than one type of learning activity directed at the objective. For example, students may read a rule of evidence, discuss a case interpreting the rule, work on problems applying the rule with a small group of students, see a demonstration of a lawyer employing the rule in offering evidence, and participate in a simulation in which the student argues about the admissibility of evidence under the rule. Progressive means that the difficulty of the issues and level of sophistication of students' performance grows during the course. For example, first students read an article about a jurisprudential theory to try to understand it, then they attempt to explain how the theory plays out in a judicial opinion, then they compare it to other theories, then they make a written argument employing the theory, then they critique and revise the theory.

The examples below, Illustrations 9-4, 9-5, and 9-6, illustrate rich, textured learning activities. These activities are aimed at three types of significant, lasting learning objectives: (1) analytical skill (elements of statutory analysis); (2) concepts and policy (public comments on proposed administrative agency actions); and (3) practice skill (negotiation).

Illustration 9-4: Statutory Analysis Example

Statutory Analysis Example

Context. Statutory analysis skills could be an important objective of any course in which statutes provide a significant part of the applicable law. This example is set in an Environmental Law course.

Objective. Students will be able to use the elements of statutory analysis to make effective arguments in this course and in practice.

Learning Activities:

- Introductory lecture. Emphasize the importance of statutory analysis skills to succeed in the course and in practice. Define six elements of statutory analysis: (1) language of the applicable statute, (2) purpose of the statute, (3) overall statutory scheme, (4) legislative history, (5) regulations interpreting the statute, and (6) cases interpreting the statute.
- Teacher demonstrates the six elements in analyzing a simple problem under the Endangered Species Act.
- Throughout the course, reading assignments ask students to identify judges' use of statutory analysis in opinions followed by in-class Socratic dialog or large group discussion of the opinions.
- Multiple assignments asking students to use elements of statutory analysis to prepare arguments based on relatively simple problems, followed by small and large group discussion of the problems in class.
- Students complete a minute paper reflecting on their statutory analysis strengths and weaknesses at the end of a class in which students work on problems.
- Students complete a practice exam asking them to use the elements of statutory analysis to make an argument in a complex problem involving the Clean Water Act.
- Large group discussion in class of a rubric or score sheet for the practice exam problem, followed by student reflection on strengths and weaknesses of their performance.
- A substantial portion of the final exam includes an essay question that requires students to use the elements of statutory analysis to make an argument in a complex problem involving the Clean Air Act.

Illustration 9-5: Public Comment Example

Public Comment Example

Context. The public comment process could be an important objective in any course with a substantial component of administrative law.

Objective. For the public comment process on proposed agency action, students will be able to (1) articulate the purpose and requirements of the process (2) critique the process, (3) identify characteristics of effective public comments, and (4) draft an effective public comment.

Learning Activities:

- Reading assignment with statutory provisions, agency regulations, and cases addressing the purposes and requirements of the opportunity for public comment on proposed agency actions.
- Assignment for students to review a sampling of public comments (posted on the course webpage).
- Large group discussion in class of the purpose, requirements, strengths and weaknesses of the public comment process.
- Assignment requiring each student to file a written public comment on a pending administrative agency action.
- Assignment that each student post the text of the public comment that they made and a paragraph reflecting on what the student learned from participating in the public comment process on the course web page.
- Assignment that each student reviews two of their fellow students' postings.
- Large group discussion in class regarding the purposes of the public comment process, the strengths and weaknesses of the process, and characteristics of effective public comments.

Illustration 9-6: Negotiation Example

Negotiation Example

Context. Negotiation could be part of a course focused on the law and skills of dispute resolution or any course with a negotiation component.

Objective. Students will be able to resolve disputes through negotiation by using an appropriate negotiation style and effective strategy, in compliance with the applicable rules of professional conduct.

Learning Activities:

- Reading assignment regarding negotiation styles, strategy in planning and conducting negotiations, and the ethical rules that apply to negotiation.
- Lecture emphasizing key points regarding negotiation styles, strategy in planning and conducting negotiations, and the ethical rules that apply to negotiation. This lecture could take place in class or, perhaps preferably, outside of class via a video or podcast.
- Assignment that each student play a virtual negotiation game online at least twice (link to the game provided by the teacher).
- Assignment that each student prepare to participate in two short negotiation simulations, one transactional and one based on litigation.
- Class in which each student participates in short negotiations (5–10 minutes for each simulation). After each simulation, pairs report their results followed by a large group debrief of negotiation styles, strategies, and ethics.
- Assignment that each student work with others in a small group (a law firm) to prepare to negotiate a more complex simulated dispute, such as pending litigation with potential liability issues and many types of potential damages.
- Before class, firms trade brief written settlement proposals.
- Class in which firms attempt to negotiate a resolution to the dispute. After 40 minutes of negotiation, firms report their results, followed by a debrief of negotiation styles, strategy, and the ethical rules that apply to negotiation.
- Each student completes a one-page reflection on the three negotiation simulations, focusing on what they learned about negotiation and their strengths and weaknesses as negotiators.

Incorporate frequent formative feedback

Feedback is central to learning. So it should come as no surprise that frequent, formative feedback furthers student achievement of significant, lasting learning goals. We address feedback throughout this book: Chapter 3 (the role of feedback in class design); Chapter 6 (feedback through students' self-reflection); and Chapter 10 (a detailed exploration of assessing students to improve their learning). Rather than repeating that discussion here, we apply formative feedback principles to our three examples of rich, textured learning experiences.

Rich, textured learning activities offer many opportunities for formative feedback. Sources of feedback include the teacher, other students, and the student herself. Feedback can occur in and outside of class. Feedback can be delivered in a large group setting, to small groups of students, or one-on-one to an individual student.

Statutory Analysis Example (Illustration 9-4)—Formative Feedback.

- Assignments throughout the course ask students to identify judges' use of statutory analysis elements in opinions and to prepare statutory analysis arguments in response to short problems. Large and small group discussions of these assignments in class give students feedback on their ability to identify elements and make arguments.
- In the minute paper, students give themselves feedback on their statutory analysis strengths and weaknesses.
- The practice exam exercise allows for several feedback options:
    - Teacher could make comments on each student's response;
    - Teacher could complete a score sheet or rubric evaluating each student's response;
    - Teacher could prepare a score sheet or rubric and have students apply it to their own responses;
    - Teacher could prepare a score sheet or rubric and have students apply it to another student's response;
    - Teacher could prepare a score sheet or rubric and conduct a large group discussion in class;
    - Teacher could meet individually with any student who wants more feedback.
- The final exam also offers multiple opportunities for formative feedback:
    - Students can review the teacher's comments on their responses;
    - Students can review the score sheet or rubric completed by the teacher;
    - Teacher could prepare a memo to students summarizing common strengths and weaknesses in student responses;
    - Teacher could meet individually with any student who wants more feedback.

Public Comment Example (Illustration 9-5)—Formative Feedback.

The assignment that each student make a public comment on a proposed agency action and post the text of the comment on the course website allows for several types of formative feedback:

- Students could engage in self feedback by posting a paragraph reflecting on what the student learned from participating in the public comment process;
- Students could provide feedback to one another by posting reactions and questions to one-another's public comments;
- Teacher could post a paragraph of feedback on each student's public comment;

Illustration 9-7: Fostering Deep, Lasting Learning Checklist

Fostering Deep, Lasting Learning

- ❑ **Foundational considerations**
  - ❑ Articulate your view of what constitutes exceptional learning in law school
  - ❑ Articulate your vision of learning that your students retain after graduation
- ❑ **Choose learning objectives that address significant, lasting learning**
  - ❑ Knowledge and analytical skills
  - ❑ Practice and relational skills
  - ❑ Professionalism, values, and identity
- ❑ **Create an effective teaching and learning environment**
  - ❑ Challenging
  - ❑ Supportive
  - ❑ Collaborative
- ❑ **Engage students in rich, textured learning activities**
  - ❑ Rich
    - ❑ Students encounter important content (knowledge, skills, values)
    - ❑ Students actively engage with the content
    - ❑ Students reflect on their learning
  - ❑ Textured
    - ❑ Multiple
    - ❑ Varied
    - ❑ Progressive
- ❑ **Incorporate frequent formative feedback**
  - ❑ Feedback from teacher
  - ❑ Feedback from other students
  - ❑ Self feedback

- Teacher could prepare a memo to students summarizing the themes that emerged from the students' public comments and the students' reflections on their learning.

Negotiation Example (Illustration 9-6)—Formative Feedback.

- The virtual negotiation game provides immediate feedback to students on the results of the negotiation and suggestions for improved performance. Students can immediately implement those suggestions by doing the game a second time.
- The large group debriefs after each of the three negotiation simulations give students immediate feedback on the results of their negotiation compared with others' results.

- The large group debriefs after each of the three negotiation simulations allow the teacher and students to provide feedback on negotiation styles, strategy in preparing and conducting negotiations, and ethical challenges.
- Students engage in self feedback through their one page reflection on the three negotiation simulations, focusing on what they learned about negotiation and their strengths and weaknesses as a negotiator.
- If students post their reflection on the course website, other students can give feedback by posting reactions and questions after reading another student's reflection.
- Teacher could post a paragraph of feedback on each student's reflection.
- Teacher could prepare a memo to students summarizing the themes that emerged from the students' reflections.

Illustration 9-7 is a checklist for fostering deep, lasting student learning.

Deep, Lasting Learning—Resources

This chapter is based largely on the following six resources. The first two books are from the higher education literature on teaching and learning.

- L. DEE FINK, CREATING SIGNIFICANT LEARNING EXPERIENCES: AN INTEGRATED APPROACH TO DESIGNING COLLEGE COURSES (Jossey-Bass 2003).
- SUSAN A. AMBROSE ET. AL., HOW LEARNING WORKS: 7 RESEARCH-BASED PRINCIPLES FOR SMART TEACHING (Jossey-Bass 2010).

These three books and one article are from the legal education literature on teaching and learning.

- MICHAEL HUNTER SCHWARTZ, GERALD F. HESS & SOPHIE M. SPARROW, WHAT THE BEST LAW TEACHERS DO (Harvard University Press 2013).
- DEBORAH MARANVILLE, LISA RADTKE BLISS, CAROLYN WILKES KAAS & ANTOINETTE SEDILLO LÓPEZ, BUILDING ON BEST PRACTICES: TRANSFORMING LEGAL EDUCATION IN A CHANGING WORLD (LexisNexis 2015).
- ROY STUCKEY AND OTHERS, BEST PRACTICES FOR LEGAL EDUCATION (Clinical Legal Education Association 2007).
- Gerald F. Hess, *Heads and Hearts: The Teaching and Learning Environment in Law School*, 52 J. LEGAL EDUC. 75 (2002).

Chapter 10

Assessing Student Learning

Introduction

Almost all teachers regularly engage in the process of assessment: *collecting information about student learning*. When we grade students' work, listen to their comments, consider students' behavior in class, or view students' comments online, we are assessing student learning; we are trying to see if our students are getting it.

This chapter focuses on designing effective assessments *at the student and course levels*. As the American Bar Association requires, effective law schools also assess programs and institutions, a process beyond the scope of this book. One form of institutional assessment—embedded assessment—draws on student work products created as part of their regular coursework. To that extent, assessments of student learning contribute to institutional assessment.

As with all aspects of teaching, an intentional approach to assessing student learning can help students develop more significant knowledge, skills, and values. Approaching assessment intentionally can also increase our satisfaction with teaching and grading. We strive to be like a colleague who said, after years of teaching, "My students now write excellent exams."

A vast amount of material is devoted to assessment—books, websites, podcasts, articles, and conferences. Much of this assessment material has developed within the past twenty years as educational accreditors, including the American Bar Association, have demanded evidence of student learning. In fact, all assessment is intricately connected to learning; you should therefore keep student learning foremost in your mind when thinking about assessment. It is not good teaching when students aren't learning.

The Assessment Cycle

Assessing student learning during the course and using that information to improve your teaching is part of the assessment cycle, as seen in Illustration 10-1. Like almost every aspect of teaching, assessment is an ongoing and recursive process. Ideally, we go through this cycle throughout every course as students perform different tasks to

Illustration 10-1: The Assessment Cycle

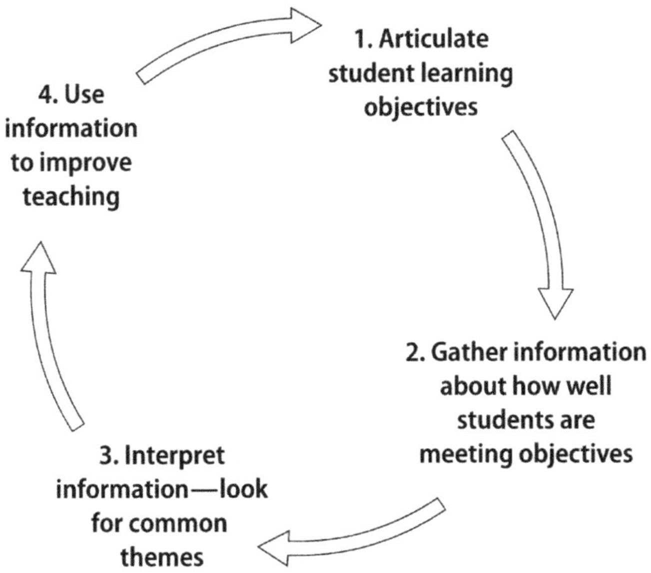

demonstrate their progress in meeting learning outcomes. Looking for trends, we see areas where most students are competent and areas where a significant number of them are struggling. We try new ways to help students learn. We give students more tasks to see if our new teaching approach helped students develop greater competency. Assessment is not easy, but paying attention to how your students are performing before your courses are over can improve your teaching considerably.

This chapter provides concrete suggestions in three areas:

1. Assessing students to improve their learning during the course
2. Assessing students to improve your teaching—using classroom assessment techniques
3. Evaluating students to assign grades

These three areas overlap—the same assessment instrument can be used to help students learn, improve teaching, improve course design, and assign grades. The key is to make assessment ongoing, effective, and sustainable. The best assessment plan must realistically account for other professional demands—such as scholarship and service—placed on law teachers. While we suggest assessment tools and methods, we don't expect or advise you to implement all of them immediately. Try the ones that resonate with you. Like all aspects of teaching, assessment is an ongoing work-in-progress.

Assessing students to improve their learning during the course

The best way to assess what your students are learning—and, hence, what you have effectively taught them—is to do it early and often. As you know from Chapter 1, students need to have many opportunities to practice showing us what they are learning so that we can give them feedback and they can improve. This type of assessment is called *formative assessment*—its main purpose is to help students learn rather than to assign grades. Having students complete a variety of assessment instruments during the course allows them to approach course material from different perspectives and achieve deeper learning. Having students engage in multiple and varied assessments also helps them develop the self-regulated learning skills that help them succeed after the course ends (see Chapters 1 and 6 for more on self-regulated learning).

Research shows that, across multiple disciplines, one of the ingredients essential for learning is an "assessment-centered" environment. In an assessment-centered environment, students have repeated opportunities to practice and receive feedback. If we want students to learn, we need to give them multiple opportunities to practice lawyering skills and get feedback on how they are learning.

In this section, we walk you through four steps in using assessment to improve student learning during the course. Illustration 10-2 identifies these important steps in the assessment process; we address each in depth below.

Illustration 10-2: Designing Effective Assessments—4 steps

Designing Effective Assessments
4 STEPS

1. Identify what you want to assess—or outcomes
2. Prepare and give assessment instruments
3. Give feedback to students
4. Use assessment information to improve teaching and course design

Thinking exercise: Consider your career. How have you benefited from having opportunities to practice and get feedback on your professional development?

Step one: Identify what you want to assess—learning goals and objectives

Ideally, before the course begins, you should have identified clear learning goals for your course and individual classes. In addition, your school may have already identified learning outcomes as required by the ABA's Standard 302. Your law school may designate your course to introduce, provide practice of, or demonstrate attainment of

Illustration 10-3: Classroom Assessment—Learning Objectives Example

Class assessment—Assignment 1

Learning objectives

1. Identify the elements of ___________;
2. Apply given facts to the elements of ____; and
3. Write coherent prose.

certain outcomes. Regardless of the state of your learning goals, go on to the next steps; often, you will better understand what you want students to learn after you see how they perform. (Examples of learning goals are in Chapters 2 and 3.)

Assume that you are only a few weeks into a course. You decide to give an ungraded assignment requiring that students demonstrate the three goals in Illustration 10-3. Be explicit about the value of testing their legal knowledge with low stakes or no stakes practice assignments. One accessible analogy you may consider to help students buy into the value of low-risk formative assessment is rooted in the preparation they undertake to pass a driving test. Even the most expert, experienced driver will probably remember the value of practicing in a parking lot with very little risk. Learning to drive by practicing in the school parking lot with orange safety cones was not a waste of their time; rather, that low-risk practice was an essential part of preparing the new driver to master their DMV test on the real road.

We have learned that such simple assignments can reveal that many students are struggling with basic legal analysis and writing skills in a course.

Step two: Prepare and administer assessment instrument

There are many different kinds of assessment instruments you can use in law school. Illustration 10-4 includes some of these.

The list of assessment instruments above is not exhaustive. Your methods of assessment will vary according to your learning goals. While the most common assessments ask students to respond to a question or solve a problem in writing, you might also ask students to engage in a simulation, prepare an oral argument, or design a graphic. You should give students the space and creativity to play to their own strengths and make use of the evolving technology available to them.

No matter what kind of assessment you are doing, as you prepare the instrument, consider the factors described below and listed in Illustration 10-5.

Answering these questions helps you focus your teaching to improve student learning and enable them to use their time more effectively. We prevent a lot of wasted time and effort—ours and the students'—if we are explicit about what we want and why we want it.

Illustration 10-4: Assessment instruments

Assessment Instruments

1. Multiple-choice and short answer quizzes
2. Analytical, issue-spotting, and advocacy essays
3. Outlines, charts, and matrices
4. Legal documents such as wills, articles of incorporation, injunctions, and statutes (or portions of those documents)
5. Journals or self-reflection worksheets
6. CALI exercises
7. Role-plays—simulations with students engaged in practice-related performances
8. Verbal presentations
9. Oral arguments
10. Web-based polling platforms or student response systems
11. Student-created slides or Flowcharts to capture legal principles
12. Image bank association charts (illustrated later in this chapter)
13. Student-created podcasts
14. Skits, movies, games, songs, artwork, jewelry, and any other creative expression

Illustration 10-5: Common Factors to Consider When Preparing Assessment Instruments

Common Factors to Consider When Preparing Assessment Instruments

- What is the rationale for this assessment?
- What do you want students to do?
- How much time will it take for students to complete?
- Will the assessment be completed in or outside of class?
- What is the assessment's content?
- Is there a particular format students should use?
- How much can students collaborate on the assessment?
- How will you provide feedback?

Provide *the rationale* for the assessment.

Make sure your students know *why* you are asking them to perform the assessment and what feedback they can expect. We usually explain our reasons when administering the assessment, e.g.,

Please prepare <u>Assignment 1</u> for next Monday. Completing this assignment will let you practice using the material we have been discussing in the past few class-

es. The exercise will also give you practice in doing what lawyers do and doing what you need to do on exams. The exercise will also help me see what you understand and what we should review.

Depending on the complexity of the assessment, consider including the rationale as part of the assessment. You also may include information about assessments in the syllabus, along the lines of:

In this class you will be completing a number of ungraded assignments. Each of these is designed to deepen your understanding of the course material. Consequently, please bring written responses to these exercises in a form that can be read by a classmate—a handwritten document or one on your laptop or tablet.

Identify what you want students *to do* and *give clear directions.*

Relate the assessment to your learning outcomes. Asking "Is this a valid contract? Why or why not?" is more effective than asking students to "Discuss the parties' claims." The word "discuss" might suggest that the student should regurgitate knowledge, rather than articulating and evaluating the arguments reasonable lawyers would make while analyzing a dispute.

Take the assessment yourself, revising your directions and the assessment based on what you learn. Remember that you may have a very clear idea of what you want students to do, but, as novices in your field, students need more clues, especially because what you want students to do may be quite different from what your colleagues ask them to do. One teacher might want students to articulate all the possible issues presented by a set of facts, while another might want to have students select the most significant issues and analyze them in depth. Help your students by giving them clear guidelines.

Take another look at the three learning outcomes in the above assessment (Illustration 10-3). Consider specifically what you want students to focus on when presented with a hypothetical problem. Do they need to identify *all* or just some of the facts that apply to the element? Do you want students to be selective about what facts they apply or should they identify as many as possible? How much factual interpretation do you expect of your students?

The longer and more complex the assessment, the more helpful it is to have specific directions or identified outcomes, such as "Identify the *best* argument this employee can make in her claim for gender discrimination." You may also find it helpful to specify what students should *not* do, such as stating something like:

Please focus on the defendant's duty of care. ***Do not*** *discuss the elements of breach, causation, scope of liability, or damages.*

Education experts would characterize such instructions as a "scaffold"; scaffolds are particularly useful for novices. As your students develop their abilities, you can gradually withdraw the scaffold until the students can handle the task on their own.

An instructional scaffold helps novice learners successfully perform challenging intellectual skills.

Evaluate how much *time* students will need to complete the assessment.

In general, students will take twice as much time as you to complete the same assessment. If you are fortunate enough to have one, ask a teaching assistant to complete the assessment and track how long it took. Ask a colleague to read the assessment and record how long it took. If students complete the assessment outside of class and it takes more than a few minutes, consider what else you have assigned students to do for that class session. If students use class time to do the assessment, budget sufficient class time for most students to complete the assessment.

Determine *when* students will complete the assessment.

Some assessments work well in class; others are better completed outside of class. Consider the other demands on your students' time. If they have graded assessments in other classes, an ungraded assessment will get considerably less attention. It is easier to figure out timing when all your students have the same courses, but, even in a large, upper-level class, you can ask for a show of hands to learn about students' other deadlines. Asking students to solve a complex problem the same weekend that 75% of the class is taking an exam in another course is unlikely to be a positive experience for you or your students.

Determine *the content* of the assessment.

Keeping your learning goals in mind, focus your assessments on the most important skills, content, and values in your courses. As you progress through the course, add complexity to your assessments. We tend to design discreet problems related to a topic. "I have a good hypo on injunctive relief for today; next class we'll work through contempt problems." Remember that the goal of having students practice is to improve their skills. Because your final exam or graded assessment will likely ask students to analyze complex facts and their relation to many different areas of the course, give students the opportunity to practice integrating different areas of the course. Embed material from an earlier section of the course in a later assessment. In designing an assessment, you may find it helpful to consult casebooks, court opinions, restatements, journals, and current events for ideas for assessment content. We also ask students to prepare problems and sample answers, embedding a concept taught earlier in the course in the problem. In the process of writing hypothetical scenarios and possible answers, students learn a lot. Ask AI to construct a hypothetical for a particular area of law; of course, you will need to carefully edit the results! Students can also design a flow chart or smart chart to demonstrate their understanding of a legal principle or rule.

When preparing an assessment, omit distractions that could impede students' performance and learning. Avoid using unexplained references or making assumptions

Illustration 10-6: Joinder Graphic Assignment

Joinder Graphic Assignment
Prepare a graphic of all or part of joinder. A graphic is a visual representation of concepts. Typical examples of graphics are flow charts and diagrams. However, a graphic could also be a picture, cartoon, board game, or many other visual representations. Use your imagination. The purpose of this assignment is to help you organize and synthesize the law that applies to joinder.

about students' cultural experiences or knowledge. For example, sports references or names of TV shows from your youth will be meaningless to many of your students. Keep the people's names simple unless you want students to consider biases and question their assumptions about names and roles.

Identify whether students should use *a particular format.*

Students benefit from having clear guidelines when they are asked to do more than supply a verbal answer. How many minutes for their presentations? Can students use props in their simulations? Should they dress up? Do you have preferences about margins, font type and size, page length, spacing, and organizational structure? (Single-spaced essays in 10-point font are hard to read.) Alternatively, you may want to leave the options wide open to allow for a greater range of student creativity. For example, you may ask students to work in small groups to create a graphic such as in Illustration 10-6 or work together to create slides to capture a particular topic.

Decide whether students *can collaborate* on the assessment.

Research shows that students learn a tremendous amount from being part of learning communities where they can brainstorm and solve problems together. However, students usually earn individual grades. To help students see how well they are progressing towards the course learning goals, have them complete at least some of the assessments individually. To maximize the benefits of collaboration, make some assessments group projects and make others hybrid, such as asking students to prepare an assessment individually and then collaborate with others on a final version. Another hybrid possibility, suggested by the cooperative learning experts, is having students take an assessment individually but awarding a bonus to all the members of a group if everyone in the group performs at or above a predetermined level, such as 80% correct.

Determine how you will provide students with *feedback.*

Many teachers fear that giving assessments will involve hours of commenting upon individual student work. There are other ways to give feedback. You could give "global feedback," where you read all assessments, get a sense of students' performance, and then comment on common challenges and successes. In class, you can select excerpts from a few sample answers and comment on the common errors reflected in these papers; make sure you emphasize how common the errors are and preserve the anonymity of the authors of the papers you use as examples. You could provide a sample answer that students can compare with their submissions. Students could review and comment upon their peers' work, and you could provide a checklist or rubric students can use to self- or peer-assess. (More on rubrics below.) If you're new at providing feedback, you can tell students that you will provide feedback and will determine the particular method after you've seen their work.

Step three: Give feedback to students

Giving feedback on assessments with the primary goal of helping students learn, rather than evaluating their performance for a grade, is known as "formative" assessment. Formative assessments are ways to give students coaching and feedback as they seek to master course goals. Evaluating students' performance primarily for a grade is known as "summative" assessment. The American Bar Association requires that law schools provide students with formative and summative assessment. This section on feedback focuses on formative assessment.

In general, give students feedback in three areas. These three areas can be pretty broad, such as "law," "facts," and "organization and coherence," with more feedback within each of the three areas. Most learners can focus effectively on three things; a list of a dozen errors tends to overwhelm. Keep the feedback organized, focused, and concise. In addition, remember the principles from Chapter 1: the most effective feedback has four characteristics:

Specific	Students learn whether their work met specific criteria and why.
Positive	Students find out what they are doing well and why what they did was effective.
Corrective	Students are given strategies to improve their weaknesses.
Prompt	Students get feedback soon and in time for the next assessment.

Provide students with *specific* feedback.

General statements, such as "Good job!" or "Needs work," don't tell students much. While an "excellent!" suggests that everything is great, novices will not automatically understand why you have concluded that their work was excellent. Moreover, a competent response usually shows a mix of skills and knowledge. Most students excel in some areas and are weak in others. Because our goal is to have students practice and get some feedback, however, general feedback is better than none at all. Students welcome any practice and feedback, even if they just get a "check," "check plus," or "check minus" on their work. If you know what you are looking for, you can quickly go through many one-page responses, putting checks on them and returning them to students in the next class.

Giving specific feedback is usually harder than giving general feedback, particularly with more complex assessments. Many teachers say, "I just know what feels like a B." You might, but your students don't have the expertise to understand *why* their performance on an assessment was above a C but below an A. Spell it out for them. It takes more time and energy the first time, but, if you build a library of effective assessments, feedback methods, and feedback instruments, you will save time and agony later. Even better, your students will learn more.

As with designing an assessment instrument, the best approach for giving feedback is to take the assessment yourself, analyze your response, and then make a list of specific things you want students to do. What are they supposed to be learning, and how will they show that to you? (Yes, you need to regularly revisit the question, *what <u>are</u> your learning goals?*) Make a checklist of what you want students to do.

Alternatively, you can read about ten sample student responses and start to generate your list from there. Start thinking in categories. Are you looking for rules? Exceptions? Factual applications? Policy? Illustration 10-7 is a sample checklist with specific information sought on an assessment.

You also can give specific feedback verbally in class. For example, you might say,

> *"Excellent! Jan just articulated a number of significant facts in analyzing this rule. Each of those facts helps show why the plaintiff was unsuccessful in this case. In practice, and on exams, it is essential to not just articulate relevant facts and give the conclusion but to also show <u>how</u> the facts apply to the law."*

This type of feedback shows everyone in the class how important this skill is and gives them a specific example. Similarly, giving students mini quizzes, using web-based response platforms, having students vote by raising their hands and then providing oral responses provide students with specific feedback. If given verbally, these techniques help to reinforce students' learning and the value of the feedback, especially if students write down the correct response or the specific feedback.

Another way to provide specific feedback without having to spend hours going over individual students' work is to give students a rubric—a grid with a set of detailed written criteria used to assess student performance. Illustration 10-8 shows a sample rubric from a criminal procedure course. Students and teachers can assess performance more effectively when they have a rubric describing specific criteria and levels of quality. It is important to emphasize to students that the rubrics capture performance on a particular assignment; be explicit in reminding students that rubric scores do not necessarily correlate with end of semester grades. Preparing a rubric initially takes time, but the benefits more than offset the investment. More about how to use and develop rubrics follows under the *Evaluating student learning to assign grades* section of this chapter.

Illustration 10-7: Sample Formative Assessment Checklist

Sample Formative Assessment Checklist

- ❑ Notes that D will have a duty of care
  - ❑ Identifies reasonably prudent person standard of care—law
  - ❑ Apply key facts to standard
- ❑ Posted speed limit—Is statute relevant?—Go through 2 part test
  - ❑ Is P in the group of people meant to be protected by the statute?
    - ❑ Apply facts to test
  - ❑ Is P's kind of harm the kind of harm that was meant to be prevented?
    - ❑ Apply facts to test
- ❑ If statute is relevant, how will courts use it?
  - ❑ Negligence per se or evidence of negligence—what effect?

Illustration 10-8: Sample Rubric

Description of what is being assessed	Levels of quality		
	Exemplary	Competent	Developing
Identifies basic and complex criminal procedural issues—"Issue Spotting" 40%	❑ Accurately identifies *all* basic procedural issues *21–30 points* ❑ Identifies *most* of the complex issues *7–10 points*	❑ Accurately identifies *most* basic procedural issues *11–20 points* ❑ Identifies *some* of the more complex issues *4–6 points*	❑ Accurately identifies *some* basic procedural issues *0–10 points* ❑ Identifies *a few* of the more complex issues *0–3 points*
Analyzes the facts 40%	❑ Accurately and explicitly shows how the law applies to important facts *27–40 points*	❑ Accurately shows how the law applies to most of the relevant facts *14–26 points*	❑ Accurately but minimally shows how the law applies to some of the facts *0–13 points*
Identifies and applies the policy for the rules of criminal procedure 20%	❑ Identifies and applies competing policy goals to facts in predicting results *14–20 points*	❑ Somewhat identifies and applies policy to facts in predicting results *7–13 points*	❑ Minimally identifies and applies policy to facts in predicting results *0–6 points*

Regardless of how and when you give feedback, we recommend that you identify no more than three areas for feedback and provide one specific example from each.

Provide students with positive feedback.

Much of law school feedback tends to be negative; we are experts at finding flaws, and we train our students to do the same. Learning to critique is important, but hearing only about what you need to do to improve can become depressing. Some students love the thrill of being critiqued and challenged. Most of us, however, learn faster when we are validated for what we do well. Research shows that learners do best in an environment where they are challenged *and* affirmed.

As a general rule, start feedback by stating what students are doing well. Students almost always do something well. Find it and name it, even if all you can say is, "Nice job using the accurate regulation" or "What is effective about this is that it is very concise—no wasted words." Another is "Great mistake! This essay did exactly what you were asked to do—make factual inferences. Let's focus on making *reasonable* inferences." Even if the student's work is excellent, identify *what* is excellent so the student can build upon it. As novices, students aren't often aware of what they are doing well.

Give students feedback about their weaknesses and *provide strategies* to improve them.

We recommend that you sandwich the specific corrective feedback in between the positive feedback. We believe in being honest and direct but also compassionate. Keep in mind that it's not easy for our students to hear that their work was ineffective; most of our students have received little critical feedback. In addition to being specific, corrective feedback is more likely to help students learn when it:

- Focuses on the work or actions, not the person;
- Avoids making normative judgments;
- Encourages students to become responsible for their learning; and
- Provides strategies to improve.

Providing feedback on a student's performance is very different from providing feedback on the student herself. Talking about the work diminishes some of the intense emotional responses that arise from receiving corrective feedback. It empowers students to see that you distinguish them from their work. Focusing on the work is a powerful, subtle shift—the spotlight is on the student's performance rather than on the student or her abilities.

Frame corrective feedback in terms of what is *effective and ineffective*. For example, "Your mock client interview would have been more effective if you had stated your advice in simpler language." Getting feedback that a performance is "poor" or "bad" or "unprofessional" or "conclusory" is unhelpful. Those words are loaded and may be based on unfounded assumptions. You may be dismayed seeing a student's ineffective performance, assume the student put in no effort, and become irritated. In fact, the student's performance may need significant improvement because the student was facing a crisis, needed additional coaching, or responded to a poorly designed assessment.

Giving students specific feedback about their weaknesses is more effective when combined with concrete strategies they can use to improve. One effective approach is to provide specific guidance on a select area. For example, a student has just engaged in a role-play where she has demonstrated how she would introduce a photo into evidence. Throughout the role-play, the student has spoken in a way that suggests a lack of confidence; each of her sentences end in the rising tone of a question. "I'm showing you what has been marked as Exhibit A? This is a photo?" Telling the student that her voice goes up diagnoses the problem; explaining how to practice deliberately lowering her voice at the end of a sentence, and then modeling a sentence for her gives her the strategy.

It can be hard to provide students with helpful strategies. Telling students that they needed to identify more issues in an assessment tells them *what* is missing but not *how* to fix the problem. A student will be more likely to improve if you suggest that the student (1) prepare a checklist to use in analyzing problems, (2) practice issue-spotting problems, and (3) compare those efforts with peers'. Colleagues and other students often have lots of ideas if you are stuck. Even if you can't provide a strategy, give feedback. Every bit helps.

To respect students' learning, we also recommend that teachers let students know when they may be in danger of failing a course. It is never an easy message, but it is far harder to have the conversation after the student earns the D or F than it is to give the student notice early on.

Give students *prompt* feedback.

The best feedback is immediate. Immediate feedback powers the learning cycle. Students learn if they can remember what they did, get the results, and adjust accordingly. Completing an assessment and getting feedback three weeks later has the opposite effect. Students may not recall what they did on the assessment and have a hard time processing the feedback. Even worse, if students don't receive feedback for a particularly long time, they may have spent weeks continuing to use ineffective study strategies.

As a general guideline, the shorter the assessment, the sooner students should receive feedback. In addition, the fewer the students, the sooner they should receive feedback. Feedback on a short quiz or hypothetical done in class is most effective when students get specific feedback during that class or the next. If students complete a longer or more complex assessment out of class, feedback within a week or so is acceptable.

Imagine that you have just collected written assessments from your 80 Remedies students. Each of them has drafted a one-page proposed temporary restraining order. You want to give them practice and prompt feedback during the course. It's 4:00 p.m. The first paper you read seems ok. You put a couple of comments on it and go to the next. The second is very different and adds helpful information. You put comments on the second, and then go back and comment on the first about the things missing. You repeat this with the third and fourth papers. It is now 6:00 p.m., you have commented on only four assessments, and you are exhausted.

You realize that, if you keep going at this pace, it will take you *38 more hours.* If you can reduce your commenting time from 30 minutes to 20, it will take you 25 hours. Even if you get it down to ten minutes per draft order, it will still take you more than 12 hours. You leave it for the morning. In the morning, though, you have another class to prepare, a committee meeting to attend, and research to complete on an article. Approaching the 76 remaining papers feels like entering the valley of doom.

Giving prompt feedback can be easier. Remember that the goal is to make assessment ongoing, effective, and sustainable. Giving feedback promptly is easier if you have prepared for it and leveraged your resources. If you have identified your learning goals, provided clear guidance to students, and know what you want to see, you will have front-loaded the feedback process. You can process students' assessments quickly; using your checklist, rubric, or sample answer, go through the papers one by one and, voilà, you're done. Even better, you can reuse the assessment and the feedback instrument next time.

You can also leverage your resources by enlisting others to help. If you have access to teaching assistants, give them a checklist, sample, or rubric and guide them on providing feedback. If students are engaging in simulations, invite practicing lawyers to your class to provide feedback. You can also enlist students. Students can read and comment upon each other's work or their own work, comparing their work with your samples, checklists, or rubrics. Students learn a lot about their own work when they review their classmates' performance. They can self-assess and, then, you can review their self-assessments. Don't do all assessments in isolation.

Teach students *how to use* feedback.

Most students benefit from guidance on how to best use feedback. (Chapter 7 includes ways to teach students to use feedback.) There are certainly tradeoffs between giving specific individual feedback and getting feedback to students promptly. We recommend that you start small, use a variety of feedback methods, and continue to reflect on what works.

Illustration 10-9 provides a list of some of the different ways you can provide students with feedback and how well each of these methods rates on the characteristics of effective feedback.

The list of feedback mechanisms discussed above is not exhaustive; web-based response platforms can be extremely effective in providing immediate feedback. Equally effective are short quizzes corrected in class using rubrics, electronically scored multiple-choice questions, online quizzes, and CALI exercises.

Illustration 10-9: Different ways to provide students with feedback

Feedback Method	Specific	Positive	Corrective	Prompt	Main Benefits ✓	Main Drawbacks ↓
Individual written comments on student work	✓	✓	✓	↓	• Very helpful for individual student—tailored to particular learning	• Takes a long time; may delay students getting feedback • Exhausting for teacher if large class or long, complex assessment
Checklists	✓	✓	✓	?	• Efficient way to provide specific feedback • Can be used later to help with future assessments	• Takes time to prepare
Rubrics	✓	✓	✓	?	• Efficient way to provide specific feedback • Provides more information than checklist	• Takes time to prepare
Teacher gives verbal feed-back in class	?	✓	?	✓	• Immediate • Takes little time	• Not as specific—verbal comments generally less specific • Engages fewer students
Students give each other feedback and self-critique in class	✓	✓	?	✓	• Immediate • Develops students' self assessment skills	• Results vary; more effective when combined with samples, checklists or rubrics • Students may need help with providing corrective feedback and strategies

Step four: Use assessment to improve teaching and course design

Commonly referred to as "closing the loop," this step involves using information gathered from assessments to reflect upon and consider ways to change our teaching and course design. The goal of this step is to continually improve our teaching practices to enhance student learning.

For example, on an Evidence midterm assessment, assume most students identify rules accurately, but fail to effectively develop and apply facts and their inferences. Assume further that applying facts is an important learning outcome in your course. If students continue to do poorly in this area on the final exam, you may want to consider making one or more changes the next time you teach the course, such as: (1) adding more opportunities for students to practice applying facts; (2) spending more class time explicitly showing students how to apply facts; (3) emphasizing the importance of this skill throughout the course; (4) finding additional materials to help students learn the skill; (5) changing the way you teach the skill; (6) redesigning the midterm to be more explicit about applying facts; or (7) weighing this skill more heavily on graded assessments. Making these changes requires energy and hard choices. If you redesign the course to spend more time on one learning outcome, it will probably mean that you spend less time on another outcome and may mean that students will perform less well in an area where they previously performed competently.

As with other steps in the assessment process, to make this step sustainable, start small and learn from the experience. In the Evidence example above, start with one small course change, e.g., you will emphasize applying facts more heavily throughout the course. On the midterm most students' performance in this skill has improved but is still not at the level you seek. You make another small change the following year, review the results, and determine your next steps. You continue this process until students are meeting important learning goals.

To make "closing the loop" effective, focus on a few learning outcomes per assessment. If you use a rubric or list of criteria and record how well students perform on each criterion, you can quickly see where most students are struggling. If most students are stating an important rule inaccurately, for example, focus your teaching and course design changes on improving students' accuracy in stating important rules. Keep one or two sample copies of different levels of student work, such as samples that are highly effective, somewhat effective, and minimally effective or ineffective. Referring to these samples the next time you teach a course helps you compare student performance and evaluate whether your teaching changes seem to be correlating with improved student learning.

Assessing students to improve your teaching— using classroom assessment techniques

Classroom assessment is primarily designed to evaluate the effectiveness of a particular class or unit of instruction. This section focuses on short, in-class assessment techniques.

With these assessments, we regularly invite students to inform us about what they are learning, what teaching methods are effective, and how we can help them learn more effectively. The focus is less on shaping individual students' development and more on getting a sense of the whole class's progress.

Even though students seem engaged and comfortable with the material, they may not have achieved the deep learning you hoped. Classroom assessment helps us identify and remedy learning gaps before the end of the semester and before graded events. Classroom assessment also reveals students' strongly held attitudes and views. We want to know:

1. Where are the students most confused?
2. Where are they excelling?
3. What are they learning and at what level?
4. What are their biases, preconceptions, and attitudes?
5. What are we doing in this course that is effective and we should continue?
6. What are we doing that is ineffective and we should stop?
7. What suggestions do students have about how we can help them learn?

This section focuses on the first four questions. Suggestions about assessing questions 5, 6, and 7, in which ask about students' perceptions of our teaching, assignments, and tests, are introduced in Chapter 2 and developed more fully in Chapter 13. Learning about students' responses to questions 1–4 can be very helpful. Students appreciate our interest in their learning, which can motivate them to learn. We learn a lot about our teaching, which gives us information we can use to improve. Many teachers also report regaining excitement about teaching from this process.

The process of using Classroom Assessment Techniques, or CATs, follows the same steps as in Illustration 10-2:

1. Identify what you are trying to assess;
2. Prepare and administer assessment instruments;
3. Give students feedback; and
4. Use assessment to improve teaching and course design.

We use CATs for easy, quick, and frequent information about student learning. CATs are shorter and simpler to administer than the more complex assessments you might give students in preparing them to master course learning goals. Co-authors of the leading book on classroom assessment techniques, Thomas A. Angelo and K. Patricia Cross, identify and explain 50 different CATs designed to apply across multiple disciplines. Their vetted CATs assess knowledge, skills, values, attitudes, self-awareness, creativity, and students' reactions to teaching, assignments, and tests. Angelo and Cross helpfully provide guidance on how long each CAT takes, how others have used it, and how to interpret data. If you are new to using classroom assessment techniques, review the suggestions in Illustration 10-10.

Illustration 10-10: Suggestions for new users of classroom assessment techniques

Suggestions for new users of classroom assessment techniques from Thomas A. Angelo and Todd D. Zakrajsek, *Classroom Assessment Techniques: Formative Feedback Tools for College and University Teachers* (3d. ed. 2024)

1. If you don't like a classroom assessment technique for any reason, don't use it.
2. Don't turn classroom assessment into a chore; go for ongoing incremental change.
3. Try the classroom assessment technique on yourself first.
4. Allow for more time than you think.
5. Give students feedback on the process: What did you learn? How will you use it to help them?

As with any assessment you give, tell your students what you are doing and why. You can give a brief explanation about CATs along the lines of:

> *Today, I am seeking information about my teaching via this three-minute exercise. This assessment is anonymous. I am looking for feedback on my performance as your teacher so I can improve, not about you as individuals. I'll review your responses after class and tell you what I have learned in the next class. Your responses will enable me to re-address concepts that are most challenging to the class.*

Specific classroom assessment techniques

Below are three classroom assessment techniques that you can quickly and easily use to assess a wide range of skills, knowledge, and values at any point in the course: minute papers, student surveys, and analysis charts. For each CAT, we include information about how to prepare it, the materials you need to administer it, samples, and an estimate of the time you will need to prepare and administer it. (Refer to Illustrations 3-2 and 3-3 for descriptions of levels of thinking—e.g., comprehension, knowledge, evaluation—and verbs you can use to assess those different learning outcomes.) If you are comfortable using electronic response devices or other web-based learning platforms, these techniques simultaneously can serve as formative assessment tools for your students and as CATs for you.

Minute papers

The name refers to the time students have to respond to a prompt. Although minute papers actually take two-to-five minutes, they are quick and easy.

Preparation: Identify a discreet prompt to which students will respond. Depending on what you want to learn, decide *when* to administer the minute question (you can do these at any point during a class session). If administered at the beginning of class and the teacher has time to skim through the answers, these minute questions provide information about what students understand going into a lesson. If most students understand the material, the teacher can proceed to build upon it. If students show misunderstanding, the teacher can summarize and redirect. Administered at the end of class, the teacher can quickly get the same information about that day's discussion and address any issues in the next class.

Materials needed: Write the prompt on the board, a slide, or handout. Some teachers like to have the prompt printed on a quarter sheet of paper; this approach reinforces the idea that students should keep their responses short.

Sample minute questions:

These questions are designed to assess students' understanding of *specific content*, usually material discussed in that class or the previous class. Tailor these for your own course.

- "What is the burden of proof necessary for a criminal conviction?"
- "Identify a major factor in determining the 'best interests of the child.'"
- "In your own words, define 'hostile work environment.'"
- "Explain the policy of deterrence in product liability."
- "How can an inventor respond to the Patent and Trademark Office's rejection of a claim?"
- "If the plaintiff's complaint fails to include facts for each of the elements of a claim, what should the defendant do?"
- "Give an example of an offer and an example of a non-offer that is similar to your offer in all trivial respects but lacks an essential feature of an offer."

Other more "global" minute questions allow students to give you information that they might not otherwise volunteer.

- "What are the three most important things you learned from today's class?"
- "What was the muddiest point of today's discussion?"
- "My biggest question/concern about what I will be asked to do on the final is . . ."

Minute questions can also be used to assess students' attitudes and confidence. They can also help students focus and self-reflect:

- "What does professional behavior look like in this class?"
- "When working in small groups, how do you want your classmates to behave?"
- "How confident are you about your ability to learn environmental law?"

- "What can you do to prepare yourself for the next assignment?"
- "How prepared were you for class today—unprepared, prepared, well-prepared, or able to teach the material yourself?"

Giving feedback: You can quickly scan through nearly a hundred short responses, taking notes on general themes and questions. You may learn different information than you anticipated. Tell students what you found: "Almost everyone had a question about federal preemption." "Most of you showed an understanding of the commerce clause." "The five most common responses were ..."

Estimated time to prepare and administer: Fifteen to thirty minutes: one-to-five minutes to generate a prompt and answer it yourself, five minutes to give it in class, five-to-twenty minutes to review the responses and summarize the main points.

Student surveys

Surveys or polls effectively gauge a range of student responses. More detailed than minute papers, you can adapt them to assess a wide variety of knowledge, skills, or values. They can be especially effective when assessing students' reactions to controversial or highly emotional issues, areas where their views could influence their understanding.

Preparation: Identify a *few* questions to which you want students to respond. Asking three–five questions is usually more effective than asking 20. You can use a Likert scale, asking students to respond to statements by checking whether they:

- Strongly disagree = 1
- Disagree = 2
- Neither agree nor disagree = 3
- Agree = 4
- Strongly agree = 5

You also can ask them to take a position on a topic. For example:

Sixteen year-olds who commit murder should be prosecuted and sentenced:

A. As adults

B. As juveniles

C. As adults or juveniles on a case-by-case basis

D. As juveniles unless the prosecutor presents evidence justifying treating the teens as adults

Materials needed: Written surveys or projected survey questions and scantron forms. You could also administer surveys online using course webpage software such as TWEN, with online learning platforms such as Canvas, or in class with technology.

Giving feedback: We recommend that you give feedback similarly to the approach suggested above for minute papers. Get a general sense of the students' responses. In that class or the next, by email, or via your course learning platform, tell the class what you learned. In a professionalism survey one of us conducted with a class of nearly 70 students, we and the students learned that almost all students thought a few students were distractingly rude. Because a few students earlier had vehemently disagreed that anyone was rude, survey results provided an excellent opportunity for the class to discuss professional behavior in law school.

Estimated time to prepare and administer: Twenty-five to thirty minutes: ten-to-fifteen minutes to generate questions and field-test them on yourself and another, five minutes to administer the survey in class, ten-to-fifteen minutes to review and summarize main points. If you have administered the survey to a prior class, you can complete these tasks much more quickly and also give students feedback on how previous classes have responded to the survey.

Analysis charts

Analysis charts, where you provide students with categories and have them fill in information, can help students connect pieces of a course. These charts can be especially effective after students have completed a section of a course.

Illustration 10-11: Sample analysis charts

Personal Jurisdiction	**Jurisdiction**	**Facts**
Identify where a court would have jurisdiction over a defendant and list the supporting facts	New York	D has business office in NY

DISCOVERY CHART—Medical Malpractice

Rule number and name	**Kind of evidence gathered**
	Medical records
	Medical examination

Pro and Con Chart

Identify three advantages to having strict liability claims and three disadvantages

Advantages	**Disadvantages**
1.	1.
2.	2.
3.	3.

Preparation: Identify multiple categories and kinds of information you want students to organize. You can ask students to complete a relatively simple chart in class to see what material they are comfortable with. Ask them to fill in the chart starting with the easiest parts. Students could also complete charts in small groups.

Materials needed: Handouts with blank sections of charts on which students can write. Alternatively, you could send the charts to the students electronically before class.

Giving feedback: You can walk around the room and look at students' charts, getting a quick sense of their responses, or you can collect the charts at the end of class and quickly review the responses. During the class, you could also have the students compare their charts with one or more classmates and then submit a group chart. Once you have a general sense of the students' responses, tell the class what you learned.

Estimated time to prepare and administer: Twenty-five to forty minutes: five to ten minutes to generate chart categories and complete the chart yourself, ten-to-fifteen minutes to administer the exercise in class, ten-to-fifteen minutes to review and summarize the main points. As with other classroom assessment techniques, if you prepare one of these for one course, you can reuse it as is or tweak for the next time, gradually building up several analysis chart classroom assessments.

Image Bank Association Charts

The "Image Bank" in Illustration 10-12 below uses the novelty of simple images to help students recall Constitutional Law justiciability principles. This ungraded assessment is an effective way to refresh student recollection of material covered in a prior class. Or the assessment tool can be used at the end of class to review material covered that day. There is no need to grade the assignment; students should also be allowed to keep the sheet as a study aid or even develop their own images to prompt a material review. With the free art available on the internet or even a teacher with limited artistic talent, you can design an image bank association chart for any course. These low-risk assessments can be used in class for a quick, painless, and fun review.

Preparation: Identify rules and information that you want students to recall. If you teach mnemonics in class to help students memorize rules or concepts, start there. Limit yourself to two or three images so you can keep the review short and sweet. Go on the web and find pictures that represent the concepts, rules or information you want to include. (There are several websites that offer photographs you can download for free.) Make a simple, two-column chart and add the picture in one column and leave the second column blank,

Materials needed: Copies of handouts with blank sections of charts on which students can write. Alternatively, you could send the charts to the students electronically before class starts.

Giving feedback: You can walk around the room and look at students' charts, getting a quick sense of their responses. When most students are done with their charts, ask for volunteers for each image. Use that time to review the responses and take a deeper

Illustration 10-12: Image Bank Association Chart

Constitutional Law — Image Bank Association Chart

Use the images on the left as "prompts" to help you recall important legal doctrines we have covered in Constitutional Law. Write your answers associated with each corresponding image in the right column. Hint: The images in this bank are associated with justiciability.

1. 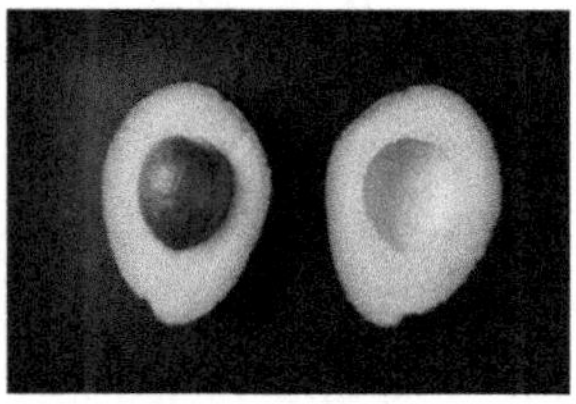	
2. 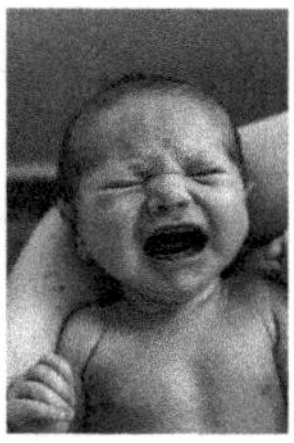	

dive on the prompt. For instance, the answers to the images in the above illustration are 1. Ripeness and 2. Capable of Repetition Yet Evading Review ("CRYER"). Instead of just stopping with "CRYER" for the crying baby image, ask the students to explain the significance of the phrase "capable of repetition yet evading review." This is good launch to test their knowledge of justiciability limits.

Estimated time to prepare and administer: Give yourself about twenty-five to forty minutes to prepare: five to ten minutes to generate the chart and another thirty minutes or so to find and insert the images. It will only take about ten to fifteen minutes in class to give students time to complete the chart and review the answers with you (depending on how many images you use). As with other classroom assessment techniques, if you prepare one of these for one course, you can reuse it as is or tweak for the next time, gradually building up several image association charts you can use for low-risk formative assessments.

Evaluating students to assign grades

Grading, or *summative assessment,* which primarily focuses on evaluation rather than student development, is the hardest type of assessment to do well. Student grades are high stakes; they can greatly affect students' opportunities in school and afterwards. Not all students do well under that kind of pressure. Consequently, unlike using assessments to help students learn during a course or employing classroom assessment techniques to help you improve your teaching, grading requires that we pay much more attention to what we are evaluating and how we are doing so.

First, some preliminaries about grading in law school. While a few law schools are progressing towards a competency system, where students earn either a "pass," "no pass," or "high pass" instead of letter grades, most schools still use letter or number grades. Given that most schools use grades, we should find ways to use grading to our students' advantage. Grades are among the most powerful learning and motivating tools we have. We can work within our institutions' required grading systems, including mandatory means and curves, and still improve our grading practices.

To preserve the integrity of the grades we assign, graded assessments must be valid and reliable. Valid grades are consistent with what we teach and what students should be learning; reliable grades are not grader or exam-day dependent.

Students should only earn a grade after having multiple and varied assessments which are fairly administered (see Illustration 10-13). No research supports the idea of determining course grades based solely on one exam given at the end of a semester. Using multiple and varied assessments requires you to do more work and perhaps even change the culture of your law school, but we urge you to give your students more than one graded assessment.

We know how important it is for students to have multiple opportunities to practice and get feedback. The same is true for graded exercises. Not all students demonstrate proficiency in the same way. For example, while some students do well on traditional, objective analysis exam questions, others do better if they are asked to use the material to apply what they have learned in drafting a client opinion letter. If we want to be fair and accurate in assigning grades, we must give students a variety of opportunities to show us their success in learning what we have tried to teach them.

In this section we address three essential characteristics of effective grading.

Use multiple assessments

Illustration 10-4 lists different types of assessments. Any number of these can be used to assign a portion of students' grades. (We address how to calculate grades below.) For example, students could earn a course grade as follows:

- 10% of their grade for class contributions (professional engagement in and outside of class);
- 30% on a midterm exam (mix of essay, multiple choice, and short answer questions);
- 10% on an oral presentation; and
- 50% on the final exam (essay and multiple-choice questions).

If this list feels too daunting, consider offering two assessments:

- 25% on a writing assignment and
- 75% on the final exam (essay and multiple-choice questions).

Illustration 10-13: Evaluating Students to Assign Grades—Essential Elements

Evaluating Students to Assign Grades—Essential Elements
1. Use multiple assessments 2. Use a variety of assessments 3. Evaluate fairly: • Test what you teach • Provide students with grading criteria in advance • Provide students with opportunities to practice meeting criteria before they are graded • Use explicit criteria to ensure consistent grading • Show students how they met grading criteria—make the grading process also a learning process

We recognize that multiple assessments may be antithetical to your school culture or a departure from your own law school experience. You may also feel personal reluctance about increasing the number of graded assessments because of the additional work it creates for you. However, failure to adopt multiple assessments makes it less likely that your grading will help your students learn or accurately reflect their learning.

To prepare summative assessment instruments, refer to the list from Illustration 10-5, Common Factors to Consider When Preparing Assessment Instruments. We also highlight a few of the particularly important factors below.

Use a variety of assessments

According to research about student learning, students perform differently on different kinds of assessments. Often students who are most articulate in class may struggle with written work; the students who ace multiple-choice and issue-spotting tests may have difficulty counseling simulated clients effectively. Because the practice of law is multi-dimensional and because students can demonstrate competency in many ways, we urge you to use a range of graded assessments. Use the list of assessment instruments in Illustration 10-4 for ideas as to the variety of ways that students can show their learning.

Evaluate fairly

To evaluate fairly, identify the specific learning goals you want to measure, establish the grading criteria you will use to evaluate student performance, and provide those criteria to students in advance. Use explicit criteria when grading to ensure grading consistency across all students' work and show students how they met those criteria.

Test what you teach

As suggested in Chapters 2 and 6, you should set your learning goals and create your assessment instruments before the class has started. If you know from the start what you want students to learn by the end of the course, you can constantly check to make sure your class sessions work towards those goals. As you construct your assessment instruments, review course outcomes to ensure that you are testing students on those goals.

Provide students with grading criteria in advance

It is only fair to evaluate students on explicit criteria that you have provided them in advance. Some colleagues reject this approach, worrying that "everyone would get an 'A'!" We have not had that experience. Every year, our students' performances have been sufficiently varied to allow each of us to produce grades well within our schools' mandatory grading requirements.

Giving written criteria in advance is not that hard; you can provide students with a list of criteria or a rubric, such as the rubric in Illustration 10-8. If you further explain the relative weight of the different criteria, students could more appropriately focus their performances based on what you say is most important. Giving students explicit criteria encourages students to be metacognitive, or reflective, independent learners (see Chapter 7). Students can also use the rubric to self-assess their own performance.

For example, if you grade presentations, you might tell students that the grading criteria and relative weights are the following:

- Content—clear, organized and coherent—50%
- Visual aids—handouts, slides, props used to enhance content—20%
- Delivery—audible, clear, varied, responsive, and within time limits—10%
- Creativity—shows innovation in presenting and engaging classmates—20%

Give students grading criteria in writing so they have this information in a tangible format to which they can refer as they prepare. Using the list above, students would know to focus less on actual delivery and more on creativity. The rubric in Illustration 10-8 also shows students explicitly the breakdown among identifying issues, applying facts, and using policy. Such rubrics provide the criteria and their relative weights, but not the content, and so could be distributed in advance.

Going through the process of articulating the criteria in writing forces us to engage in the same process that we go through when we identify specific learning outcomes. We have to name what we mean by "analyze the following problem." Usually, we find out that we are expecting far more from students than they—or we—realize.

Law students often spend lots of time struggling to understand new material *and* what the teacher wants. By providing them with clear criteria, past graded assessments, sample rubrics, and examples of student work, we give them that guidance.

Provide students with opportunities to practice meeting criteria before they are graded

As we urge you to do in the earlier portion of this chapter, give students plenty of practice and feedback before you administer the final graded assessment. Practice exams, quizzes, paper drafts, and mock performances—coupled with feedback—promote student learning and allow them to be fully prepared for graded assignments. Grading students on their performance when they have had no opportunities to practice just isn't fair.

Use explicit criteria to ensure consistent grading

Grading without explicit criteria can be unfair and is usually inefficient. Absent such criteria, teachers in every discipline are notoriously inconsistent in grading complex student performances. A single teacher might score the same test differently at different times, and teachers who verbally agree on standards often widely fluctuate in their evaluations of student work. In contrast, when teachers have explicit criteria, such as rubrics, they mostly grade consistently and reliably. In addition, teachers can maintain high expectations by modifying criteria according to the level of the course.

Having a rubric, checklist, or scoring guideline also makes grading far more efficient. One of the hardest things about grading is spending lots of energy worrying about whether we graded Exam #123 using the same standards as we used for Exam #72. The order in which we grade assignments, our energy level, emotional state, and health may affect how we interpret students' work. When we have explicit criteria, though, we know what we are looking for, and we are much more consistent. Yes, creating a checklist or rubric takes time, but the early investment pays off significantly during the actual grading. And once you make one rubric, the next ones are much easier.

Show students how their work met grading criteria—make the grading process a learning process as well

Students usually receive their grade weeks after they have completed an assessment. For most students, the grade is where it ends. Students may be delighted or disappointed, but, usually, they have little clue why or how they earned the grade. Some teachers will meet with students to show them the criteria they used to grade the assignments but won't allow a student to keep the student's copy of assessment or the student's response.

Structure your graded assessments so that they also are opportunities for formative feedback; make a graded assessment a learning experience. If the graded assessment occurs before the end of the semester, hold a review session to go over the exam or spend time in class reviewing it. Allow students to see the checklists or rubrics you used to assign their grades. Ask several students who have done well for permission to share their work as examples. Let students learn what good exam answers can look like.

Even if you want to reuse part of an exam, consider having a window of time, say two or three weeks, when students can view their exams, your comments, scoring sheets, and sample answers.

Talking to students about grades

Talking to students about their exam results and grades can be difficult. Students may be upset, frustrated, and angry, even in instances in which they earned a B+. Some of your students may have negotiated grade increases when they talked to their college teachers; they may have similar expectations in law school. We have found the six practices below help make these discussions manageable and productive.

1. *Meet with students in person.* It is easier to read body language, empathize, and try to help students learn when you meet with them in person. Talking about grades over email, zoom, and the telephone is sometimes unavoidable. In those situations, it helps to have students initially let you know what their questions are and then schedule a time to talk or have an electronic exchange.
2. *The 48-hour blackout rule.* Talk to students only after they have had their graded assessment results for 48 hours. The time gives everyone a little breathing space.
3. *Have students review all materials and prepare questions before meeting with you individually.* Asking students to review their graded assessment, the scoring criteria, and any other feedback before they meet with you makes the experience much more manageable and specific. Some professors require students to complete and submit a "Goals Sheet" that captures feedback on memos or assignments and student plans for improvement prior to scheduling a conference to review grades. If students are given a rubric and challenge your evaluation of their ability to meet criteria, ask them to show you where in their assessment the criteria were met, "Help me understand where the exam answer analyzes the policy behind patent law reforms."
4. *Almost never change a grade; if you do, only do it slowly and very carefully.* Your school likely has rules about grade changes. We never change grades unless there has been a computational error. We've been known to make mistakes in our math, no matter how closely we have double-checked. Because grades are high stakes, once they are released, most of the class will soon know about the grade change. If you learn of a mathematical error, review that assessment and score sheet *and* the practice that may have contributed to the problem. Also be aware of whether your institution requires you to report a grade change to the Academic Dean. Some schools require that you receive permission in advance—and only after sharing the mathematical error. Further, if the error happened more than once, consider how to fix the problem for all students.

5. *Limit the number of weeks in which students can talk to you about a graded assessment.* We are referring to talking about the particular graded assessment, not to talking about student learning in the course. One reason for this policy is our limited memories. Having recently graded the assessments, they are relatively fresh in our minds. After a few weeks, though, we become less effective in talking to students about their individual efforts. The second and more important reason for imposing a time limit on such discussions is that the students also forget: the sooner they review the assessment, the greater its potential as a learning exercise.
6. *Try to make the meeting a learning experience.* We encourage students who wish to meet with us to self-assess their studying and preparation process before the meeting; one explicit goal of the meeting is to help students discover ways to improve on future assessments. Related to this critical goal is an equally important point: Do not get defensive. When students are asking about grades or their evaluation, some are truly trying to understand the material better. Even those who are trying to push for a higher grade should encounter a professional, thoughtful instructor open to helping students learn—even from their mistakes.

Writing test questions and directions

Because of the high stakes involved and the problems that emerge if a graded assessment has flaws, you cannot be too careful in constructing your test questions and directions. Sometimes, we ask teaching assistants to field-test our graded assessments. Almost always, we have a colleague review them. As the author of a graded assignment, you know what you want students to do, but students frequently answer questions in different ways than we anticipate.

Provide *ultra-precise* directions. We can't emphasize this recommendation enough. It may take more paper, but giving students plenty of white space, using bullets, numbers and different forms of emphasis will help them succeed. Write directions in plain English, using sentences of 25 words or less and paragraphs of 4–8 sentences. Unless you intend an ambiguity, students should have no doubts about what you expect them to do.

If possible, give students the directions *before* the graded assessment event, i.e., review the instructions together in class the day or week before the assessment event This practice can reduce a lot of needless stress because your students will know what they will be expected to do and are aware of the exam's format, number of questions, time allotted, and format requirements. It will also help you correct any unintended ambiguity or conflict in the instructions. Also make sure students know what materials they can bring to the exam room and use. You must also ensure that your instructions conform to any institutional requirements.

Determine how much time to allow

Few of us do our best under high pressure. The same is true for our students, particularly when we give them little practice. Accordingly, as we suggested above, take and time any graded assessment—then give your students twice as much time as you needed.

If the assessment has time constraints, give students suggested amounts of time for each section. For example, how many minutes do they have to complete a series of multiple-choice questions? How many minutes per question? Tell them. Students have a hard time budgeting their time; these suggestions help keep them on track. The same is true for any other assignment. It may seem obvious to you that a student should spend 75% of the time on 75% of the test's points, but explicit directions help.

Giving take-home assignments

Take-home assignments have advantages and disadvantages. If you give these assessments, we recommend that you either give students a lot of time, such as handing out the assessment a week before it is due, or giving students 8 to 9 hours, particularly if the assessment counts as a large part of students' final grade. When faced with a 24 to 72-hour, high-stakes assessment, some students panic for the whole time, barely sleeping and ending up more stressed than they would be if they had 8 or 9 hours to get the assessment done. In addition, in today's AI-enabled context, you also need to think through the possibility that students will be tempted to use AI; be explicit about your AI use expectations and the consequences of any violation of those expectations.

Content

Humor is best avoided on assessments. Many teachers get creative with puns and witty phrases. These choices don't help. We love using humor in the classroom, and humor has been found to enhance learning, but using it on a graded assessment can be distracting.

Other distracting content is also best avoided. Perhaps you need to test rape on a criminal law exam, but, if the goal is understanding and applying the law, there are lots of other crimes that will not provoke a powerful and negative emotional response in students who may have been raped or abused. When possible, keep the content realistic and related to practice. Students may use graded assessments as writing samples; having to prepare a license agreement using the law from the fictional planet Marculon is a needless distraction.

Use names carefully. Avoid names that sound the same, such as Deanna and Doreen. The name of every person in a question should have a name that sounds different from any other person. We like using one-syllable names that start with "P" or "D" when we want to make it clear who the plaintiffs and defendants are. Because we don't have learning goals that relate to the parties' names, the names should be as simple as possible. Also use realistic names of corporations, towns and statutes.

Consider graphics in addition to text when designing assessment content. A photo, map, or other visual can help students more quickly understand the scenario you want them to analyze.

Talk to colleagues and check out different websites to get ideas about graded assessments. We recommend you never write your exam alone.

Designing rubrics and grading assignments

There are many ways to develop a rubric and evaluate student work. Almost all of us have some form of a "rubric" in our head whenever we grade student work; the goal is to make these criteria transparent so that we can improve our grading and our ability to enhance student learning. If you are new at grading law school exams and haven't developed a rubric or scoresheet in advance, you can still prepare one after the students complete their graded assessments. Below is one method we've used in preparing and applying a rubric. (For shorthand, we are using the term "exam" to mean a graded assessment.)

- Start with students' completed exams.
- Identify how much time you have until you will submit grades. Remember that giving feedback sooner is more effective for student learning.
- Read about ten exams quickly, developing checklists for what is effective and ineffective. Start your checklists as soon as possible after the exam ends. Waiting doesn't make grading any easier, and you will be more stressed. If you must, clean off your desk to make a clear space, but don't indulge your procrastination inclination for more than a few hours. If you want to "chunk" your workload, consider grading a group of five exams in the morning and another five in the afternoon.
- Read through a few more exams, refining the checklists. Analyze the checklists—what are common themes? What do the effective exams have that the ineffective answers don't?
- Determine how to weigh the different effective components—is spotting sophisticated issues more important than spotting basic issues? How important is the number of issues the students have spotted? How important is the number of facts the students have used in their analysis? How important is the quality of the students' efforts to explain the significance of the key facts?
- Draft the rubric or scoring sheet. Consider this first effort a draft; you may need to change it as you go—students always surprise us.
- Consider including a "bonus" category; if a student does something really well that makes the exam really thoughtful and rewards what you have taught in class, you can use the "bonus" category to award extra points.

- Use the draft rubric to score ten exams. Revise the rubric as necessary. Set aside these first ten exams.
- Keeping a list tracking exam numbers or names, score exams using the rubric.
- If the exam has more than one part, such as three essays, grade all students' Essay #1's. When you have scored all Essay #1s, grade the Essay #2s. This approach helps reduce "drift," where a student's performance on one part of an exam influences your evaluation of another part of that exam.
- Vary the order in which you grade the exams. If you graded the first essays starting with low exam numbers, grade the second essays beginning with the middle or highest numbers.
- Use a pencil or erasable ink pen if grading by hand.
- Consider using a bank of comments if grading online.
- Take breaks every hour, even if only for a few minutes to stand and stretch—even if you don't think you need it. You'll be more efficient in the long run.
- When you have finished grading all your exams, revisit the first ten you graded. If their scores reflect what you would assign now, having worked through the entire set, you are good. If you have changed your approach (such changes usually are quite slight if you have a detailed rubric), revise the grades. If you notice significant discrepancies, review the next ten, revising accordingly. Keep going until you find that the scores you gave the first time are consistent with the ones you give the second. Sound hard? Yes. But we want to be fair. If you have a detailed scoring sheet, you will find you are far more consistent.
- Total all the scores. Review the handful of highest and lowest scores.
- Look for trends in scores. Notice where students are doing well and where their scores as a whole reflect that they have struggled. Store that information with your notes on the course so you can consider how to help students avoid those errors the next time you teach the course.
- Submit grades.
- Once you have submitted your grades, you may want to identify a few students who earned high scores on different parts of the exam. Request their permission for you to use their unidentified answers as samples of high-quality student work.
- Make a page of notes for yourself about the grading process to help you the next time. What worked? What did you learn? What do you want to remember for the next time you design and use a rubric?

We encourage you to engage in the recursive assessment cycle. Gather information from students about their learning, interpret information, and make changes to your teaching. Repeat.

Checklist for assessing student learning

Illustration 10-14 is a checklist you can use as you work through the assessment process.

Illustration 10-14: Assessing Student Learning Checklist

Using assessment to improve student learning and your teaching

- ❑ **Identify discreet learning outcomes**
    - ❑ What knowledge, skills, and values do you want students to show they are learning?
- ❑ **Prepare and give assessment instruments including CATs**
    - ❑ What is the *rationale* for this assessment?
    - ❑ What do you want students *to do*?
    - ❑ How much *time* will it take for students to complete?
    - ❑ Will the assessment be completed *in or outside of class*?
    - ❑ What is the assessment's *content*?
    - ❑ Is there a particular *format* students should use?
    - ❑ How much can students *collaborate* on the assessment?
    - ❑ How will you *provide feedback*?
    - ❑ How can you use student performance to improve your teaching?
- ❑ **Give feedback to students**
    - ❑ **Specific.** Students get information about specific criteria.
    - ❑ **Positive.** Students find out what they are doing well.
    - ❑ **Corrective.** Students learn about their weaknesses and have strategies to improve.
    - ❑ **Prompt.** Students get feedback while the assessment is fresh.
- ❑ **Evaluating students to assign grades**
    - ❑ Use multiple assessments
    - ❑ Use a variety of assessments
    - ❑ Evaluate fairly:
        - ❑ Test what you teach
        - ❑ Provide students with grading criteria in advance
        - ❑ Provide students with opportunities to practice meeting criteria before they are graded
        - ❑ Use explicit criteria to ensure consistent grading
        - ❑ Show students how they met grading criteria—make the grading process also a learning process
- ❑ **Engage in ongoing assessment**

Assessing Student Learning—Resources

Law School Assessment Resources

- Kelly Terry, Gerald F. Hess, Emily Grant, and Sandra Simpson, Assessment of Teaching and Learning: A Comprehensive Guidebook for Law Schools (Carolina Academic Press 2021).
- Lori E. Shaw & Victoria L. VanZandt, Student Learning Outcomes and Law School Assessment: A Practical Guide to Measuring Institutional Effectiveness (Carolina Academic Press 2015).
- Olympia R. Duhart, *The "F" Word: the Top Five Complaints (and Solutions) about Formative Assessment,* 67 J. Legal Educ. 531, 2018.
- Olympia R. Duhart, *"It's Not for a Grade": The Rewards and Risks of Law-Risk Formative Assessment in the High-Stakes Law School Classroom*, 7 Elon L. Rev. 491, 2015.
- Sophie M. Sparrow, *Describing the Ball: Improve Teaching by Using Rubrics—Explicit Grading Criteria,* 2004 Mich. St. L. Rev. 1.

Higher Education Assessment Resources

Designed for higher education in general, the five books below provide excellent fundamental and detailed guidance about multiple levels and kinds of assessments.

- Trudy W. Banta & Catherine Palomba, Assessment Essentials: Planning, Implementing, and Improving Assessment in Higher Education (2d ed. Jossey-Bass 2014).
- Peggy L Maki, Assessing for learning: Building a Sustainable Commitment Across the Institution (2d ed. Routledge 2010).
- Linda A. Suskie, Assessing Student Learning: A Common Sense guide (3d ed. Jossey-Bass 2018).
- Barbara E. Walvoord & Virginia Johnson Anderson, Effective Grading: A Tool for Learning and Assessment (2d ed. Jossey-Bass 2010).
- Barbara E. Walvoord, Assessment Clear and Simple: A Practical Guide for Institutions, Departments, and General Education (2d ed. Jossey-Bass 2010).

Chapter 11

Teaching and Learning Gems

This chapter is an eclectic collection of ideas that have worked well for us in our courses. In big and small ways, these ideas have helped us improve our teaching and our students' learning. These ideas advance core principles of teaching and learning that make up the heart of the preceding chapters.

We recognize that some of these ideas will not appeal to every teacher. No idea works for everyone. We encourage you to ignore the ideas that do not appeal to you and to adopt the ideas that you think will work for you and your students. We also believe that each of these ideas can be improved upon, so please go ahead and make them better.

Eleven ideas follow:

1. First day ideas
2. Daily prompts
3. Learning and using students' names
4. Variety in calling on students
5. NextGen bar-style tasks integration
6. Teaching doctrine entirely through multiple-choice questions
7. Writing skills for the final exam and law practice
8. Short quizzes
9. Podcasts
10. Graphic arts and beyond
11. What is a good class? Or a bad class?

1. First day ideas

The first days of a course are important for all sorts of reasons. The first day begins the process of building an effective teaching and learning environment. We transmit course norms and expectations to students by what we write in the syllabus, say in the first class, and have students do on Day One. Students quickly form opinions about the course, the teacher, and their fellow students. Here are three ideas for getting the course off to a solid start.

Building community— teacher and student introductions

One important aspect of a course's teaching and learning environment is the community that develops among teachers and students. An online format in which teachers and students do not share the same physical space can present special challenges in creating community.

To build community at the beginning of a course, students and teachers can introduce themselves during the first week. There are all sorts of ways these introductions could happen—via a 30 second video, a 30 second podcast, a half page of text, or a questionnaire. Prompts for the introductions could include some of the following: Educational background? Work/life experiences? How do you learn best? Interests outside of school? Teachers and students can post their introductions via the course management system. Encourage students to view one another's responses.

Teachers and students will learn quite a bit about one another simply by viewing the responses. And teachers will learn about students' experiences, expertise, and interests that teachers can weave into the course during the semester. To maximize the benefits of this exercise, teachers can create bonds with students by responding to the student introductions. In a small class, the teacher could send a quick email to each student commenting on student introduction. Teachers could do the same in a large class, but it will take significant time. Another way to respond to students in a large class is by summarizing themes from the introductions and sharing them with the class. In large classes, there may be groups of students with the skills and experiences to build a house, form an orchestra, field a competitive sports team, converse in a dozen languages, etc.

One final twist on this idea is to offer students the opportunity to tell you confidentially via email anything they think is important for you to know about them. Typically, not many students respond to this invitation, but those who do respond often disclose information that is very helpful for you to know to help those students succeed.

Learn something significant on day one

A critical measure of success for a course is the quality and quantity of student learning. One way to motivate students is to design the first class to try to ensure that students learn something significant on day one. The significant learning could be a concept, theory, skill, or aspect of professionalism.

Here's an example. In a Civil Procedure course, assign a one-page problem for the first class. The problem tells students to assume they are two years out of law school, practicing in a small law firm. They receive a phone call at home from a friend, Carl Young. Carl is distraught. He is calling about a disaster that has befallen his 23-year-old daughter Lynn, who was injured while working at an outdoor store when an indoor climbing wall partially collapsed. Carl goes on to describe Lynn's injuries, hospitalization, statements by the store manager, and actions by the EMTs who responded to the event. The problem ends with a prompt for the students—"What are the first questions you have for Carl?" (We adapted this idea from materials created by Professor Philip G. Schrag of Georgetown Law.)

Gerry takes up this problem during the last 10 minutes of class. Students eagerly offer many questions they have for Carl. Most of those questions deal with underlying facts, potential liability, possible financial remedies, and other "lawyerly" questions. Gerry commends students on their questions and then shared his first question for Carl by writing on the board in huge letters—"HOW'S LYNN?" Many students are stunned. This exercise provides a chance to briefly make a point about the importance of maintaining our humanity in law school and in law practice. Over the years, many former students have commented that they never forgot that bit of day one.

Perform your message

A common and useful part of day one includes teachers describing for students their expectations and the way class will run during the course. Better yet, the first class can model those expectations and methods. Perform your message.

For example, to keep students motivated and to accomplish a range of learning goals, tell students the class will use a variety of teaching and learning methods. Consequently, the first class should include a variety of methods, such as brief lecture, questioning, small group discussion, and writing.

In classes with less than 30 students, emphasize the importance of active engagement by every student in every class. The first class could include a problem and discussion that requires each student to speak on day one.

2. Daily prompts

Two of us were members of faculty engaged in curriculum design for a new law school. As part of the design process, we gathered data from lawyers and judges regarding the knowledge, skills, and values essential to success in the legal profession. The faculty assigned each important concept, skill, and value to one or more required courses. The faculty expected teachers of required courses to incorporate those concepts, skills, and values in their course goals and to find ways to teach them effectively.

We were experienced teachers and quite comfortable incorporating concepts and skills in our course goals and class sessions. Although we had made professional values part of our courses in the past, we had been less intentional and systematic in teaching values than concepts and skills. To help ensure that values goals did not fall through the cracks in the busy day-to-day life of our courses, we used a simple device—daily reminders.

The daily values reminder

Two of the professional values assigned to the first-year Civil Procedure course were respect and responsibility, The Civil Procedure teacher wrote the words "respect" and "responsibility" in dark letters on a sticky note and stuck the note to his office computer. The Torts teacher had the values assigned to Torts appear on her computer.

The effects of the daily value reminders were dramatic. The reminders prompted both teachers to ask themselves questions throughout their courses:

- What have we done to help students achieve the assigned value goals this week? This month?
- Have we demonstrated the assigned values in our interactions with students?
- Have we clearly articulated the importance of the values for success in the legal profession?
- Have we given students opportunities to practice these values during the course?
- How can we assess whether students are meeting the values goals?

Both teachers concluded that the daily reminders prompted them to incorporate the assigned values in their courses much more intentionally and thoroughly than in the past.

Other daily prompts

The mechanism for daily reminders can be simple and flexible. The reminders could be on paper or electronic on a phone, computer, or tablet. All that really matters is that the reminder appears regularly and prominently to the teacher.

To avoid daily reminders from becoming oppressive, limit the reminders to 1–3 items at any time. Some reminders are appropriate for the entire length of the course. Others may be appropriate for a discrete portion of the course.

Many important aspects of our teaching could benefit from daily prompts. Consider the examples below.

- Motivation: How can we help students strive to achieve the goals of the course? How can we stay motivated to work hard to make the course a success?
- Inclusion: What can we do to make every student feel welcome, supported, and respected? What can we do to help every student succeed in our courses?
- Active Learning: How can we keep students actively engaged in class? What types of methods require students to write, speak, perform, reflect, etc.?
- Formative Assessment: How can we give students feedback about their learning throughout the course? What types of formative assessment devices are appropriate for our courses: Multiple-choice questions, short answer quizzes, analytical essays, outlines and charts, oral arguments, journals, etc.?

3. Learning and using students' names

We foster a more welcoming, inclusive, and positive learning environment when we use students' preferred names. To facilitate students' engagement with each other, try to help them learn and use their classmates' names. With remote online synchronous classes, this is relatively easy; students can be asked and reminded to include their full screen name and, when possible, have their cameras on.

Using name tents in face-to-face classes

As recommended in Chapter 5, Teaching the Class, one way to learn and use students' names is to have students in face-to-face in-person classes receive printed "name tents" at the beginning of the term. Students can bring their name tents to all classes, or at least until everyone in the course knows each other's names. (See Illustration 5-1: Name Cards.) Encourage students to keep their name tents in their textbooks as a bookmark so they can bring them to class.

On the first day of class, before the class starts, teachers can go around the room with a handful of heavy black markers and ask students to write their preferred first name on the back of each name tent, if it's not already there. Explain that name tents should be clearly visible not just to the teacher, but to their classmates around them. If their name tent gets turned around when they move, one side of the tent will almost always be visible. Students should also be invited to put their pronouns on their name tents if they are comfortable doing so. Explain that everyone in the course should use everyone else's names. Use a name tent for yourself (hang from your podium when you start class) and consider making one for any service animals that are in class (if the human companion is comfortable doing so).

At the beginning of class, remind students to take out their name tents or make a new one using the markers and paper left in the front or side of the classroom. In smaller courses, most students learn everyone's names within a few classes; once everyone can name each person in the class, they can ditch their name tents. In larger classes, once the class is several weeks into the semester, students may protest having to put out their name tent, stating that the teacher already knows their name. Respond that unless everyone knows all their classmates' names, the class will continue to use them. Faced with that challenge, students acknowledge not everyone in the course knows all their classmates' names and they continue to use them.

Roll call

On the first day of class, whether online, hybrid, or face-to-face, call roll. Before you do so, ask students to raise their hands when their name is called, respond verbally with a "here" or "yes," correct any mispronunciations, and state their preferred names. Speaking all names aloud allows the whole class to hear each student's name, hear their classmates' preferred names if different than the school's posted names, and have a visual and verbal cue about their classmates. When the teacher calls out each student's name, the teacher should also locate the student in the physical classroom or in the video gallery, make eye contact, and try to pronounce their name correctly. Going through the list of enrolled students also allows the teacher to learn which students are absent, and which students need to be added to the roster.

As you go through roll call, briefly annotate your list of students, noting pronunciations, different preferred names, and other brief items. To help students pay attention and listen, roll call starting at the end of the alphabet. Roll call takes a few minutes, but it's worth having all students' names spoken aloud at the beginning of the semester to help make them feel seen. Using their names lets them know they are not just a number.

Seating chart

Seating charts are also helpful in learning and using students' names. There is no need to memorize which student sits in which seat. However, it can be helpful to designate numbered sections on a classroom seating chart. For example, with a class of about 70 students, you could mark off 12 sections of seats on the classroom seating chart. Use similar numbering sections regardless of the classroom to make it easier to remember, such as always starting with section 1 on the top far left, section 2 in the mid-level far left, section 3 below section 2, etc. For each of the 12 sections, list the 5–6 students who sit in that section. It can be much easier to remember the 12 sections and then the cluster of students who sit in that section than trying to remember where each of the 70+ students sit.

Annotated student names and photos

As the semester continues, you may choose to annotate your student lists and photos, adding information that helps you remember each student. Sometimes these are notes about students, what the student said about themselves in their introductory video or survey, or other things that can trigger your memory. Try to use their names as often as possible during class. While harder without the classroom context and clues, you can also try to use their names when you see them outside of class.

4. Variety in calling on students

Questioning, dialog, discussion, and problem analysis are common methods in many law school courses. When using these methods, teachers make choices about how to call on students. Cold calling is at one end of the spectrum and calling on volunteers is the other end. There are many choices in between. Below are brief descriptions of eight ways to call on students. As big believers in variety, we use many of these methods in every course. These methods apply in both synchronous online and brick and mortar formats.

Cold call

Cold calling gives students an incentive to prepare for class. It furthers a core goal as a teacher—creating an environment in which all students and the teacher prepare well for every class. But some students find cold calling to be very stressful, and they perform poorly when called on, even if they are well prepared.

Teachers who use cold calling must decide how to choose the students to be called. Some teachers effectively use a random method, such as a random number table or a stack of cards with students' names that is shuffled before every class. Instead, making a conscious choice before each class about which student to call allows the teacher to ensure that the students called in each class represented a mix of gender and race and that every student is called multiple times during the course.

Cool call

At the beginning of class, we sometimes parcel out responsibility for taking the lead on cases or problems—"Sanaz, I would like you to take the lead on the *Harris* case; Fran, please take the lead on Problem 2.2; Juan, please take the lead on problem 2.3; etc." This method gives the students some time to gather their wits and often results in higher quality student responses. We recognize that cool calling has a downside—those students may lose focus on the rest of the class as they get ready to respond. No method is perfect.

Dual call

We sometimes call on two students to take the lead on a case, problem, or question rather than a single student. Dual call can work with either cold call or cool call. Having a dialog with two students can provide a more complete and nuanced discussion than a dialog with a single student.

Write call

Some questions are important enough that the teacher is willing to spend significant class time (5–10 minutes or so) on them. Pose the question orally and in writing via a slide, for example, and say, "Please generate a brief written response to the question. You have 60 seconds." Almost every student will produce a written response. Not *every* student—no method works for everyone. Then you may cold call several students—"Li, please tell us what you wrote; Andre, please tell us what you wrote; etc." Then you could solicit other views from volunteers. As a result of the time to write, many students can produce more complete and thoughtful responses.

Group call

Group call comes into play after students work in groups to analyze a problem, complete an exercise, or discuss a question. The teacher can then cold call an individual or a group—"Alex, summarize the analysis your group produced" or "Group 5, what was the first step in your analysis." Follow up by calling on another student or group to respond or by opening the discussion to all groups—"Did any other group analyze the problem differently?" or "Does any other group have a different perspective on this question?"

Panel call

Some teachers divide their students into panels by splitting the class into thirds, for example. One panel is on call for a particular class session. The teacher then uses cold call or some other calling method with individual students in the panel. The advantages of panel call can be that the panelists are very well prepared for the class and the other students are free of the stress of cold call for that class session. Some teachers are not comfortable using panel call because they believe that it undercuts a core goal of all students preparing well for every class. Other teachers use panel call effectively. We believe strongly that when teachers find methods that work for them and their students, they should keep using those methods.

All call

For issues that are very important to the course, particularly if the issues are complex and lend themselves to many different perspectives, we sometimes ask every student to weigh in. For example, in Environmental Law after spending two weeks on the National Environmental Policy Act, students can be asked to "Identify one strength, weakness, or beneficial amendment for the National Environmental Policy Act." The teacher can pose the question or problem orally and in writing and tell the students that each will be asked to give a 20 second response. To get things rolling, identify one student to begin—"Alex, when you are ready, I am going to begin with you." All call should be used sparingly—once or twice during the course—because it takes significant class time. A 20 second response from 30 students takes 10 minutes of class time. For courses with enrollments over 30, the method can be adapted by having students discuss the issue in small groups and asking every group to weigh in; it is essentially an all group call.

Vol call

Calling on volunteers is part of most teachers' repertoire. Advantages of this method include that volunteers are comfortable responding in class and are prepared to speak. Vol call can be problematic if it is the sole method for calling on students. The exclusive use of Vol call may provide less incentive for every student to prepare for class and the same group of students may dominate the discussion.

One technique to expand the group of students who will volunteer to respond to questions during class is for the teacher to use sufficient "wait time," the amount of time that passes between the teacher asking a question and calling on a volunteer. Some students are ready to respond within a second; another cohort of students will be ready after five seconds; and even more students will be ready to volunteer after ten seconds. Silence is a powerful tool during class. One of the most difficult practices for new teachers to master is the ability to sit with silence. It is important to allow this to happen sometimes; resist the urge to fill the space by answering your own questions. Simply by allowing a bit of silence after posing a question, we can expand the number of students willing to volunteer a response.

5. Bringing NextGen Bar-style tasks to our courses

With the NextGen Bar Exam on the way (and whatever California decides to do), law professors will be under increasing pressure to teach skills connected to the doctrinal areas tested on the bar exam. In Contracts, those skills include negotiating contracts, reading contracts, identifying contractual ambiguities, and drafting contract provisions. The following ideas reflect efforts to integrate the teaching of these skills in a contracts class, without sacrificing doctrinal coverage.

1. **Negotiating Contracts Idea**: This idea has been used in both Contracts and Contract Drafting. Have students elect five representatives to serve as negotiators to negotiate the terms of the course, i.e., the number of assessments, the weight of each assessment, expectations for class preparation and participation and the consequences for students being unprepared, the teaching methods to be used, etc. It is helpful to provide students with a template that identifies the topics to be covered (including the mandatory university and law school provisions). The teacher should meet with the negotiating team to work out a deal, and, afterwards, debrief the negotiations, including the tricky power dynamics. (As is often the case in the real world, one party has more power—the teacher is still grading the students.) You can also opt to hold a signing ceremony once the deal is finalized and drafted where all the students sign the contract and everyone enjoys a glass of sparkling cider.
2. **Reading Contracts in Contracts Idea**:
   a. Have students read about the common types of contract provisions (recitals, covenants, conditions, boilerplate, etc.).
   b. Give students a contract that includes at least one very ambiguous clause. Have the students prepare for class by identifying the types of provisions in the contract and explaining their effect.
   c. In class, ask them a series of questions—some short answer and some essay—that require the students to share the provisions they identified and explain the effect of those provisions.

d. About six weeks before the final exam, give them a contract from which you will draw questions for your final exam. Promise to include an essay question, a short answer drafting exercise, and five multiple-choice questions based on the contract. Embed many more issues that run as much as the entire gamut of the course as possible so that students study as much of the course as possible as they review the contract. Encourage the students to review the contract with their peers and encourage them to mark it up. Promise to provide an unmarked copy for the final exam.

3. **Identifying Contract Ambiguities**: Students often struggle in identifying patent contractual ambiguities. Some of that struggle is akin to the struggle people have in identifying both the older woman and the younger woman in the famous drawing that appears to be each depending on how you look at it.

To help students develop this skill, the teacher could have them read about the types of ambiguities (patent, latent, and contract gaps) and the ways a contract provision can be ambiguous (the words or phrases are subject to two plausible meanings, grammatical ambiguities—typically unclear modifiers, and conflicts between terms). Use the group-pair-solo technique to have students move towards independence. One option is to give students five patent contractual ambiguities reflecting each of the possible ways a term can be ambiguous and have students work in small groups to identify the two alternative, plausible meanings for each one. Next, have them work in pairs with five more patent contractual ambiguities, again asking them to identify the plausible alternative meanings, and conclude the class with each student trying a final set of five patent ambiguities and identify the plausible alternative meanings.

4. **Short Drafting Exercises in Contracts Idea**: Some topics in Contracts particularly lend themselves to being taught with a focus on drafting. Before the first such exercise, teach students some basic drafting principles, drawing heavily from a contract drafting text such as Tina Stark's, *Drafting Contracts: How and Why Lawyers Do*

What They Do. The subjects that work best for short drafting exercises include: (1) having students draft a liquidated damages clause for a hypothetical client with the instruction that the clause must be so clearly valid that it will not possibly be challenged in court (which usually requires the students to say no to one of the client's requests), (2) having students draft a simple and unambiguous express condition for a hypothetical client, and (3) having students draft a one-page demand for assurances to address a performance issue a hypothetical client is facing. Provide rubrics for each and grade each on a pass-fail basis. Students can then legitimately expect that the final exam will include one short drafting question.

6. Teaching doctrine entirely through multiple-choice questions

A few of the authors have used this method on occasion for two reasons. First, there is evidence that students learn a subject more deeply when they try to answer a multiple-choice question about the subject even before they do anything (read, discuss, etc.) to learn it. Second, as we say elsewhere in this book, implementing a variety of teaching and learning methods is a positive end in and of itself.

Create two or three bar exam-like multiple-choice questions (or even use former bar questions that are in the public domain) that assess knowledge of a new topic, such as the measure of damages for conversion for a remedies class, for instance. Students answer the questions and then learn the relevant doctrine as the teacher and students debrief each question. As long as the teacher explains what he or she is doing and why, students appreciate the variety, and they appreciate that the technique saves them some reading time.

7. Exercising writing skills for final exams and law practice

When students prepare and attend class, many students feel they "get it" because they can understand and identify the important points in texts, follow 90 percent of the class discussions, and respond to most of the teacher's questions when asked. Many of them, however, cannot always effectively show their understanding in organized, accurate, and clear prose. For that, they need many opportunities to practice spotting issues, applying facts and policy, drawing logical inferences, identifying assumptions, making judgments, and evaluating legal solutions connected to substantive law—*in writing.* Unless students can translate their thinking into words on the page, they will struggle on exams and in practice as new lawyers.

We can engage students in writing legal analysis without having to provide all students with detailed individual feedback by following a few steps.

Assign short practice writing exercises

To help students practice course-related written analysis, give them a writing assignment of 250 to 1000 words. Assigning writing early in the term informs students about our expectations for their written work, which may vary widely by teacher, subject, and course learning goals. To make the assignment focused on their learning, give the assignment almost no value, e.g., one or two percent of the course grade. Having some value encourages students to complete the assignment; having a very low value allows them to make mistakes without being heavily penalized. If the students complete the assignment on time and follow all directions, they earn full points. You could also reserve the right to deduct points who do not make a good faith effort.

Give explicit directions for writing assignments

To ensure all students complete the same assignment, have an equal opportunity to do well, and learn efficiently, be explicit about the specific questions to which you want them to respond. This includes things like telling students how precise they need to be about rules, whether they need to advocate or predict, apply policy, identify and refute counterarguments, use detailed facts, make logical inferences, use a particular format, or adhere to word limits. We want students to practice writing answers to specific questions and follow directions, rather than spending energy trying to figure out what we want them to do.

Provide guidance to students about how much time you expect them to work on the assignment. Plan on students needing three or more times as long as it would take you to complete the assignment effectively. Remind students that writing legal analysis usually takes at least twice as long as we think, even for experienced lawyers, and requires more effort than reading and taking notes to prepare for class. Suggesting the amount of time to allocate for a writing assignment helps students plan and manage their time more effectively and allows them to practice being efficient for final exams.

Sophie learned this lesson the hard way when one student submitted 27 pages and another spent eight hours on what she intended to be a simple torts assignment. Now Sophie writes a sample response before asking students to complete the assignment; doing so helps her figure out exactly where she wants students to focus their efforts and usually requires her to significantly modify—usually shorten—the assignment and provide them with a sense of how long they should expect to spend on the assignment.

Another way to help students manage time expectations for assignments is to survey them on how much time they took to complete assignments and share the survey results—captured in a few charts—with the class. Revealing the time range and identifying the average can help students better manage their pace and progress in relation to the rest of the class. Students who are putting in minimal effort may self-correct once they see that they are outliers; likewise, students who are spending an unreasonable amount of time on an assignment may strive to become more efficient.

Invite students to ask questions about assignments

Students often don't know what questions they have until they start writing about a topic. Before an assignment is due, encourage them to post questions and share your answers with all students. Making your responses to their questions available to everyone (1) helps students who are too shy or scared to ask you questions; (2) guides students who have questions when you don't have time to answer them; (3) saves you time by not having to respond individually to the same questions; (4) gives you a written record of your guidance; and (5) allows you to refine your directions the next time you give the assignment. Be sure to set a reasonable cut-off time for your questions so you are able to answer the questions well ahead of the due date and give students a reasonable opportunity to make changes. Also consider limiting the number of questions each student can submit so you are not overwhelmed by their requests. This limit also forces students to be more thoughtful about reviewing the resources you have provided before they ask you questions they can answer themselves.

Have students share their work with their classmates

Students learn a lot from seeing their classmates' writing. Those with strong organizational skills can try to emulate their classmates' in-depth legal reasoning; students with detailed legal rules and nuances can learn from a classmate's more in-depth fact applications and reasonable inferences. In addition, because they read their classmates' responses to the same question they have worked through, students often realize how important clear organization and coherent prose are to helping their readers effectively grasp their analysis.

Direct students to post their assignments to a course discussion website or small group forum where some or all their classmates can see their work. Having their work visible to their classmates encourages students to pay more attention to what they are doing. Students may not care about their teacher's opinion, but most care deeply about their peers' opinions. Letting students know in advance that they will be reviewing their own and possibly their classmates' work against specific criteria further motivates them to take the assignment seriously.

Have students compare their own or a classmate's work with a sample answer

Many students briefly read their teacher's sample, think they understand how it differs from their work, and believe they will now write better answers. Alternatively, students may dismiss the teacher's sample because it reflects unreasonable performance expectations for a student. To help students learn more deeply from a writing assignment, give students criteria to use when comparing a sample with their own or a classmate's work. Having to use explicit criteria guides students in assessing their own and others' work. Ask students to note what they learned from a writing assignment and offer to meet with them individually. Few may follow up on the offer; however, by engaging in writing and carefully reviewing their own and others' work most students identify what they need to do differently.

8. Give students short quizzes

As with realizing what they don't know when students write an answer to a problem, students also learn what they don't know when they take quizzes. Because students learn a lot from their mistakes, and because their answers reveal important information about where they are struggling, teachers should consider giving students several short multiple-choice quizzes during a semester. These quizzes could assess students on multiple levels. Some questions test foundational knowledge all students should know, some test students' ability to apply rules to new factual situations, and some require students to analyze slightly more complicated problems.

These quizzes are low-stakes, closed-book assessments, generally worth less than three percent of a course grade. The goal is for students to take them seriously but allow them to take risks and make mistakes. They are also worth only a few points in their overall grade because they are being quizzed on foundational rules and applications, not sophisticated analysis. Stress to students that these quiz questions are meant to serve as the equivalent of mastering basic math functions. Just as students should know simple addition, subtraction, multiplication, and division without having to use a calculator, they should know certain foundational material without having to look it up. Even if they don't have to memorize a wealth of substance for their state's bar exam, there are certain concepts all lawyers should know.

All multiple-choice quizzes instruct students to choose the best answer. When designed well, some of the answer options will be correct but not the best answer, forcing students to look more closely at the facts, the call of the question, or applying the correct rules. Students are directed to take quizzes within a limited time, usually around two minutes a question, and, if they have time left over, note the reasons why some answers were better than others.

When time permits, after students have completed quizzes individually, they take them again in small groups and must agree on a single answer to each multiple-choice question. The group quizzes are also closed-book, but students have the benefit of harnessing their colleagues' brains. A ton of learning happens when students need to collectively decide on the best answer. They argue over rules and facts, parse the questions and answer options closely, and debate the meaning of sentences, phrases, and words. Every student in the room is engaged. Rarely does one student alone have all the right answers, and even when they do, they must sufficiently articulate why they are right and convince their group colleagues of their analysis. Working in groups, students see that there are other ways to view problems and quickly realize that the loudest and most opinionated person in the group isn't always right.

Once the correct answers are revealed, students write their group's score on a whiteboard in the front of the room. While the group score may not factor into the students' grades, students are both relieved when other groups don't have perfect scores and delighted when their group does well.

At the end of the group quiz, students also identify which questions they want to go over in class. This makes the process more efficient; rather than reviewing each question, only spend time on those that students still struggle to understand. Writing good quiz questions is hard, so reuse them, tweaking them each time.

9. Experiment with podcasts

Podcasts can be used in a variety of ways to support teaching and learning. First, the teacher can assign podcasts that discuss or critique cases. Students can listen to the podcast in place or in addition to the case, depending on the coverage demands. These assigned podcasts can be part of homework. Or the teacher can play an excerpt of a podcast in class and ask students to post questions or comments in real-time on a platform such as Padlet so everyone can see all the posts on the shared screen.

Teachers in seminars or workshops could also ask students to produce their own podcast by interviewing an expert on their seminar paper topic or workshop field. By using Zoom, students can create their own podcast on the "hot topic." The teacher could then require that the student design a flyer advertising the podcast and the class could build its own YouTube channel featuring these legal podcasts. Potential experts could include law faculty, local attorneys, and national experts who are willing to participate in a 15-minute student interview on a Zoom recording. This work helps identify other policy considerations that might inform a seminar paper or workshop product, highlights the value of expansive communication skills, and may spark a passion for the topic being discussed.

A newer way to incorporate podcasts has emerged through the rise of Artificial Intelligence, which can create a podcast out of an essay or article. This feature might be helpful to students as they are given an opportunity to hear a discussion of their own seminar paper draft. This feature could help students—especially auditory learners—identify holes in their analysis. It could also help them flag areas in their draft that they unintentionally overemphasized. When incorporating AI this expansively, however, make sure you are conforming to your law school's guidelines regarding the use of AI. Also spend time reviewing the ethical and professional considerations with students—or even bringing in someone from the local ethics board or a bar grievance committee to highlight the risks and rewards of using this technology.

10. Graphics, arts, and beyond

Most of our courses have learning goals that include some combination of doctrine, theory, analytical skills, performance skills, and professional values. To achieve those goals, we ask our students to interact with a variety of material in and out of class—textbooks, legal documents, stories, articles, course webpages, pictures, videos, slides, podcasts, websites, flowcharts, concept maps, etc. We choose those materials to support teaching and learning activities, which we hope leads to significant learning for our students.

What if we have students create learning materials?

Why do this? First, most courses include major units with complex concepts, frameworks, and skills. Students can solidify and deepen their learning by producing a graphic, story, or video that illustrates the applicable doctrine, framework, skill, or professional value. Second, the materials created by students can help their peers learn as well. Third, some students feel that legal education systematically beats creativity out of them. When we encourage students to apply their creativity in our courses, many students produce spectacular results. Finally, student-created materials can be lots of fun for us and our students.

A graphics, arts, and beyond assignment

A good time to use the graphics, arts, and beyond assignment is at the end of a major unit in a course. Below is a generic version of the assignment.

Graphics, Arts, and Beyond

Prepare a visual or auditory representation of [insert subject matter here]. Your representation could be a graphic, an artistic expression, or something else. Examples of graphics include flow charts, concept maps, and diagrams. Artistic expressions include photographs, paintings, drawings, slide shows, cartoons, plays, poems, stories, songs, videos, animations, etc. Other representations could include games, objects, etc. Use your imagination. The purpose of this assignment is to help you organize, synthesize, and demonstrate [insert subject matter here].

Time and Space Limits

- Graphics, photos, paintings, drawings, stories, poems and similar expressions—one page.
- Video, audio, animations, and similar expressions—two minutes.
- Slide shows—five slides.

You can complete this assignment on your own or in a group of up to four students. The only grading criteria are whether you complied with the time and space limits and made a good-faith effort to represent [insert subject matter here]. This assignment is worth 10 points. You should all earn 10 points on this assignment. Prizes will be awarded for expressions that best demonstrate [insert subject matter here], most help your peers learn, are especially creative, or any other category that seems appropriate after I review your work.

Learning from the assignment

Most students actively engage and put significant effort into the assignment. The assignment pushes students to organize and synthesize an important part of the course. Then the process of creating a graphic or artistic expression helps students solidify their learning.

The teacher can facilitate more learning from the assignment in several ways. For instance, review the student products and correct any obvious misunderstandings. Next, arrange for students to review one another's products. In a brick-and-mortar format, students should bring their graphics and expressions to class and spend 15 minutes viewing each other's work. In an online format, have students post their products and review and comment on one another's work. Select graphics and expressions that are especially helpful and share them with the entire class.

Teaching and learning environment benefits

The assignment can make significant contributions to maintaining a positive teaching and learning environment. Most students delight in viewing one another's graphics and artistic expressions. Creative and artistic students have an opportunity to shine. And the students who are not so creative seem to enjoy seeing and hearing what their more artistic classmates produce.

When you introduce the assignment, acknowledge that some students may struggle with limited artistic talent. You could disclose your own lack of artistic range (if applicable) and lighten the stress by offering an award certificate for "Boring Flow Chart #48." Gerry once had a student admit that when he introduced the assignment she groaned internally because she believed she lacked artistic ability of any sort. When she was a child, her mom had to complete art projects for her. In response to the assignment, she produced a boring flow chart on a purple piece of paper. Gerry gave her an award certificate for "Most Pathetic Attempt at Creativity." She was thrilled.

Though some students may struggle with producing something more creative than a flow chart, other students have produced clever games, elaborate mobiles, hilarious songs, Oscar-worthy short videos, enormous cakes with graphics in the frosting, and beautiful drawings. The advent of AI and other technology certainly makes it easier for people to produce something creative. And do not underestimate a law student with a sense of humor. In Gerry's class, one year the assignment was due the day before Halloween. A student walked into the classroom, slapped an 8.5 by 11-inch piece of paper on a table, placed a graphic carved into a pumpkin atop the paper, gave Gerry a stern look, and said, "See. It fits on one page." Gerry raised his hands in surrender.

Allow students to create alternative assessments

Some of us have also incorporated creative projects billed as "alternative assessments" to offer students a chance to demonstrate their knowledge through a project they create. Cognitive scientists have found a deep connection between learning and novelty, and alternative assessments leverage this connection by challenging students to illustrate a legal doctrine or rule through unique projects that they design. This type of assessment also engages tactile learners who benefit from hands-on activities. Because these assessments rely heavily on subjective evaluation and some students are more anxious about the prospect of compelled creativity, you might consider making the alternative assessments optional. Worried about participation? The prospect of earning extra credit on a midterm or final exam offers enough incentive for most of the class to participate. If staged together as part of a review, the entire class can also benefit from the final projects.

If offering alternative assessments, the teacher should give the class at least two weeks to submit a project. When used in Constitutional Law, for instance, students could be asked to design a project that reflects a unique, concrete approach to teaching a Constitutional Law concept. Students are evaluated both for creativity and instructional value. Showcasing samples ahead of time is highly recommended—though this will be difficult the first time the teacher implements this practice. (Teachers could use a few samples or creative teaching tools that they or their Teaching Assistants made to help students understand the assignment.)

Create a clear rubric or checklist to review ahead of time. Encourage students to focus on a discrete subject covered in class; do not award points for general images or projects related to American history. Reserve the right to grant partial or no credit to submitted projects. You may also consider group projects. Once the projects are submitted, they can be showcased to the entire class. Olympia has hosted "The Best Con Law Day Ever" for students in a hall where the alternative assessments were on display. Students were offered donuts, and she led an interactive final exam review. The alternative assessments had just come in the day before, and the room was set up to resemble a science fair. (The projects had not yet been graded.) Students who participated had made creative projects that reinforced the doctrinal law covered in class. They were especially encouraged to design an alternative assessment about a subject that was difficult for them to understand.

A wide range of alternative assessments came in. They included: board games ("Conlopoly" and "Con Law Land"); Bill of Rights hand-painted jewelry and explanatory brochure; movies made on iMovie; books of poetry about *Marbury v. Madison;* a Con Law Recipe book featuring lemon bars and homemade bread (think Lemon Test and *Lochner);* rap songs about justiciability; a hand-built due process dollhouse (a room on privacy, marriage, voting, etc.); Commerce Clause Crossword puzzles; an MTV Cribs-version of the Big House of Due Process; and a hand-sewn jumbo Equal Protection pyramid pillow with accompanying analysis. The exam review was conducted in the middle of the room, and afterwards, the class was given 30 minutes to explore the alternative assessments. In addition to being instructive, the Best Con Law Day Every helped allay student anxiety a week before finals started. It also was a good venue to field the last day of questions before exams began.

What is a good class? Or a bad class?

In our lives as teachers, some days seem better than others. Most of us teach class sessions that we consider to be particularly good or bad.

Thinking exercise: Take a couple minutes to think about class sessions you taught in the past that you think were particularly good or bad. Why do you consider those sessions to be successes or failures?

In teaching and learning workshops over the years, we have asked many law teachers to describe good class sessions and bad class sessions. Descriptions of good classes include statements like these:

- My students and I were thoroughly prepared for class.
- My students were actively engaged throughout the session.
- Class discussion was lively and included many different student perspectives.
- Everything clicked.
- Students came up with insights that I didn't expect.
- Students and I learned more than I had hoped.
- We worked together, had fun, and moved the ball forward.

Descriptions of bad classes included:

- Teacher errors—incorrect statements, muddled explanations, inadequate responses to questions, confusing directions for exercises, poorly phrased questions, etc.
- Low levels of student preparation, engagement, and interest.
- Teaching/learning methods that fall flat, including technological failures.
- Students leave class more confused than when they came to class.
- Student behavior or comments that are disrespectful, confrontational, or hurtful.
- Teacher behavior or comments that are disrespectful, confrontational, or hurtful.

We have personally experienced every aspect of law teachers' descriptions of good days and bad days in the classroom. And we have felt the joy and suffering that accompanies those days. Perhaps you have as well. Over time, we have tried to develop a set of criteria to assess what constitutes a good day and bad day in class. So far, we have three criteria: (1) the teacher's subjective, personal reaction to the class; (2) the level of students' learning; and (3) the effects on the teaching/learning environment.

Teacher's subjective reaction

In the immediate aftermath of a class session, many teachers have strong subjective reactions based on our assessment of our own performance and of students' responses to the class. Did the teaching/earning activities "work"? Did we ask effective questions? Were we organized and clear? Did we make significant errors? Were students prepared, engaged and interested? Did they enjoy the class? Did we? Did anything bad happen?

For part of our teaching careers, our subjective reactions were the primary factor in our assessment of the quality of a class session. Over time, we began to doubt the value and validity of this factor. We came to realize that our subjective reactions to the class may have no relationship to students' experience of the class or to their learning. Yet our subjective reactions are not irrelevant. Teaching is an intensely personal endeavor. Our subjective reactions have a significant effect on our morale and motivation, which influence our future performance as teachers. However, we have come to believe that our subjective reactions to class are the least important of the three factors.

Students' Learning

A more important factor has become the level of students' learning from a class session. Did students learn the concepts, skills, and values that we hoped to teach that day? How deep and lasting is their learning? If most students gained significant learning from the class, then our feelings about our performance and our thoughts about their engagement or interest don't matter much. Likewise, if significant learning does not take place, we should take little comfort in our view that the class was lively, creative, and fun.

It is easy for us to say that the level of student learning is our primary criterion for evaluating the value of class sessions. It is more challenging for us to act accordingly. The best way for us to know what our students are learning is to include significant formative assessment in our class sessions—quizzes, writing exercises, "clicker" questions, minute papers (for example, students each identify in writing three things they learned in class that day), practice exams, student performances, etc. In addition, we should routinely gather feedback from students on the impact of various teaching and learning methods on their learning.

Teaching/Learning Environment

The effect of the session on the teaching/learning environment is as important to us as the level of student learning because the teaching/learning environment is foundational to effective teaching and student learning throughout the course. Healthy teaching/learning environments feature mutual respect among teachers and students; high, uniform, mutual expectations; support, collaboration, and inclusion; and active engagement and enthusiasm from teachers and students. We build the teaching and learning environment with our students one class session at a time. So, at the end of each class, we try to assess whether anything happened to enhance or hinder the environment. For example, a high level of preparation by us and our students coupled with an effective exercise could result in an especially active session. On the other hand, a disrespectful comment or gesture, by us or a student, even if unintentional, could dampen enthusiasm and alienate some students.

An Example

In Civil Procedure, Gerry devotes one class session to appeals—the final judgment rule and its exceptions. He created an Appeal Jeopardy game that takes up the entire session. Students collaborate enthusiastically in teams. They work hard during the class to come up with answers (each in the form of a question, of course). Student participation is energetic and widespread. Fantastic class, right? Well, Gerry's subjective reaction is that many, though not all, students love the class, as does Gerry. The collaborative, active, enthusiastic nature of the session enhances the teaching/learning environment. And the level of student learning? Based on students' performance on exam questions dealing with appeal issues, Gerry rates the level of learning as average. Many, though not all, students learn the basic doctrine and some students gain a good grasp of the underlying policies. Gerry has seen no evidence that students learn any significant skills or values in the class. So, all things considered, a pretty good, not great, class. After evaluating the class session, the challenge for Gerry is to make adjustments to the class that lead to greater student learning.

Thinking exercise:

(1) Think again about "good" and "bad" classes you have taught in the past. Apply the three criteria. We hope the criteria help you develop a more nuanced view of what constitutes good and bad teaching days.

(2) Identify and apply additional criteria that you think are particularly appropriate for your classes.

(3) Identify one change that could improve each class.

Chapter 12

Troubleshooting

The design of this chapter is quite different from the other chapters in this book. In this chapter we identify ten teaching challenges commonly experienced by law teachers and offer our ideas for addressing those challenges. Consequently, each of this chapter's subsections describes a challenge and then suggests ways to address it. We have created this list of challenges based on comments teachers have made to us at teaching workshops we have conducted and at law teaching conferences at which we have presented (collectively we have conducted more than 500 such workshops and presentations), from questions raised by law teachers with whom we have privately consulted, and from outstanding law teachers that we have studied. Of course, our list of challenges is impossibly non-exhaustive; to assist you in dealing with the challenges we have not identified, we conclude the chapter with the common themes we identified in thinking through the challenges and writing the chapter.

Challenge 1: Coverage vs. Active Learning

The challenge

This challenge can be expressed in a variety of ways, but it boils down to three assertions: (1) coverage is an important goal for law teaching; (2) active learning methods use up more classroom time than passive learning methods; and (3) consequently, law teachers who create active learning experiences must sacrifice essential coverage.

Addressing the challenge

We have doubts about all three premises. First, doctrinal coverage is but one of many important goals in law school. To prepare students for practice, their legal education should include doctrine, theory, skills, and professionalism. In practice, good lawyers do not rely on their memory of doctrine they learned in law school.

We also doubt that law teachers of any subject actually cover all the important doctrine in that field. Law school casebooks include only a subset of all the doctrine in a field, and few law teachers get through every doctrinal point in the casebooks they use.

In the context of bar-tested courses, based on what we know about brain science, some degree of coverage does matter. Students benefit from frameworks that help them later learn the topics in the bar review course outlines; however, there are no studies confirming even the framework hypothesis, and most studies have not found a strong correlation between merely taking bar-tested courses and bar pass results. Even if we were to assume coverage is helpful for bar passage, students remember longer and better the things they learn more deeply through active learning experiences; consequently, it is just as plausible that active learning-focused law teachers provide greater support for bar takers even if they are sacrificing some coverage. We do know that students are likely to forget most of what they learn in our classes within a few months after the final exam; thus, the greater long-term retention and understanding produced by active learning is worth a sacrifice of coverage.

The notion that active learning inherently requires a sacrifice of coverage is also questionable. In flipped classrooms, for example, students do the reading, watch videos, and listen to podcasts before class and do active learning exercises during class time. The students' preparation for class can ensure the desired coverage, and the active learning in class can produce greater short-term and long-term recall. Teachers can also inspire their students to read their assignments more closely and for greater understanding by administering short daily reading quizzes at the beginning of each class session. In this way, the students are more likely to learn most of the basic concepts before the class session starts. Other teaching techniques similarly help the students learn core concepts by having students take tests on their readings individually and in groups and then applying those concepts to more complex scenarios. More generally, if students know they will have to use what they read in class in an active learning exercise, they are more likely to do the deep, critical reading that correlates with retention of course material.

Challenge 2: Laptops in the Classroom

The challenge

Some students who use their laptops in class seem to engage less in class discussions. Others seem more likely to allow themselves to be distracted by less than ideal uses of their laptops, such as games, email, social media, and shopping. For many law teachers, computer screens feel like a barrier between the teachers and their students. Students who use laptops and type quickly have a tendency to treat note-taking as a form of dictation, a goal that distracts from the actual learning.

Addressing the challenge

While the four of us do not ban laptops in our classes, there is increasing evidence that, unless a student has a disability that requires the use of a laptop, requiring students to take notes by hand instead of typing their notes may improve their learning. There seems to be something in the process of listening and writing by hand that creates a stronger memory trace; perhaps, because students cannot take notes by hand fast enough to convert the process to one of taking dictation, they must focus on the key points and therefore engage more deeply with those points. Two of the twenty-six people we studied for WHAT THE BEST LAW TEACHERS DO (Harvard University Press 2013) ban laptops in their classrooms.

We choose not to ban laptops because we believe that many of the problems commonly asserted as reasons for banning laptops can be addressed by best practices in teaching. For example, teaching students best practices in note-taking, such as the Cornell Note-Taking System, in which students strive to both take notes and reflect on their learning process as they do so, naturally and effectively moves students away from transcribing the class. Similarly, active learning activities during which students must talk to each other, write, solve problems, and otherwise engage make it much harder for students to be distracted by the other possible uses of their laptops. In addition, teachers can direct students to use their laptops in class for productive purposes, such as finding examples that illustrate concepts, conducting research, or drafting documents.

Challenge 3: Unprepared or Unmotivated Students

The challenge

This discussion addresses two, closely-related issues and a third more general issue. The first issue focuses on how we choose to react when one of our students is unprepared. The second issue focuses on that rare occasion when many students are unprepared. The third issue addresses what law teachers can do if their students seem generally under-motivated.

Addressing the challenge

We start with two key takeaways from WHAT THE BEST LAW TEACHERS DO. Those two takeaways offer important preventive measures that law teachers can do to minimize student unpreparedness and disengagement. Students we interviewed repeatedly told us, "I would never be unprepared for _______'s class because she prepared for class so hard and cared so much about my learning." In other words, our effort and engagement often correlates with our students' effort and engagement. Second, when we interviewed the subjects for the study, we discovered that they all devote considerable time and effort to thinking through how they will motivate their students to learn. For example, one professional responsibility teacher would start each class by reading from the disciplinary reports from her state bar, often finding violations of the concepts the class was learning that day. Two of our subjects interviewed the lawyers who handled the cases they taught; the students reported feeling on the edge of their seats waiting for their unique insights their teachers had tracked down for them. A civil procedure teacher distributed recent newspaper stories that raised the concepts he was teaching each day; he distributed the stories to his students to read before class and explain, at the start of class, the relevance of those stories. Relevancy is important to all learners and influences motivation, but it is especially important to adult learners.

We regard the single, unprepared student as the easiest issue. On the one hand, publicly embarrassing or berating the student is a significant mistake; teachers who do so often lose not only the unprepared student but many others as well. On the other hand, simply ignoring an unprepared student communicates that we do not care about preparation, which may create a risk that more students will be unprepared. Our preference is to let students know, in our syllabi and on the first day of class, that we expect students to diligently prepare for class but do not believe in publicly embarrassing unprepared students. We explain that, instead, we will privately contact any unprepared student and address the issue. We consistently follow through by contacting those students. We have found that the most effective way to do so is to send an email that says something like, "I noticed you were not fully prepared for class today. I have no doubt you are capable of more. What can I do to better inspire you to prepare for my class?"

We suspect that, absent unusual circumstances, more widespread unpreparedness is rare. Unless you know for certain, it is probably better to assume that the students you happened to call on that day happened to be the unprepared students than to assume no students or only few students were prepared. Moreover, even if the unpreparedness is widespread, the reasons for the unpreparedness likely vary. Consequently, we suggest you start by sending emails along the lines suggested in the prior paragraph. If we really believed we had a persistent problem of student unpreparedness, we would address it by getting feedback and suggestions from the students. We may invite students to provide anonymous feedback in writing and then devote five or ten minutes of class to an open discussion. The key to having a successful open discussion of such an issue is to assume students' good faith, avoid accusations, and take some ownership of the problem.

If your students do seem generally under-motivated and unprepared, it is worth finding new ways to motivate the students. Ask them for input into the teaching methods that motivate them. Find relevant current events. Have students do personally-guided field trips in which they find examples of key concepts in the course in the real world. If you are comfortable with more radical approaches, try engaging students by having them compete to learn the concepts via a Jeopardy Game or put them in teams and have the teams compete to answer multiple-choice questions that review key concepts.

Challenge 4: Disrespectful Students

The challenge

This challenge can involve students being disrespectful to the law teacher, a faculty administrative assistant, a teaching assistant, or classmates. The literature and our colleagues' experiences suggest that faculty members and students of color and women are more frequently subjected to disrespectful student behavior than are white male teachers and students.

Addressing the challenge

We have a syllabus-based suggestion for addressing this challenge and a general teaching suggestion, both of which we hope will minimize your experience of such issues. However, because you may nevertheless encounter disrespectful students, we also offer a suggested process for addressing the issue and a final suggestion for addressing persistently problematic students.

We recommend setting expectations for respectful discourse in your syllabus. This approach may be most effective if you allow students to set the expectations for their interactions with you and each other. (Students nearly always include respectfulness, and, if they don't, you can ask them about their expectations in terms of respectful interactions). Those law teachers who set the expectations themselves can and should communicate in the syllabus an expectation that students respond respectfully to the teacher, administrative assistants, teaching assistants, and each other.

Our general teaching suggestion is that you do everything you can to model the behaviors you expect of your students. Be extraordinarily well prepared. Be respectful of the students who disagree with you. Be positive and kind. Assume the best of your students. Admit errors. Think of yourself as modeling the behaviors you desire from your students.

Our suggested process to address disrespect in the classroom involves multiple steps, and you may want to consider, if you have had past problems with disrespectful students, that this will be your process for addressing such matters:

1. Pause. Let the words hang there in silence; catch your own breath so you can manage the situation calmly and authentically.
2. Move the discussion outside of the class while also communicating that you are holding the students accountable. Ask the student to stay after class, i.e., "[Insert student's name], can you please stay after class? I'd like to discuss your last comment with you privately."
3. Assume good faith. When you do speak with the student one-on-one, even if you believe that the student's manifestation of disrespect is the product of explicit or implicit bias, start with an assumption of good faith. Because the ultimate goal of any response to disrespectful behavior is to change that behavior in the future, a response that labels the student's behavior in a way that causes the student to be defensive (e.g., "that was a sexist thing to say") decreases the likelihood the student will change the behavior.
4. Don't assume it is personal. Bad student behavior is nearly always about the student and not the teacher.

5. Describe the behavior, your reaction to it, and why you reacted that way: "When you said or did [insert specific description], I [or the other student whom you observed being disrespected] felt [describe your response, e.g., angry, frustrated] because [explain why you felt that way, e.g., because your statement assumed ..., because you spoke before (insert disrespected student's name) had finished her thought, because you interrupted (insert disrespected student's name)]".
6. Reference the class policy. "As you may recall, my syllabus says, '[quote the relevant portion of your syllabus.]'" Take extra care to reference the class policy ahead of particularly challenging topics.
7. Make a specific demand: In the future, when you feel like [saying or doing] [insert what the student said or did], I want you to [insert specific desired new behavior.]

If all these suggestions fail with a persistently disrespectful student, get help. Have a trusted colleague sit in on your class and give you an insight into what is going on. If your school has an Associate Dean of Faculty Development, ask that person to observe your class to offer you feedback. Invite someone from your university's Teaching and Learning Center to meet with you or visit your class. Consider talking to a number of colleagues, including those in student services, to gain ideas for how to work with the student and how to relate showing respect in class to behaviors related to success in practice. You may also want to ask a trusted former student or a teaching assistant for insight.

Challenge 5: Getting Lackluster or Poor Student Evaluations

The challenge

Over the years, many law teachers have approached us for help when they believed they taught a class well yet received poor or lackluster student evaluations. While we are familiar with and recognize the limits of student evaluations, we do not believe they are meaningless, and we therefore believe that certain types of efforts to improve student evaluation scores are worthwhile.

Student evaluation scores are not meaningless because, generally speaking, if students conclude that a teacher is excellent or poor, an expert in teaching evaluating that teacher would be likely to independently reach the same conclusion. Thousands of empirical studies of student evaluations conclude that, in general, they are valid and reliable measures of teaching effectiveness. However, women and minorities consistently receive lower student evaluation scores, and recent studies suggest that students' impressions of teachers in the first three minutes of a course seldom change by the end of the semester or year. While all these limitations on student evaluations give us pause, we decided to identify this issue as a problem and offer suggestions because we also know that law schools often rely heavily on student evaluations in evaluating teaching effectiveness. And we know that many law teachers who experience poor student evaluations feel upset or embarrassed by them.

Addressing the challenge

Please see Chapter 13 for a general discussion of addressing student evaluations.

All of the practices, attitudinal, and relational behaviors described as being characteristic of good teachers detailed in Chapter 1 also positively influence student evaluations. We emphasize five such behaviors below. It is important, as you consider these recommendations, that you keep in mind that the first few minutes of the first class session are critical; first impressions matter. A lot.

First, manifesting respect for students and your investment and confidence in their ability to learn can make a huge difference in students' initial and continuing impression of you. Students who perceive that you care to know them as individuals (both their names and their interests) are more likely to interpret the things you do as reflecting your efforts to help them learn. Students who believe you do not respect them or believe they can be successful are likely to feel insulted and disrespected, even if you adopt a wide variety of teaching practices aimed to help them learn. One example from the people we studied for WHAT THE BEST LAW TEACHERS DO illustrates this point. Some of the teachers had class-by-class syllabi from which they never varied; others adjusted their assignments every week to reflect student progress. The students who had the teachers who never wavered from their planned syllabi told us that their teachers respected them so much that their teachers made sure they stuck to their syllabi so their students could manage their time. The students whose teachers' syllabi varied said their teachers respected them and wanted them to succeed so much that they adapted their lesson planning to the students' needs. Both groups of students interpreted their teachers' conduct in light of their belief that their teachers wanted them to succeed. In other words, the critical factor was students' perception that their teachers respected them and cared about their learning.

Second, authenticity can make a big difference in students' perceptions. Some of the people we studied for WHAT THE BEST LAW TEACHERS DO have wonderful senses of humor; others never crack a joke in class. What the students identified and focused on was their teachers' sincerity. They described their teachers as authentic, sincere, "very real," etc. In contrast, teachers who try to teach the way they were taught, even teachers who try to imitate their own favorite teachers, invariably struggle to win over their students.

Third, law teachers' preparation for class, on the first day of class and throughout the semester, makes a huge difference in student perceptions. When students believe their teachers have worked very hard to prepare for class, they are more likely to forgive errors, work hard, value their learning, and invest themselves in unfamiliar learning activities.

Fourth, teachers' passion for their subjects and for student success can influence student evaluations of our teaching. One of us once listened as our daughter's geometry teacher explained -during the first three minutes of her back-to-school presentation—why she loves triangles. Her excitement about triangles convinced the parents in the room that she must be a good geometry teacher—anyone who was that excited about triangles could inspire any child to learn geometry. Teacher excitement conveys the message that something in the class is worth being excited about. Students from elementary school through law school identify the teacher's passion or enthusiasm as a critical characteristic of effective teachers.

Fifth, it is important to avoid making the particular kinds of mistakes that most frustrate students. Return all exams, papers, and assignments promptly. Delay in getting feedback aggravates students. Assign students an amount of class preparation that is reasonable for them and reasonable for you to cover in the following class session; students get frustrated when they have too much reading to do their best work on their assignments or when you skip materials you required them to read for class. Show up on time for class, start class and end class on time, and do everything you can to avoid cancelling a class session. (If you must cancel a class session or miss a grading deadline, be transparent about the causes and apologetic about your failure.) And, of course, avoid yelling at students, embarrassing them in class, and speaking to them in a condescending tone.

Please note that none of our suggestions involve lowering standards or expectations, spoon-feeding, or grading easier. Making classes easier has, at most, a minimal effect on student evaluations and harms learning. Moreover, students consistently give their highest ratings to teachers with high expectations and to courses that they perceive as the most challenging.

Challenge 6: Widespread Poor Student Performance on Final Papers or the Final Exam

The challenge

One of our favorite articles on teaching referred to grading as the "dark night of the soul." Grading is often painful, even for excellent teachers. No matter what we do, some students do not learn. Dr. Benjamin Bloom (famous for Bloom's Taxonomy), in fact, argued that teaching succeeds if 80% of the students learn 80% of what we hoped they would learn. Unfortunately, even when students do learn 80% of what we teach, they do not always learn the particular 80% we wished they had learned. Here we focus on those devastating instances when too many of our students fail to learn what we hoped they would learn.

Addressing the challenge

A large number of problems can potentially cause a widespread failure to learn, ranging from errors in teaching, overestimations of students' entering skills or knowledge, mistakes in selecting course materials, flaws in our assessment instruments, or unachievable expectations. Consequently, it is helpful to start by enlisting a colleague to help you review the exams, your syllabus, your student evaluations, and any other relevant data. Invite a teaching expert or someone from your university's teaching and learning center to review your materials and sit in on a few class sessions.

Do not assume your exam or final assignment was flawless. All four of us, especially early in our careers, constructed exams that could not possibly be finished in the allotted time. Earlier in this book, we encourage you to make it a regular practice to show your exams or paper assignments, well before students will see them, to a colleague who teaches your subject. We also suggest you have one or more teaching assistants try out the exam or assignment and give you feedback. Even if you adopted those suggestions for the particular assessment that stumped your students, we encourage you to reconsider the exam and make sure the students' performance issues were not a function of exam design, such as an unintended ambiguity in the facts.

Seriously consider and identify the skills and knowledge you are assuming your students bring to your classroom. Try creating lists of each. Ask colleagues who teach the same students whether your assumptions are reasonable. If you discover your students have gaps in necessary knowledge or skills, you can do some backfilling. For example, you could create recordings paired with short, pass-fail multiple-choice tests to make sure your students learn necessary background knowledge.

Consider having a colleague interview your former students. The students may have insights not available from any other source. For example, they can compare your assignments to their assignments in other classes, identify strengths and weaknesses in your teaching practices, and help you pinpoint flaws in your course materials.

Closely reviewing your students' actual work products is probably most important. Look for patterns of errors. For example, in reviewing a set of poor exam answers, we might ask: Did the students miss a lot of issues? Did they spot the issues but not know the law? Did they struggle to use the facts? Did they not understand the theory or policy? The answers to these questions should guide your choice of responses. If you have a good rubric, the task of determining patterns in your students' errors will be easier.

Your results will guide your next steps. For example, if your students struggle to spot issues, they may need concentrated instruction focused on the skill of issue spotting (called "pattern recognition" by learning experts). Similarly, if your students inaccurately state the law, you may need to create learning activities that help them deepen their understanding and improve their memorization of the important doctrine. Students who struggle to perform legal analysis need training in the skill and practice and feedback in performing it. You may even need to work on all three.

Think of your teaching as a continuous improvement enterprise. No one does it perfectly, and most of us improve over time. Each assessment is an opportunity to collect data about your effectiveness, to make changes as needed, and to improve. Your students' less-than-optimal performances therefore are an opportunity for you to become a more effective teacher.

Challenge 7: Doing Multiple Assessments without Killing Yourself

The challenge

You've read Chapter 10, Assessing Student Learning, and believe that you need to administer multiple formative and summative assessments to improve student learning. You understand that practice and feedback helps students determine how to improve, and using multiple assessments allows you to assess a wider array of skills and knowledge and improve the accuracy of your conclusions about the students' success in learning the course material. The real challenge is implementation. Providing feedback, particularly individualized feedback, can take hours of work, and, and the workload is exacerbated if the teacher is also grading the students' performance. In a class with 75–100 students, the burden seems insurmountable.

Addressing the challenge

We have divided this discussion into two segments: (1) ideas for reasonably providing formative feedback in a large class, and (2) ideas for reasonably providing summative feedback in a large class. Keep in mind, however, that pre-final summative feedback also serves as formative feedback.

The following is a list of ideas for providing formative feedback that imposes manageable burden on the law teacher:

- Administer an essay question and then provide the students with a model answer to compare their answers;
- Administer an essay question and then provide the students with a rubric they can use to self-evaluate the work (the teacher can confirm that each student has used the rubric to evaluate the essay);
- Administer an essay question and then provide the students with a rubric they can use to peer-evaluate a colleague's work (the teacher can confirm that each student has used the rubric to evaluate a peer's essay);
- Administer an essay question and then review a sample student answer in class;
- Administer an essay question and then lead a class discussion of how the students should have answered the question;

- Administer an essay question for participation points and use Teaching Assistants to evaluate using the rubric you provide. Be sure to calibrate the Teaching Assistants by reviewing the same two student papers together and comparing the feedback you provide; and
- Provide practice multiple-choice questions with answers and explanations.

The list of manageable-burden summative assessments is equally lengthy:

- Administer one or more short multiple-choice tests;
- Administer short (one paragraph) free response questions (be sure to limit the length of your students' responses);
- Have students answer an essay question as a group (assuming groups of six students and 100 students, the teacher would only need to review less than 20 exams);
- Have students draft one or two contract clauses, will provisions, discovery requests, affirmative defenses, etc.; and
- Have students find real world examples (internet posts, newspaper stories, etc.) of the legal concepts they are learning and write up an analysis of the legal implications.

Challenge 8: Addressing Controversial Topics in Class

The challenge

Most law school courses raise controversial issues. Constitutional law is an obvious example of a subject that can and does give rise to disagreement, but courses in contracts, property, tax, torts, and most other subjects can raise thorny issues of race, class, gender, politics, and privilege. These issues create several, related challenges. How do we encourage free discussion and give all views a chance to be aired while keeping the focus on our core learning goals? How do we protect students from personal attacks or comments that are gratuitously disrespectful? How do we manage our own reactions to upsetting student remarks? How can we effectively interrogate public policy and legal doctrine with civility and respect?

Addressing the challenge

Ignoring or suppressing discussion of controversial issues is probably the worst choice. If you allow free discussion of even one policy issue, your failure to permit discussion of an issue about race or gender or politics, because you are concerned students will be upset, has the potential to send a message that you regard the issues you are ignoring as unimportant. Rather than ignoring such topics, acknowledge your worries about the potential for discord, ask the students to be sensitive to each other, and then open up the subjects. The remainder of this discussion focuses on our suggestions for managing the discussion effectively.

If you believe there are any topics about which students may become agitated, it is important that the class agree to expectations for respectful communication. Ideally, involve your students in (1) setting those expectations and (2) discussing the value of different perspectives to the learning process. You may also want your students to engage in an exercise in which each of them imagines another student saying something with which the student disagrees and planning how she or he will listen and respond respectfully.

If you wish to set the expectations yourself, your expectations might include: (1) listening respectively (and repeating the key point of the person who just spoke) before speaking; (2) assuming good intentions of others and avoiding personal attacks or global statements about affinity groups; (3) speaking only to add new points rather than to repeat previously made arguments or communicate agreement with a previous speaker; and (4) thinking through how your words might be heard before speaking—even if that means that you volunteer to speak and then wait 10–15 seconds before speaking. If you decide to include an expectation that students should only speak to add new points, give your students an opportunity to communicate agreement in some other way, such as by snapping their fingers.

You also may need to set other types of expectations. For example, consider imposing a time limit on the duration of the discussion or on how long each student may speak. Likewise, your students need to know that you are managing the discussion and using the discussion to further course goals. Some teachers find it helpful to give students space to be upset, allowing students to decide to leave the room for a moment to collect their emotions.

Our next set of suggestions for dealing with heated discussions are more ideas about what you can do during the discussion. In facing challenging issues, we first need to be aware of our own responses. In these situations, students especially need to see us model calm and constructive leadership. Think of yourself as someone responding to a health emergency or 911 call. The first rule is to stay calm. Take a deep breath. Try to disengage for a minute and consider the view of the classroom dynamic from above the class. What just happened? Why might a student have reacted that way? We can name the challenge, use silence, and ask students to pause and reflect on what just happened in the classroom. "I see that many of you are uncomfortable with the opinion just stated, that health insurance should never cover the cost of an abortion. Before we continue, let's pause for a minute to think about why some of us might hold that view." We want students' to learn how to listen to controversial views and to try to understand others' perspectives.

As noted above, it is critical that you make sure you retain control of the discussion; students responding to students is often a sign of a good discussion—unless the emotions have gotten out of hand. Some teachers find it helpful to give students time to write about an issue, either before launching into the issue or if the discussion gets heated. It is helpful, before letting students evaluate or respond to the arguments on a topic, to have the students identify all the possible arguments and what a supporter of each argument might say to defend his or her argument. Likewise, having students volunteer to defend an argument with which they disagree can be a powerful learning tool for future lawyers.

You may be concerned that addressing controversial issues will take up valuable class time that could be otherwise used to help students learn. We suggest that understanding others' perspectives and learning how to address controversy with respect and dignity is an important learning objective in any class. If you have created a positive classroom environment, anticipated issues in advance, and seek to have students learn from these discussions, you will have done your students a service.

If a student does become particularly upset, we make it a point to contact the student after class, ask the student how he or she is doing, invite the student to talk to us about concerns or just share their reaction, and otherwise provide input.

Our final thoughts return to the idea of doing your best to manage your own emotional reactions to a discussion. It is always a mistake to yell at or otherwise berate a student based on a comment the student made in class. You can and should, of course, enforce agreed-upon expectations, such as listening respectfully and avoiding personal attacks or global assumptions about affinity groups. We suggest you be transparent as you can (e.g., "I am finding myself feeling agitated, but I want to make sure everyone in this room feels respected and feels safe to make arguments with which I disagree, so I am ... [explain what you are doing to manage your feelings and encourage discussion, such as waiting 20 seconds to collect your thoughts and starting by summarizing the key points you just heard]").

Challenge 9: Being Asked a Question That You Are Unable to Answer in the Moment or Making a Mistake in Class

The challenge

At the outset, it is worth noting that being unable to conclusively respond to a student's question or making a mistake in class is not limited to new or inexperienced law teachers; we believe that, if we are doing our jobs well, we all have both types of moments throughout our careers. While we believe that preparation and experience minimize both types of challenges, we see *a complex, perceptive student question for which there is no easy answer as a success*. We also believe not only that mistakes are inevitable but, in fact, are more likely if we are taking the healthy teaching risks essential to growth as a law teacher.

Addressing the challenge

The very best thing we can do to respond to most questions for which we do not have a ready answer is to copy the approach used by teachers we studied for WHAT THE BEST LAW TEACHERS DO. The teachers we studied typically (1) acknowledged that they do not have a ready answer to the question ("I had not thought about that; thank you for raising."); (2) showed delight that a student asked a question for which they do not have a ready answer; (3) offered a tentative answer, making it clear not only that their answer was tentative, but also speaking aloud their process in generating their answer (modeling how a lawyer thinks through knotty questions); (4) promised to get back to the class with a more definitive response; and (5) did get back to their students in the next class with a more definitive response, identifying and congratulating the student who asked the question.

Mistakes are even easier to address. We find it easiest to just admit the mistake, correct the error, and move on as if nothing significant has occurred.

The approaches we recommend have two common features. As we have suggested throughout this chapter and throughout the book, authenticity works. If we are transparent about the limits of our knowledge, students feel more connected to us and perceive us to be so confident about our expertise that we are comfortable acknowledging our limitations. Moreover, if students perceive that we work hard to help them learn, and we put a lot of care and commitment into our teaching, they readily forgive our errors and failings, especially if we take responsibility for them rather than hiding or obscuring them. Likewise, respect for students works. When students feel we respect them enough to celebrate their insightful questions, find answers to those questions, and acknowledge our errors, they invest themselves more in our classes and feel better about their learning experiences.

Challenge 10: Students Do Not Read: (1) the Instructions on Exams (2) Assignment Instructions, (3) Emails, or (4) the Syllabus

The challenge

We very commonly hear complaints about students failing to read things their law teachers wanted them to have read. Generally, the missed information relates to deadlines and formatting and results in students making excuses for submitting late assignments or work products that fail to comply with stated expectations.

Addressing the challenge

We think it is helpful to consider our exam and assignment instructions, our emails, and our syllabi as containing information we want our students to learn. This conceptual approach suggests a few simple practices would help. First, as is true of any piece of information we want our students to remember, merely telling our students is often insufficient. Repetition and variety were common teaching practices among the teachers we studied for What the Best Law Teachers Do, and repetition and variety can help students internalize deadlines and instructions. This information should be available to students in writing in the syllabus, in a handout, or both. And we can remind students of this information orally or in writing on the board or on a slide. Second, students tend to remember the things on which they know we will test them. Telling students they will have a closed-syllabus test on the syllabus or a closed instructions test on the instructions gives students an incentive to remember this information. More generally, if students understand they will be held accountable for deadlines, and you follow through and do hold them accountable, they will quickly adapt. Third, adult learners tend to respond to expectations they regard as meaningful. You can explain to students that meeting deadlines and complying with instructions are fundamental aspects of professionalism. To the extent you can create formatting rules consistent with your local court rules and direct your students to those local court rules, you can accomplish your goals while also getting your students to see the importance of local rules.

Conclusion: Common Themes

As our responses to all of the challenges addressed in this chapter reflect, addressing most of the challenges law teachers face involves applying the principles discussed throughout this book. Core principles of good teaching, including respect for students, caring about their learning, preparation, creativity, focus on learning goals, authenticity, and integrity are generally relevant to producing learning and specifically relevant to addressing the challenges commonly faced by law teachers.

Chapter 13

Developing as a Teacher

The central aim of this book is to produce significant student learning by designing, delivering, and assessing law school courses and classes. An underlying premise is that teachers play a meaningful role in students' learning. This chapter focuses on our continued professional development as teachers. How can we enhance our students' learning by continuing to improve our teaching throughout our careers?

Sustaining a teaching practice

Empirical research demonstrates that university professors are motivated primarily by the intrinsic rewards of academic work, including teaching. Faculty want to feel competent and have a sense of self-determination. The need for self-determined competence leads us to engage in activities that interest us, provide challenges, and lead us to learn and achieve. Self-determined competence spurs us to seek feedback on our performance and new strategies to improve our teaching.

Although continued professional development as teachers can provide great satisfaction and reward, we acknowledge the institutional and personal obstacles. Many law schools value research and publication over teaching excellence. If the quantity and quality of publications is the primary criteria for tenure, promotion, and salary increases, many faculty members will choose to exert more effort on scholarship than teaching. In addition, faculty misconceptions about teaching and learning present obstacles.

Misconceptions include (1) if you know the content well, you can teach well; (2) you should master one teaching technique that suits your style and stick with it; and (3) good teachers are born, not made. Research debunks all of these myths:

(1) effective teaching requires knowledge of content coupled with pedagogical skill;

(2) no single teaching method works well for every student or accomplishes every educational goal; and

(3) successful teachers learn how to teach and continue to improve their skills throughout their careers.

Illustration 13-1: Ongoing Teaching Development

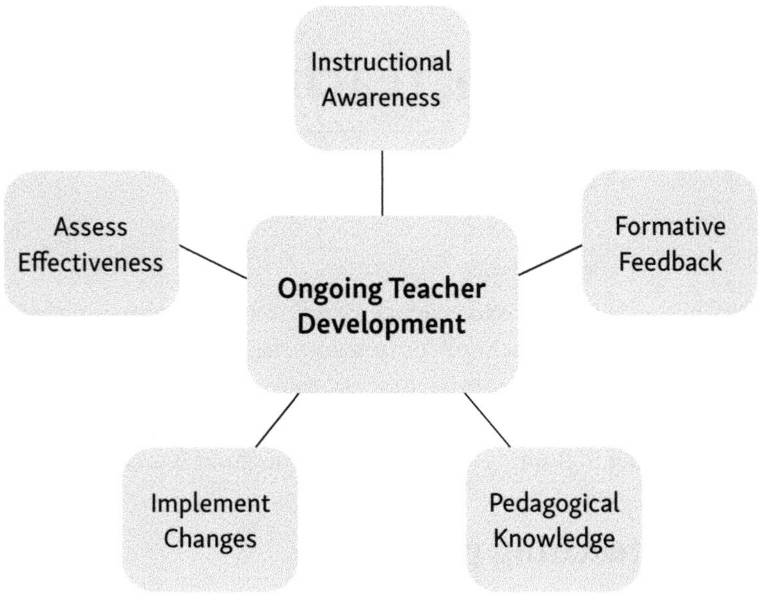

Finally, continuing to develop teaching skills, a complex human activity, is not easy. As we learn more about teaching and learning, we may uncover shortcomings in our current philosophy and practice. We often make mistakes when we try new methods. Sustained development in teaching requires hard work and perseverance.

The challenges and rewards of ongoing efforts to improve teaching apply to all faculty, not just new teachers or those who are struggling in the classroom. All of us can enhance our effectiveness through reflection, feedback, and innovation. Most models of teaching development are cyclical and involve several stages: instructional awareness, formative feedback, pedagogical knowledge, implementing changes, and assessing effectiveness.

Instructional awareness

An essential step in the process of improving instruction is to increase our understanding of our own teaching philosophy and practices. What do we believe are the purposes of legal education and our roles as teachers? What are our assumptions about teaching and learning? What behaviors do we exhibit when we interact with students in and out of the classroom? Are our teaching methods consistent with our educational philosophy?

Formative feedback

Formative feedback is critical to improving teaching and learning. To make effective changes in teaching, we need to know our current practices' strengths and weaknesses and their effect on students' learning. We can gather that information from ourselves, students, colleagues, and consultants.

Pedagogical knowledge

Deeper understanding of student learning and teaching methods can help us put the feedback we receive in context. We can gain valuable insights from research and scholarship about learning theory, student motivation, and factors that inhibit or improve learning. Knowledge about students and learning provide a foundation from which we can examine our current educational philosophy and practices. Likewise, the extensive literature on teaching methods, instructional design, educational technology, and assessment of student performance informs our choices about appropriate adjustments in our teaching.

Implementing changes

Teaching improvement occurs through changes in our teaching philosophy, attitudes, and behavior. Numerous resources are available to assist us at this stage—books, articles, websites, and videos on teaching; discussions with colleagues; working with consultants. To be effective, these changes should be incremental and systematic. A good start in teaching improvement could entail one or two small changes implemented throughout a course. For example, incorporating more small group activities and more ungraded feedback for students throughout the semester would be an ambitious, but achievable, teaching development agenda.

Assessing changes

The final stage is for us to evaluate the effectiveness of our teaching improvement efforts. Did our changes in philosophy, attitudes, and practices improve our teaching and our students' learning? We can gather this information from the same sources for formative feedback—ourselves, students, colleagues, and consultants. This information forms the basis for the next cycle in our teaching development.

Types of teaching development activities

Many types of faculty development activities are available for teachers who want to increase their effectiveness. We surveyed law teachers throughout the United States regarding their participation in twenty-two types of activities to improve teaching. The chart below summarizes the percentage of faculty members who engaged in each type of faculty development activity in the five years preceding the survey.

These faculty development activities fall in five categories. Teachers can:

- Engage in self-assessment and reflection;
- Read and produce scholarship on teaching and learning;
- Gather formative feedback from students during and after the course;
- Collaborate with colleagues in discussions about pedagogy and class observations; and
- Attend and present at workshops or conferences on teaching and learning.

Illustration 13-2: Engagement in Faculty Development Activities to Improve Teaching

Faculty Development Activity	Percentage of Respondents
Thinking about effective teaching methods before and after class	97%
Reviewing student evaluations of own teaching after the course	95%
Talking with colleagues about teaching	94%
Reviewing students' performance on exams, papers, and assignments	93%
Reading articles on teaching and learning	82%
Reviewing teachers' manuals	75%
Observing a colleague's class and providing feedback	58%
Gathering and reviewing feedback from students about own teaching during a course	51%
Attending a workshop on teaching and learning at own institution	51%
Having a colleague observe your class and provide feedback	46%
Attending a session at AALS Annual Meeting on teaching and learning	43%
Making a presentation on teaching and learning	33%
Reading books on teaching and learning	33%
Reviewing institutional data on student engagement and learning	25%
Attending a national or regional conference or workshop on teaching and learning	24%
Writing a journal or newsletter article on teaching and learning	17%
Reviewing a videotape of own teaching (alone or with others)	17%
Reviewing student performance on bar exams	15%
Reviewing websites on teaching and learning	15%
Reviewing a videotape of another's teaching (alone or with others)	11%
Keeping a journal about teaching	9%
Conferring with a consultant about own teaching	5%

Each of these categories of teaching improvement activities is discussed in the sections below. Also included in those sections is the survey respondents' assessment of the effectiveness of each type of faculty development activity on five dimensions:

(1) increasing their awareness of their own teaching practice and philosophy;

(2) increasing their knowledge of teaching and learning principles;

(3) improving their level of confidence in their teaching;

(4) increasing their enthusiasm or passion for teaching; and

(5) making changes in their teaching practices.

Thinking exercise: Make a list of the teaching development activities you employed in the last five years. Assess the effectiveness of each type of development activity on your list according to the five dimensions above.

Self-assessment and reflection

Many faculty members provide their own faculty development through self-assessment and reflection. The most common teaching development activity for respondents to our survey involved thinking about teaching methods before and after class.

Self-study and reflection can help us become more aware of our teaching assumptions and behaviors, articulate a coherent teaching rationale, and make informed changes in our instructional practices. Most teachers have deeply ingrained assumptions about teaching and learning, which affect teaching behavior. To grow as teachers, we must identify our current assumptions and behavior that may be hindering our effectiveness. Our observations and reflection can reveal patterns of behavior, habitual responses, underlying motivations, and aspects of our teaching that need improvement. Reflective teachers can explain the rationale behind their teaching. That rationale can give us confidence and serve as the foundation for our teaching choices. As a result of examining assumptions and developing a rationale, reflective teachers modify their plans, attitudes, and actions in the classroom. We can model critical thinking for our students by openly questioning our assumptions, articulating our rationale for our actions, and explaining to students the changes we make in our pedagogy.

These benefits of reflective practice are supported by empirical research. Our survey respondents concluded that reflection on their teaching before and after class is effective in increasing their awareness of their teaching philosophy and practices, improving their level of confidence, and increasing their enthusiasm and passion for teaching. Further, law teachers rated reflection (thinking about teaching and keeping a journal about teaching) as the faculty development activity most effective in producing changes in their teaching practices.

A variety of self-assessment techniques can help teachers build and maintain a reflective practice:

- Completing the student rating instrument for each course;
- Filling out a teaching inventory;
- Keeping a teaching journal;
- Reviewing a video of their teaching; and
- Constructing a teaching portfolio.

Completing the student rating instrument for each course

Course evaluation forms can help teachers engage in self-assessment. We can analyze our teaching behaviors by completing the same course evaluation form that the students fill out at the end of the term. The results can be revealing. According to empirical research of university faculty, most teachers' self-assessments of their strengths and weaknesses agree with their students' assessments. We can complete the form in the middle of the course in time to make mid-course adjustments. Then we can complete the form again at the end of the course, compare our ratings to the students ratings, and make appropriate changes the next time we teach the course.

Filling out teaching inventories

Inventories help teachers assess the presence, absence, and extent of instructional behaviors. Inventories adapted to legal education allow us to assess our teaching in the context of seven empirically derived principles for enhancing learning:

- Encouraging student-faculty contact;
- Fostering cooperation among students;
- Encouraging active learning;
- Giving prompt feedback;
- Emphasizing time on task;
- Communicating high expectations; and
- Respecting diverse talents and ways of learning.

Try completing the inventory about cooperation.

Keeping a teaching journal

An excellent tool for reflection is a teaching journal. By writing regularly in a journal we can develop the habit of reflection and reap many benefits of reflective practice.

Journals are a useful device for creating a comprehensive account of our experience. In a journal we can record problems, successes, strategies for improvement, and ideas for subsequent classes. Journal entries made around the time of our experiences are often more accurate than our recollections months after the events. Journal writing helps us clarify our assumptions and theories about teaching and learning, evaluate the effectiveness of instructional practices, and identify alternative methods to try in the future. Further, teaching journals are tools for setting goals, planning individual class sessions, and restructuring courses. We can use journals to analyze problems and work through the strong emotions that accompany teaching. Writing in a journal can help us deal with our disappointments, fears, and failures. Finally, journal writing can be a vehicle for us to integrate our personal and professional selves and to engage in a lifelong, reflective learning process.

Illustration 13-3: Sample Faculty Inventory

Good Practice Encourages Cooperation Among Students

Assess your teaching practices on each item with the following scale:

1 Very often
2 Often
3 Occasionally
4 Rarely
5 Never

____ I ask students to tell each other about their interests and backgrounds.
____ I encourage students to prepare together for classes and exams.
____ I structure out-of-class team projects.
____ I ask my students to provide feedback on each other's work.
____ I ask my students to explain difficult ideas to each other, including to other students whose backgrounds and viewpoints are different from their own.
____ I encourage students to join at least one campus organization.
____ I use small group discussions and exercises in class.
____ I model cooperation and collaboration in my dealings with administrators, staff, and faculty members.
____ I help students understand the value of cooperation and collaboration in law practice.

Law teachers who keep a teaching journal rated it as the single most effective faculty development device for prompting actual changes in teaching behavior. Yet only 9% of our survey respondents kept a teaching journal. Why? Keeping a teaching journal is not easy. It takes time, energy, and discipline. And journal writing does not fit well for every teacher; some of us are more comfortable talking about our experiences than writing about them.

Teachers are more likely to engage in journal writing if they find it to be enjoyable rather than a chore. Several practical aspects of the journal writing process can make it more fun and valuable:

- **Space.** Find a comfortable place to write free of distractions—in the office with the door closed, in a coffee shop, or at home in a comfy chair.
- **Time.** Schedule time for journal writing; for example, twice a week for thirty minutes or after each class for ten minutes.
- **Format.** There are many options to fit individual preferences—bound journal books, three ring binders, an artist's sketchbook, a computer, tablet, or phone.

- **Commitment.** Put journal time on the calendar and treat it like a professional commitment. But don't let guilt get in the way—if we miss our journal time, so what? Write again later.
- **Trust the process.** Don't censor. Insight and progress can follow paragraphs of bland, uninspired writing.
- **Content.** Free-writing in which we describe and explore our experiences is a common form of journaling. An alternative is to write in response to a prompt. Illustration 13-4 contains prompts from Stephen Brookfield's Becoming a Critically Reflective Teacher. Take a few minutes to respond to the questions in writing.

Reviewing a video of teaching

Video can be a powerful device for assessing and improving our classroom communication skills. A video of a class provides accurate, reliable, audio and visual feedback of several areas of our classroom performance:

- Verbal communication—clarity of speech, volume, verbal tics;
- Visual aids—legibility of board work, visual impact of computer presentations;
- Nonverbal behavior—eye contact, movement, gestures;
- Questioning—types of questions we ask and how we handle student responses; and
- Other presentation skills, including organization, flow, pacing, and variety in methods.

Despite the value of video in faculty development, many teachers are reluctant to be recorded. Conducted before the COVID-19 epidemic, only 17% of our survey respondents reported viewing a video of their teaching. Their reluctance may have been due to anxiety about the recording and review, which can reveal communication glitches and dramatically illustrate to teachers the disparity between their self-image and the behavior they see on video.

Several techniques can minimize the anxiety and maximize the value of video review.

1. Select a "typical" class to record. Explain to students that the purpose of the video is to provide feedback on your teaching, not to record their performance. If using a video operator, ask them to try to focus on both you and the students if possible.
2. View the video soon after the class while the class is fresh in your mind. View a portion of the video once to get used to seeing yourself on video and to get over the natural tendency to focus on minor distractions—Do I really sound like that? Look like that? Have those mannerisms?

Illustration 13-4: Reflective Inventory

What am I proudest of in my work as a teacher?
What would I like my students to say about me when I'm out of the room?
What do I most need to learn about in my teaching?
What do I worry most about in my work as a teacher?
When do I know I've done good work?
What's the mistake I've made that I've learned the most from?

3. View the video a second time focusing on specific strengths and weaknesses rather than the minor distractions (voice, appearance) that have little to do with effective teaching.
4. Use a checklist to help you assess significant components of teaching, such as organization, visual aids, clarity of presentation, questioning, student participation, and classroom climate.
5. Use the video to generate detailed data on specific aspects of your teaching. For example, record every question you ask and analyze the clarity and depth of each question. Or keep track of what is happening at one-minute intervals—teacher talk? Student question? Student comment? Exercise?
6. Review the video with a trusted colleague who can provide a fresh perspective on your teaching and suggestions of potential modifications in teaching practices.
7. Choose one or two aspects of your teaching to address in response to the feedback from your review of the video.

Constructing a teaching portfolio

A teaching portfolio is an extensive, reflective type of self-evaluation designed to foster ongoing teaching development. The portfolio can address our teaching as a whole or can focus on a particular course. The portfolio contains evidence, our reflections, and plans for further development. For example, a portfolio directed at a particular course could include the following.

(1) Introduction—a brief description of the course/s and the students;

(2) Your teaching philosophy for the course;

(3) The course design—a description of course learning objectives, teaching and learning methods, materials, and assessment scheme;

(4) Evidence of student learning;

(5) Selected course documents such as syllabus, slides, handouts, exercises, web page, exams, quizzes, student work product, your feedback to students, video of teaching, student ratings of the course, and peer review reports;

(6) Your reflections on the course design, student learning, course documents, student ratings, and peer observations; and

(7) An action plan for improving teaching and learning in the course.

The process of constructing a portfolio of our teaching can improve our effectiveness as we think deeply about our teaching, rethink practices, and plan for continuing development.

Scholarship on teaching and learning

Numerous print and electronic resources in higher education, including legal education, are available to facilitate self-directed faculty development. Journal articles, books, newsletters, videos, podcasts, and websites address the theory and practice of teaching and learning. Law teachers regularly engage in this type of development—over 80% of our survey respondents reported reading journal articles on teaching and learning and 33% read books on those topics. Reading and viewing these resources can help us improve our teaching in several ways—by causing us to reflect on our instructional practices, by giving us ideas, and by inspiring us to take reasonable risks and exert the effort needed to improve teaching and learning. We react differently to these resources throughout our careers. Each of us has read material on teaching and learning that we found uninspiring and unhelpful yet reread the same material later in light of our new experience and discovered critical insights. The references at the end of each chapter in this book provide a gateway to that literature.

Producing scholarship on teaching and learning by writing journal and newsletter articles can be a highly effective faculty development activity. Our survey respondents rated producing scholarship on teaching and learning among the top five most effective development activities in increasing awareness of their own teaching practice and philosophy, increasing their knowledge of teaching and learning principles, and increasing their enthusiasm and passion for teaching.

Formative feedback from students

Feedback from students about our teaching and their learning is an important part of faculty development. Over 90% of our survey respondents engage in two types of activities involving students: reviewing student evaluations after the course and reviewing students' performance on exams, papers, and assignments. In addition, about 50% of the respondents gather feedback from students about teaching effectiveness during the course.

Student evaluations

The most common method of assessing teaching in legal education, and higher education in general, is written student evaluations at the end of the course. Our focus is not on using student teaching evaluations to make retention, tenure, promotion, and salary decisions. Instead, we address the role that student evaluations can play in teaching development.

Extensive empirical research in higher education demonstrates the value of student evaluations for faculty development. Approximately 80% of college teachers report that student evaluations provide useful feedback that leads to improvements in teaching. Analysis of dozens of studies reveals a persistent positive effect of written feedback from students on subsequent teaching effectiveness. Written student comments can provide us with formative feedback and helpful suggestions for improvement in areas such as our clarity, delivery, organization, punctuality, fairness, demeanor, empathy, and availability outside of class.

Despite the potential benefits of end-of-the-term student evaluations for faculty development, some law teachers are reluctant to use them for development purposes. Their reluctance may come from a lack of confidence in the value of student evaluations and the pain that comes from reviewing negative comments. Our survey respondents did not rate reviewing student evaluations among the ten most effective faculty development methods on any of the five teaching development dimensions. The following ideas may help maximize the usefulness of student evaluations and minimize the discomfort from negative comments.

- Before reading student evaluations, write your prediction of what they will contain.
- Look at the numerical evaluations and read quickly through the comments to get an overall sense of the students' reaction to the course. The first time through the evaluations, many teachers focus on the lower scores and negative comments.
- Review the numerical evaluations a second time to analyze the results. Compare the scores on each item to scores from the previous time or two that you taught the course. Create a chart with these scores and pay attention to the trend in the scores.
- Review the comments a second time to identify themes rather than focusing on isolated comments. Write down several categories of positive comments. Identify in writing one or two areas where the students made negative comments or suggested improvement. Compare the positive and negative themes to comments in previous student evaluations.
- Choose an area or two to address the next time you teach the course. Make incremental, not wholesale, changes.

- Try to ignore mean comments, such as "I learned nothing in this course" or "Professor X should be fired." These types of comments reflect the commentator's problems, not our teaching.
- Read your evaluations with a trusted colleague or two who are reading their evaluations at the same time. Share mean comments. Laugh about them. There is power in camaraderie.
- Have a colleague or consultant review your student evaluations. Another set of eyes can help us see the positive aspects of the evaluations and assist us in identifying trends, themes, and appropriate adjustments to make in the future.

Thinking exercise: How do you currently use your students' end of the course evaluations of your teaching? How could you make more effective use of those evaluations to improve your teaching?

Student learning outcomes

Although over 90% of our survey respondents reported that they reviewed their students' performance on exams, papers and assignments, few respondents found the review to be a particularly effective teaching development activity. We note that our survey took place before the ABA Accreditation Standards dealing with learning outcomes and assessment that took effect in 2016. Perhaps those standards will provide an impetus for more effective use of student learning outcomes as a teaching development tool.

Every student performance in a course provides an opportunity for teachers to assess student learning and make appropriate adjustments to the course. Exams, papers, quizzes, student presentations, drafting exercises, problem responses, contributions to online discussions—graded or ungraded— help us determine how well our students are learning important doctrine, theory, skills, and professional values. It may be appropriate for us to make adjustments to the course design or delivery to bolster student achievement of particular learning outcomes either during the remainder of the course or the next time we teach the course.

Feedback from students during the course

Many devices for gathering formative feedback from students during the course are excellent faculty development tools. Our survey respondents rated "gathering and reviewing feedback from students about their own teaching during a course" as an effective means of improving teaching in three ways: improving their level of confidence in their teaching, increasing their enthusiasm and passion for teaching, and making changes in teaching practices. The classroom assessment methods described in

Chapter 10 help teachers gather feedback from students about their learning and make reasonable adjustments in teaching methods during the rest of the course to maximize students' learning. Additional means of gathering formative feedback include written questionnaires and student focus groups.

Teacher-Designed Questionnaires. Teachers can design short written questionnaires to obtain detailed feedback from students during the course to improve teaching. We can ask students for feedback about any aspect of our courses—teaching methods, materials, instructional technology, online formats, exercises, class environment, etc. The questions can be open-ended, close-ended, or a combination of both. We can do this once during the course or periodically throughout the course. Illustration 13-5 contains three examples.

Keep the questionnaire process simple. Here are some guidelines.

- Design the questionnaire. Either load it on your course management system in a way that allows students to respond anonymously or prepare a one-page, hard copy of the questionnaire.
- Explain to students the purpose of the questionnaire—to gather feedback to make your teaching and their learning more effective.
- To maximize the number of student responses, give the students five minutes in class to complete the questionnaire. Give students time at the beginning or in the middle of class; giving students time at the end of class may make some of them spend less time on the survey so they can leave class earlier.
- After class, review and summarize the responses, focusing on themes rather than isolated comments.
- Within a week, report back to students about common responses and at least one change or suggestion you intend to implement based on their feedback. This last step—implementing a change or suggestion—is critical. If we take this step, many students will view the teacher and the course more positively. If we fail to take this step, some students will resent the process.

Teachers who use questionnaires during the course can experience several types of benefits. First, students' responses should provide specific feedback and suggestions to improve teaching and learning. Second, the process of seeking feedback from students and implementing reasonable suggestions shows our deep respect for students. Many students will respond by working hard to achieve the goals of the course. Third, the formative feedback process is collaborative—we share responsibility for the success of the course with our students. Respect and collaboration are two important elements of a positive teaching and learning environment. Finally, the questionnaire process demonstrates a critical life-long, professional skill—welcoming and profiting from constructive feedback.

Student Focus Groups. We can gather formative feedback from students by using focus groups. One method is to use 30 minutes of class time to get feedback and ideas from small groups of students on how to make teaching and learning in the course

Illustration 13-5: Teacher Designed Questionnaires

Please assess the effectiveness of the following for your learning:

Whole Class Zoom Sessions
(1) Very Effective (2) Effective (3) Somewhat Effective (4) Ineffective
Comments:

Breakout Group Sessions
(1) Very Effective (2) Effective (3) Somewhat Effective (4) Ineffective
Comments:

Video Lectures
(1) Very Effective (2) Effective (3) Somewhat Effective (4) Ineffective
Comments

For the Clean Water Act assignment, please rate the following:

Clarity of the instructions: (1) Very Clear (2) Somewhat Clear (3) Unclear

Level of challenge: (1) High (2) Medium (3) Low

What would help improve your learning from the Clean Water Act assignment?

What teaching/learning methods have been most effective for you in this course?

What teaching/learning methods have been least effective for you in this course?

What other teaching/learning methods should we try in this course?

more effective. We can ask the groups to create four short lists of activities and behaviors: (1) those the teacher should keep doing; (2) those the teacher should stop doing; (3) those the teacher should start doing; and (4) those the students should be doing. The groups should include a brief explanation for each list. The teacher should collect the lists, summarize the results outside of class, and report back to the students with the results and ideas to make teaching and learning more effective going forward.

A more structured way to gather feedback from our students is through a student advisory team—a group of students who meet periodically with the teacher throughout the course. The students' role is to provide feedback to the teacher about their own learning, to solicit comments from all students in the course on the effectiveness of particular instructional methods, and offer suggestions to improve teaching and learning in the course. The teacher's role is to listen to students' feedback and to respond appropriately, which could include implementing reasonable suggestions during the course, working with the team to modify the suggestion, implementing the suggestion in future versions of the course, or explaining why the teacher will not implement the suggestion. It is common for some team members to be skeptical about the Student Advisory Team process until we respond to their suggestions. The best way to motivate team members is for the teacher to immediately implement a suggestion from the team.

Empirical research supports the value of Student Advisory Teams in legal education. Most team members report that their participation improved their attitude toward the course (98%), the teacher (94%), themselves as learners (82%), and law school in general (82%). In addition, most team members believe that the Student Advisory Team process improved the course (94%), their learning (84%), and the teacher's effectiveness (92%).

Despite the data confirming the benefits of Student Advisory Teams in law school, they are not appropriate for every teacher. Success of the Student Advisory Team process depends in part on the teacher's belief that students should share responsibility for course design and delivery with the teacher, that students can give accurate feedback on their learning and the effectiveness of teaching methods, and that they can provide useful suggestions for improvement. Even for teachers who hold these beliefs, Student Advisory Teams present significant challenges. The feedback is raw and honest—sometimes hard for the teacher to hear. The Student Advisory Team is unlikely to succeed if the teacher is unwilling to share control of the course by implementing reasonable student suggestions. (For detailed instructions on the Student Advisory Team process see Gerald F. Hess, Student Involvement in Improving Law Teaching 67 UMKC L. Rev. 343 (1998).)

Collaborating with colleagues

Our colleagues are valuable teaching development resources. Over 90% of our survey respondents talk with colleagues about teaching as one form of faculty development. Around 50% have observed a colleague's classes to provide feedback or had fellow teachers observe their classes for development purposes. Finally, colleagues with expertise in teaching and learning can provide individual coaching.

Discussions with colleagues

Talking with colleagues about teaching and learning is a common and effective type of development activity. In our survey, law teachers rated this activity as effective on every dimension of teaching development:

- Increasing their awareness of their own teaching practice and philosophy;
- Increasing their knowledge of teaching and learning principles;
- Improving their level of confidence in their teaching;
- Increasing their enthusiasm or passion for teaching; and
- Making changes in their teaching practices.

Discussions among colleagues about teaching and learning can occur in a variety of circumstances. Private conversations between two teachers in a faculty office are commonplace. These conversations between trusted colleagues can uncover common fears and problems, bolster our morale, and motivate appropriate changes in teaching practices. It is especially important for junior faculty members to feel comfortable having these conversations with more senior colleagues. Some of us find colleagues at other institutions that share our passion for educational excellence and engage in monthly phone calls about teaching and learning. Productive interchanges about pedagogy can occur in small groups, for example, at a lunch brown bag discussion. Discussion groups are more likely to lead to instructional improvement if they focus on a particular topic, such as ways to facilitate active student participation in class or how to maximize student learning online.

Peer observations and feedback

We can help one another improve teaching through peer observations and feedback. Although approximately half of our survey respondents had participated in class observations, they did not find the process to be particularly helpful—class observation and feedback did not rate in the top ten most effective teaching development activities on any of the five dimensions. Perhaps the following five ideas will help make peer observations and feedback more effective.

1. Characteristics of effective peer observation programs. The authors of Collaborative Peer Review identify common characteristics of effective peer review programs at colleges and universities. Participation in the program is voluntary. The program is not remedial—faculty members with a wide range of teaching experience and expertise participate. Participants decide for themselves what aspects of their teaching they would like to address. Class observations are reciprocal—colleagues switch roles as the observer and the observed—which creates mutual vulnerability and shared responsibility. The colleagues work together throughout the term and develop trust and mutual respect. The results are confidential and completely separate from the summative evaluation of teaching for purposes of tenure, promotion, and salary.

2. Three-Step Process. A three-step process can facilitate effective peer review. First, the colleagues meet for a pre-observation conference. They discuss their approaches to teaching, goals for the course as a whole and class to be observed, material for the class, expectations for student preparation, what students will do during the class, and the teaching methods to be used. Most importantly, they tell one another the specific types of feedback they would like to receive, such as organization, clarity, use of visual aids, types of questions, handling student responses, level of student engagement during class, etc. Second, the pairs visit each other's classes and gather the requested feedback. Third, the colleagues meet for a post-observation conference after the class or the next day. Those discussions should include the specific feedback requested in the pre-observation conference, the strengths and weaknesses of the class, the extent to which the goals for the class were accomplished, and an exploration of alternative methods to improve teaching and learning in future classes.

*3. **Descriptive, data-driven feedback.*** Effective feedback is descriptive and data-driven. Descriptive feedback is non-judgmental. For example, "Your instructions for the small group activity were ineffective" is judgmental; "approximately half of the small groups were confused by the instructions and spent time trying to clarify them" is descriptive. Or, "Your flow chart activity worked well" is judgmental; "all of the students appeared actively engaged in your flow chart activity" is descriptive. A particularly useful type of feedback is data gathered during the class on important aspects of teaching and learning. For example, a colleague could keep track of the students who speak in class. How many students spoke? How many men? How many women? How many students of color? Many faculty members are surprised by the results. The colleagues can use the data to strategize about active student participation in future classes.

*4. **Peer review of course documents.*** In addition to classroom visits, colleagues are ideally situated to help one another with course design, materials, and evaluation instruments. Peers can provide formative feedback on syllabi, course web pages, readings, and other assignments. Colleagues can be especially helpful in reviewing the materials related to evaluation of student work: quizzes and tests (both graded and ungraded); paper and presentation assignments; student responses to quizzes, tests, and assignments; and the teacher's feedback to students on their performance. Reciprocal review of syllabi, materials, assignments, and tests should have the same supportive dynamic as reciprocal classroom observations.

*5. **Peer review instruments.*** Checklists can facilitate all aspects of formative peer review. COLLABORATIVE PEER REVIEW and PEER REVIEW OF TEACHING include helpful checklists for pre-observation conferences, classroom observations, post-observation conferences, and many types of course documents.

> **Thinking exercise:** Identify a colleague with whom you would like to collaborate for a semester in reciprocal classroom visits. Do you feel comfortable committing to observing this colleague and being observed two or three times next semester? If so, give it a try.

Individual coaching

Teaching development consultants can be national "experts" from outside of the institution, members of a college or university teaching excellence center, or faculty members from within the law school with expertise in teaching and learning.

Consultants can coach an individual teacher through a four-phase instructional improvement process.

- **Data collection.** The consultant interviews the teacher about the teacher's course goals, methods, and materials. The consultant and teacher discuss the teacher's concerns about teaching and consultation objectives. The consultant gathers information through a self-assessment completed by the teacher, classroom observation, review of materials, student teaching evaluations, and formative feedback from students.
- **Data analysis.** The consultant organizes and summarizes the data. The teacher and consultant examine the data summary to determine the teacher's strengths and weaknesses. They identify specific areas of the teacher's instruction to address.
- **Improvement strategy.** The teacher and consultant agree on an objective for change in the teacher's behavior or attitude. The consultant acts as a resource to help the teacher choose an improvement strategy, select new methods to try, or identify appropriate training.
- **Feedback.** The consultant observes the teacher's instructional changes and provides feedback on their effectiveness. The consultant helps the teacher make appropriate refinements in the improvement strategies.

Empirical research in colleges and law schools establish the effectiveness of individual coaching. For college teachers, the four-stage consultation process resulted in better teaching performance according to student evaluations. Those improvements persisted over time. Although only 5% of the law teachers who responded to our survey reported working with a consultant, they concluded that the consultation was a very effective teaching development activity. The consultation increased teachers' awareness of their teaching practice and philosophy, increased their knowledge of teaching and learning principles, and resulted in changes in teaching practices.

Teaching workshops and conferences

Teaching effectiveness workshops rank among the most popular faculty development efforts in higher education and are also common in legal education. Approximately half of law teachers responding to our faculty development survey report attending a workshop on pedagogy at their own institution or a session on teaching and learning at the Association of American Law Schools' annual meeting. About one quarter of the respondents attended a national or regional teaching conference.

Among the twenty-two activities assessed in the faculty development survey, attending a national or regional conference or workshop was among the most effective. Attending these conferences was rated as the most effective in three dimensions: (1) increasing a teacher's knowledge of teaching and learning principles; (2) improving a teacher's confidence in teaching; and (3) increasing a teacher's enthusiasm and passion for teaching. In the two other dimensions—increasing awareness of a teacher's own teaching practice and philosophy, and making changes in a teacher's own teaching practice—attending teaching conferences was rated among the top five most effective teaching development activities. Attending workshops on teaching and learning at their own institutions or sessions on pedagogy at an AALS annual meeting were rated a bit lower than national conferences, but fall in the top half in all five dimensions.

The value of attending national or regional conferences is further supported by a survey that we conducted five years after an AALS teaching and learning conference. Most of the respondents reported that their attendance at the conference increased their reflection on teaching methods (97%), knowledge of teaching and learning principles (96%), awareness of their own teaching philosophy (95%), confidence (71%), and enthusiasm for teaching (70%). In addition, 93% of the respondents implemented changes in their teaching practices as a result of the conference. Attending conferences benefited the institution, not just the individual teacher. Respondents reported increases in talking with colleagues about teaching and learning (79%), influencing colleagues to implement changes in their teaching practices (53%), making presentations about teaching and learning (43%), influencing the school to emphasize improving teaching and learning (41%), and writing articles and essays about teaching and learning (33%).

Fostering a culture of teaching and learning

How can a law school create and maintain a culture of teaching and learning? It can employ the same methods that institutions use to foster a culture of scholarship: criteria for appointment, tenure, and promotion; separation between development and evaluation; administrative support; faculty leadership and motivation; institutional reward structure; community, collegiality, and collaboration; scholarship redefined; and continuous process.

> **Thinking exercise:** To what extent does a culture of teaching and learning exist at your institution? As you read this section of the chapter, identify elements of a supportive teaching culture that currently exist at your institution. What would need to happen to enrich that culture? What role would you be willing to play?

Criteria for appointment, tenure, and promotion

Most universities and law schools define the faculty role to include at least three elements—scholarship, teaching, and service. At most institutions, service is subsidiary to teaching and scholarship. The relative weight that an institution gives to teaching and scholarship in appointment, tenure, and promotion decisions demonstrates its commitment to quality in those two areas. If teaching and scholarship have equal weight, faculty will be motivated to excel at both. Schools that value teaching make candidates' aptitude for and experience in teaching a significant element in hiring decisions. Likewise, institutions communicate their commitment to teaching excellence by rigorously assessing teaching through both peer and student evaluations as part of the reappointment, tenure, and promotion process.

Separation between development and evaluation

Law schools evaluate faculty members' performance for purposes of retention, promotion, tenure, and compensation. That summative evaluation process usually assesses performance in all portions of a faculty member's role, including teaching. Rigorous, summative evaluation of teaching can help ensure that personnel decisions are made fairly. However, there is general agreement among researchers that the summative evaluation process has little positive effect on teaching.

Unlike summative teaching assessment, the purpose of which is to judge performance, teaching development activities are designed to improve teaching through formative assessment. At its best, the formative assessment process gathers data and diagnostic feedback, which suggest changes in pedagogical policies and practices to enhance teaching and students' learning. Although the summative and formative processes may gather data from the same sources, including the teacher, peers, and students, the processes should proceed independently. Nearly all faculty development scholars and researchers agree that it is unwise to use the information collected for formative assessment when making personnel decisions. Teaching improvement requires data, feedback, practice, and readjustment, free from the fear that the information will be used against the teacher in the reappointment, tenure, and promotion process.

Administrative support

Successful teaching development requires senior administrators' clear commitment and support. The law school dean and associate deans should communicate to the faculty, students, and alumni that teaching excellence is a core value of the institution. The dean should give teaching improvement activities the same high visibility that accompanies scholarly achievement. The administration needs to provide financial support for teaching development. Even a modest annual investment can fund significant activities and resources:

- Library resources such as books, videos, journals and librarian time to support teaching and learning;
- Workshops on pedagogy led by educators from outside of the institution (faculty are often willing to learn new techniques from an outside "expert" even when they reject similar ideas from colleagues);
- Travel and registration fees for faculty to attend national and regional teaching and learning conferences; and
- Consultants to provide coaching, especially for junior faculty as they encounter the steep learning curve and anxiety that can accompany their pre-tenure years.

Many law schools have an associate dean for faculty development. To foster a culture of teaching and learning, the responsibilities of this position should encompass both scholarship and teaching or there should be a separate associate dean for teaching development. One of the associate dean's roles is to work with faculty members to plan teaching development activities. An excellent way to start the planning process is to survey the faculty to determine the activities that would most interest and engage the faculty in a given year. The associate dean for teaching development could coordinate a teaching mentor program for new faculty as well as a peer review and mentoring program for adjunct faculty.

Faculty leadership and motivation

Although administrative support is an important part of a teaching culture, faculty development activities that are designed and imposed by the administration may meet with a cold faculty response. Instead, teachers should play leadership roles in all phases of the faculty development effort: planning, design, delivery, and assessment. Faculty involvement in program design, delivery, and guidance increases faculty commitment to the program's success. High levels of faculty input and ownership in faculty development programs correlate with greater faculty participation, satisfaction with the program, and changes in faculty attitudes about teaching.

Faculty participation in teaching development activities should be voluntary. Requiring faculty members to engage in teaching improvement activities will likely lead to resistance and resentment. When teachers are motivated to participate in teaching development, their commitment to implementing instructional changes and to continued improvement are stronger.

Faculty members should be in control of their own faculty development. Teachers not only should decide whether to participate in teaching development activities, they should choose the extent and nature of their participation:

- Which teaching development activities will be most valuable for them—workshops, discussions with peers, individual reflection?
- What aspects of their teaching should they address—active learning methods, evaluation of students, instructional technology?
- What sources should provide feedback about their current teaching practices—students, peers, video, consultants?
- What changes should they make in their teaching—cooperative learning, variety in methods, systematic course and class design?

Institutional reward structure

Law schools support and encourage scholarship with summer stipends, course reductions, release time, awards, and preferential scheduling. The same rewards can support teaching development and increase faculty members' incentives to work on improving their teaching. Institutions should support faculty members who choose to devote their sabbaticals to course development and teaching improvement. Schools that are serious about teaching excellence as a significant factor in tenure and promotion decisions will use the teaching development process and institutional reward structure to help faculty members succeed.

Community, collegiality, and collaboration

A central goal of a faculty development program should be to create and maintain a sense of community around issues of teaching and learning. A critical first step in establishing effective teaching development programs is to help faculty members listen to and respect one another. Teaching development programs can open lines of communication among faculty members as they discuss teaching, provide feedback for one another, and support their instructional innovations. Increased communication and collaboration can improve faculty morale and, consequently, faculty commitment to effective teaching and learning.

Most law schools build a culture of scholarship by hosting brown-bag discussions where faculty present scholarly works-in-progress. The same simple process can help law schools establish a culture of teaching and learning. Law schools can host teaching and learning discussion sessions on a biweekly or monthly basis. As with scholarly presentations, faculty could volunteer to lead sessions on topics such as active learning, discussion techniques, instructional technology, student motivation and engagement, course design, and testing and grading. A portion of a video of a faculty member's class could be the spark for a lively brown bag session. Invite adjunct faculty members to participate as well. Faculty should be encouraged to try new techniques and debrief their instructional innovation efforts with their colleagues.

The participation of good and excellent teachers in faculty development activities helps foster a positive teaching culture. Their involvement sends the message that effective teaching is not innate, but is instead a set of knowledge, skills, and attitudes that must be developed through ongoing effort. The participation of passionate, effective teachers can make the discussions about teaching, learning, and students more positive, rather than focusing on the negative comments sometimes expressed by struggling, disengaged teachers. If excellent teachers are enthused with the development activities, it counters the perception that teaching development is "remedial" and encourages less confident teachers to participate.

Scholarship redefined

Faculty productivity in publishing doctrinal law review articles and making presentations on substantive topics is highly valued at most law schools. To foster a teaching culture, presentations and journal articles on pedagogy deserve the same value. Scholarly activities should be evaluated on the same set of criteria (depth of research, quality of writing, originality of ideas, etc.) regardless of the topic.

Presentations and publications on teaching and learning are effective faculty development activities. In our faculty development survey, respondents rated both activities as effective on all five dimensions. Making presentations on teaching and learning was especially effective in improving teachers' confidence and increasing their enthusiasm for teaching. Writing a journal or newsletter article on teaching and learning was especially effective in increasing respondents' passion for teaching and their awareness of their own teaching philosophy and practices.

Continuous process

Teaching development should be an ongoing process, not a one-time event. By offering a flexible mix of development activities throughout the year, the law school helps faculty members maintain collaborative relationships, share new ideas on teaching and learning, and build a teaching community. Improving law professors' teaching skills involves substantial time and effort from teachers, not quick fixes. Empirical research demonstrates that teaching development programs are more likely to have lasting effects if they continue for more than a semester and include follow-up activities, such as refresher training, reports to colleagues on instructional changes implemented, or assessment of the effects of new teaching techniques on student learning.

Illustration 13-6 is a checklist you can use to guide your continued development as a teacher.

Illustration 13-6: Teaching Development Checklist

Teaching Development Activities

- ❑ **Self assessment and reflection**
  - ❑ Thinking about effective teaching methods before and after class
  - ❑ Filling out student ratings forms during and after each course
  - ❑ Completing inventories on teaching practices
  - ❑ Constructing a teaching portfolio
  - ❑ Keeping a teaching journal
  - ❑ Reviewing a video of your own teaching
- ❑ **Scholarship on Teaching and Learning**
  - ❑ Read books, articles, newsletters, and websites on teaching and learning
  - ❑ Produce books, articles, videos, and podcasts on teaching and learning
- ❑ **Formative feedback from students**
  - ❑ Reviewing student evaluations of your teaching after the course
  - ❑ Analyzing your students' performances and learning outcomes
  - ❑ Gathering feedback from students on your teaching during the course (questionnaires, student focus groups)
- ❑ **Collaborating with colleagues**
  - ❑ Talking with colleagues about teaching and learning
  - ❑ Observing a colleague's class or course documents and providing feedback
  - ❑ Having a colleague observe your class or course documents and provide feedback
  - ❑ Receiving individual coaching on teaching strengths and weaknesses
- ❑ **Teaching workshops and conferences**
  - ❑ Attending a national or regional conference on teaching and learning
  - ❑ Attending a workshop at your institution on teaching and learning
  - ❑ Making presentations on teaching and learning at conferences or workshops
- ❑ **Evaluation criteria for teaching development activities**
  - ❑ Increasing your awareness of your own teaching practice and philosophy
  - ❑ Increasing your knowledge of teaching and learning principles
  - ❑ Improving your level of confidence in your teaching
  - ❑ Increasing your enthusiasm or passion for teaching
  - ❑ Making changes in your teaching practices

Developing as a Teacher—Resources

This chapter is based on the following books and articles from the legal education and higher education literature.

Books

- STEPHEN D. BROOKFIELD, BECOMING A CRITICALLY REFLECTIVE TEACHER (1995).
- NANCY VAN NOTE CHISM, PEER REVIEW OF TEACHING: A SOURCEBOOK (2d. ed. 2007).
- LARRY KEIG & MICHAEL D. WAGGONER, COLLABORATIVE REVIEW OF TEACHING: THE ROLE OF FACULTY IN IMPROVING /COLLEGE TEACHING (1994).
- MICHAEL B. PAULSEN & KENNETH A. FELDMAN, TAKING TEACHING SERIOUSLY: MEETING THE CHALLENGE OF INSTRUCTIONAL IMPROVEMENT (1995).
- KELLY TERRY, GERALD HESS, EMILY GRANT & SANDRA SIMPSON, ASSESSMENT OF TEACHING AND LEARNING: A COMPREHENSIVE GUIDE FOR LAW SCHOOLS (2021).
- MARY ELLEN WEIMER, IMPROVING COLLEGE TEACHING (1990).

Articles

- Gerald F. Hess, Michael Hunter Schwartz & Nancy Levit, Fifty Ways to Promote Teaching and Learning, 67 J. LEGAL EDUC. 696 (2018).
- Gerald F. Hess & Sophie M. Sparrow, What Helps Law Professors Develop as Teachers: An Empirical Study, 14 WIDENER L. REV. 149 (2008).
- Gerald F. Hess, Improving Teaching and Learning in Law Schools: Faculty Development Research, Principles, and Programs, 12 WIDENER L. REV. 443 (2006).
- Gerald F. Hess, Learning to Think Like a Teacher: Reflective Journals for Legal Educators, 38 GONZAGA L. REV. 129 (2003).
- Gerald F. Hess, Student Involvement in Improving Law Teaching and Learning, 67 U.M.K.C. L. REV. 343 (1998).

Appendices

The following pages provide examples of how we have implemented the various principles discussed in the book. We have organized this Appendix in the same way we have organized the book. All material in the Appendices are available to download at

caplaw.com/TLBD3e

(Note: There are no appendices for Chapters 1, 6, 9, 11, and 12.)

Index